From Broken To Becoming

Tell Your Story.

This Is Where the Healing Begins.

Penned by Mel Joy

© 2021 Penned by Mel Joy

From Broken to Becoming

All rights reserved. No part of this publication may be reproduced, stored in a retrieval system or transmitted in any form or by any means, electronic, mechanical, photocopying, recording or otherwise without the prior permission of the publisher or in accordance with the provisions of the Copyright, Designs and Patents Act 1988 or under the terms of any license permitting limited copying issued by the Copyright Licensing Agency.

Published by: Penned by Mel Joy

Book Design by: Daniel Alexander Roca

Cover Art by: Penned by Mel Joy

A CIP record for this book is available from the Library of Congress Cataloging-in-Publication Data

ISBN (Paperback): 978-1-7371159-3-9

ISBN (EPUB): 978-1-7371159-7-7

This book is dedicated to my mom

Thank you, mom. Your strength and faith in your own beliefs inspired the strength and faith I find in my own.

You will never know how deep my admiration of you goes. Your guidance and wisdom (though sometimes ferociously fought) has made me the woman that I am today. Strong, with deep convictions, yet light-hearted, wise, and warm.

I am caring, because I have watched you care for others. I am giving, because I have watched you sacrifice throughout your life. I sing and dance through my sorrows, because you taught me how to make the most of every moment, no matter what we faced. I am forgiving, because I watched you tend to the souls that broke you. I am compassionate and empathetic, because I watched you try to understand that everyone has their own demons to bear. I am optimistic and hopeful, because I have watched you push through the pain, determined to keep your joy. I am fierce, because I watched you fight for what you deserve. I am strong-willed, because I watched you break through the barriers and limitations others set for you in your own life. I am resourceful, because I watched you make the most of what we had.

You taught me the value of persistence and hard work. You taught me to go after what it is I need and want in my life without fear. You taught me that the needs of others matter, but in the end, I must be full in order to give. You taught me how to find what fills me, even in the emptiest places. You are my hero.

Contents

- i   INTRODUCTION
- iii   PREFACE
- ix   PROLOGUE

- 1   PART I - THE STORY
  - 2   Cracked Walls in a Glass House
  - 7   Sister, Sister
  - 9   Little, Lost, and Led
  - 17   Through the Eyes of a Child
  - 22   The In Between
  - 28   The Path to Healing
  - 32   The Storm Before the Calm
  - 41   Walking the Fire
  - 41   to Become the Flame

- 44   PART II - THE PRAYERS
- 104 PART III - THE REVELATIONS
- 238 PART IV - THE BECOMING
- 270 EPILOGUE
- 272 ABOUT THE AUTHOR

Introduction

I believe in God, the Divine, the Creator of all that is seen and unseen. I believe that He lives in all things. He is energy. He is matter. He is both feminine and masculine. He is all that exists, has existed, and will exist. I believe in the Holy Spirit, the presence of my ancestors, and that God's angels walk with us at all times.

He is the universe to me, the still small voice, the light that lives within me. He is my greater wisdom, my ancient knowledge, my spirit guide in all that I do. He is the beginning of who I am and the end to where I am headed.

He is the Higher Power, the Sacred Divine, the Lord of All Light. And while I have written about my journey with God, this book is not written in conformity to religious practices, nor does it align with what common religion is. This book is written entirely based on my own personal relationship with the Divine. It is my journey from darkness into a light that I have learned burns brightly within me. It is my testimony to how His power has changed me from a lost and broken soul to one that shines from the inside out and impacts the world around me.

It is a testimony to how my own failures, perceptions, and emotions lead to tower moments that were divinely orchestrated to bring me to revelation that has the power to change my life if I am willing to see it for what it is. It is a journey into the trappings of my own mind that kept me blinded to all that is out there for me and kept me deaf to His voice that was leading me to where I needed to be.

He is the Great Teacher, the Guiding Light, and the Wisdom for All Ages. He is. Through Him, I am.

Through my own testimony, may you find the light within you that has been hidden but is waiting to burn brightly into the world around you.

Mel Joy

Preface

I am writing this book in the middle of a pandemic, a pandemic that has shaken the world and changed people, their way of living, their beliefs, and the way they function around others. The pandemic has changed the way people respond to authority, how their voices will be heard or silenced. It has brought out passion for causes that have been burning on the inside of them for years, for they recognize the fears that have kept their passions silenced and hidden from all who know them. It has created division within their families, their nations, their systematic structures, and the world. They have learned the importance of questioning the cultural and systematic structures that have shaped their communities and societies in ways that challenge their own personal, innermost beliefs. For the first time in their lives, they realize that their life matters outside all of this, that life itself matters outside all of this.

The experience has created fear and doubt, but at the same time has given them back a deeper hope for all things that should have, and now do, take priority over all the shallow cultural things that used to matter. The pandemic created the opportunity for time; for themselves, their families, and created a need for reconnecting to who they really are and all who really matter. People have begun to look within themselves and question the things that have mattered before the pandemic, and what really matters in the end. They have begun to see the meaning of life and the meaningless ways they lived their lives before all this. Everything they are discovering inside them is changing everything around them, and they are learning to find a freedom to live life fuller, despite the attempts by those in their circles and societies to contain and restrain them.

In this sense too, because of the tragedies and experiences I have gone through, I see my own personal pandemic at my core, and I too, am changing the way I see life, myself, lessons from my past, what my present needs to be, and my reason for living. I am discovering who I am and learning how to shine again from the inside and learning how to affect others around me from all the things that make me unique and beautiful.

This book is my testimony. It is my story in its raw form, from the traumas of abuse in my childhood, to the tragic deaths of my brothers, to the isolation and struggle in my blended family that led to separation and divorce, and how God took all of this and made everything beautiful from "my" own ashes.

The following pages are my thoughts, prayers, and God's gentle guidance in each moment. They demonstrate our conversations and influence of the Holy Spirit during some of my darkest times. It is written with prayer and thought followed by the verses and messages that I was led to in those moments. It is written with deep heartfelt longing for answers and guidance followed by a message that I received online, or in church, or by a simple sentence someone spoke to me. They are written with an opening to my daily entry with the most prominent thought of the morning, followed by a message written to myself, without really knowing what I was writing in the moment. They are the gentle nudges often derived from a message I am hearing or simply just divine guidance at a moment when I need it most.

<u>Part One</u> will begin with my story that started my journey to healing and wholeness.

<u>Part Two</u> will reflect my journal entries filled with prayer, and the random messages that came from the deep heart prayers that led me to that journal entry, in that moment, and from that deep heart cry.

<u>Part Three</u> will be the revelations that came from automatic writing, where I stopped speaking my need, but my need in those moments were being spoken directly to me.

<u>Part Four</u> will be the becoming of who I really am. It is my hope that through this process, you will discover your truth and learn to love who you really are too, and the life you are called to live.

It will be a blend of my journal entries during my struggle for peace and joy, to the inspired Word of God in my life that has astonished me and amazed me more times than I could count. As you read through, you will recognize the changes in my writing, in my level of awareness, but most importantly, in the way God begins to communicate healing and restoration to a soul that just about gave up.

When I started this book, I was lost, desperate, hurting, numb, and in complete darkness. I was in the middle of grief beyond anything I had ever experienced in my life. I was drowning in weakness and sorrow. I was struggling to move through life for I could no longer hold it all together and pretend that everything was okay. I was going through relationship issues in my home, and in my blended family that pushed me deeper into my darkness. I labeled myself rejected, neglected, alone, and afraid.

Through writing this book, I found that I had experienced these feelings for most of my life. You will come to know my childhood tragedies of abuse and neglect, and the struggle that pursued me all of my adult life. You will come to know the addictions that I had to supplement what I was lacking, and the strength that brought me out of it all.

This book has been born out of grief, loss, abuse, neglect, separation, divorce, loneliness, darkness, and sorrow carried for most my life until I reached the end of my rope. This book was born from all this, and has brought me hope and healing, forgiveness and self-worth. It has changed my perspective on how I see my past, my present, and my future. Writing this book has been a journey to finding a wholeness I never knew I could have. During the process of writing this book, I have cried a million tears of pain, of joy, of gratitude, and of peace. Yes, I have cried all of these things. And through the tears, He reached me.

I truly believe that if we allow ourselves to talk to God expecting a real relationship with real back and forth communication, and a heart that believes that He speaks, He will. He speaks through His Word. He speaks through random, chance encounters with other people. He speaks through events in your day. He speaks through everything, and everyone, (believers and non-believers alike) all the time. He speaks to you if you are just willing to listen.

Not everyone believes that God still communicates with people, but I do. There are so many stories in the bible, so many verses, so many different words, that there is no way that every single time I pray about something very specific, and randomly flip open the bible, it takes me directly to guidance specific to my "type" of need and circumstance. I couldn't even begin to tell you what books or chapters or versus cover what, nor in what order they fall. All I know is that I reach for the Word, and the Word reaches for me. EVERY time. It NEVER fails.

Call me crazy. I don't care. I have a real relationship with the Father, the Son, and the Holy Spirit God, and He speaks to me daily.

He speaks through a gentle nudge, a gut feeling, a thought that just won't leave. He speaks through our dreams, and just a firm knowing. He is not the voice of choice in your head. The messages are clear, with biblical foundation, specific to your prayers, and hopes, and worries. And they are never self-centered, but rather, have a greater cause – usually a choice you never even considered.

His messages correct you, guide you, and give you wisdom beyond your own understanding. Why on earth would I tell myself I am wrong, when all I want is to be right sometimes? Even when I firmly believe that I am right in a situation or argument, he corrects me and shows me different ways to look at things – usually not my own way.

His Spirit guides me through some really tough stuff, and no one could tell me otherwise. I have come out of the darkest corners of grief and learned some valuable lessons along the way. There is still so much uncertainty about where God is leading me, but I am following in full faith, knowing that this is the path He has placed me on to turn my pain into purpose.

My hope in writing this book is that you too may find peace amidst your chaos and see how God works when nothing seems to be working. May you hear His voice in these pages that helps you break through your own barriers, limitations, and break out of your own desperation and into peace and joy that cannot be shaken nor taken away from you.

May it inspire you to live fully, freely, and finally find the love in yourself for who you are in your own eyes. May it push you and propel you to see the beauty in your own becoming. May it guide you through the emotional challenges you are experiencing and will experience through your own transformation as you begin to fight for your own inner freedom. May it whisper your worth into your own heart. May it connect you to the God who validates who you are. May it reignite the light within you that you begin to shine in your own eyes. May it trigger your fight for you.

May it inspire you to tell your own testimony, so you find freedom from those bondages and you learn it is easier to set them down than to carry them any further. May you find the beauty in your own story and see the blessings in your own breaking. May your self-imposed burdens be removed, and you learn to live like you're worth it! Because you are.

For those of you that are battling grief so embedded in who you are now, that you can scarcely remember who you were before…there is hope. No words in this book can ever change what has happened to color your world black, but may you find my story a small piece in your puzzle where the Light can begin to bring back the vibrant colors that your soul longs to see again.

For those of you who have never known grief that steals every ounce of strength you thought you had, nor experienced moments where overwhelming loss drains your soul unexpectedly, and robs you of much needed peace, may my story help to inspire you to help others that you may know who are currently lost in this deafening darkness.

It is not easy putting these words down because I am forced to feel. I am forced to relive the hardest days of my life. I am forced to remember how both of my brothers died in vivid detail. I am forced to live through their deaths all over again. I am forced to face my isolation and the loneliness during the struggle. I am forced to live through my troubled marriage, the war in my head of what it could be, and what it really was. I am forced to hear my inner screams as I learn to sing beyond them. I am forced to face the fact that I have had to face this alone. I am forced to see the me that I no longer recognize. I am forced to feel and face all of this all over again, but I know that I cannot heal until I do.

Thank you for walking through this journey with me.

October, 26 2017

I woke up this morning at 4:40 and heard the calling to rise, to read, to write. For months now, his voice has come to me in many forms, and each one, urging me to write. I closed my eyes, relaxed my mind, opened my heart, and opened my bible to a random page. This is where he brought me.

Timothy 4:14

Do not neglect the gift that is in you, which was given to you in prophesy with the laying of hands of the eldership. Meditate on these things. Give yourself entirely to them, that your progress may be evident to all. Take heed to yourself and to the doctrine. Continue in them, for in doing this you will save yourself and those who hear you.

Much has happened in my life that brought me to this point where I was opened up enough to hear His messages, and much has happened in my life after this message came to me that sent me on a dark journey, running full force from what He had called me to do, and from the door that would lead me to peace. It is now May 2019. This is the story of my journey from nothingness, through deep, shattering grief, and to a love that held onto me until I was ready to heal.

Prologue

This book begins 5 years after my brother Jerry died. The story is that he took his own life in the jungles of Guam. I am still working through this story and all the emotions that go with the unknown. I experience anger, resentment, deep sorrow and sadness, regret, and at times, a thirst to avenge him. But God. I put this tragedy in the hands of God because to be honest, I am hardly in my right mind to make clear decisions on how to handle those that I feel are responsible for his death in some way. At times, I too, hold myself accountable, and this is hard to live with. Jerry's story will be told in these pages and the impact that both his life and his death had on me and those of us who love him that are now left behind.

This will also be the story of my brother Gilbert. He died two years later at the hands of two strangers, during a planned carjacking, and they took his life in the most brutal way possible. His death, because of the senselessness and his suffering, sent me on a deep and dark journey into the depths of grief like I have never known before. I still suffer from PTSD, and there are triggers I battle daily, some that hit me with the intensity of a rolling boulder, some that sneak up on me at unexpected moments, and others that I seem to have a bit more control of. Either way, losing each of my brothers broke me and brought me here, to a place of healing, and out of the darkest darkness anyone could ever know. Had it not been for key people and events that were placed along my journey, I may have stayed in that living hell.

Throughout the book, there will be inserts from my journal, along with my conversations with God. The good, the bad, the ugly, in its realness, and sometimes, complexity. Emotional turmoil is never easy, but add the battle with God to grief, and you get a big giant mess of screaming in anger, a shattered soul crying to no one and The Only One at the same time, and a lonely girl, lost in the trappings of her sorrow. It's been a long road that she walked alone, and no one, not one, could have walked it with her. At times, you will see the lost girl in these pages, and at other times, you will see her hope written in all its colors, and at times, you will see the Spirit of God carrying her through this journey. You will see healing. You will see peace, ever-growing. You will see God moving in her life, stirring her soul, and bringing her to a place of wholeness once again.

Life after death goes on, and these pages will also show the daily tragedies I have faced while dealing with my darkness. I can honestly tell you that I had no power in this battle. I barely had the will to want to win. But God! And so, it begins; the journey from nothingness, through deep, shattering grief, and to a love that held onto me and brought me to healing and wholeness like I had never known before.

Thank you to all those who loved me through this. To those who took the time to make me laugh, to lift me up, and to demonstrate a soft kindness, during the hardest times of my life. You will never know how these small moments were instrumental in helping me out of the dark.

If for a moment, you could put yourself in my shoes,
Would you? And could you?
If for a moment, you could feel the pain of my past,
How long do you think that moment could last?

If for a moment you could see the tears I have cried,
Do you think you could see the ones I have buried inside?
If for a moment you could hear the screams in my head,
The ones of abuse, and the ones of the dead,
The ones of rejection, and the ones of neglect,
The ones of cold silence, knowing that's all you have left.

Would you? And could you?

Not many people could stand in my place,
Long enough to truly relate,
To the terrors inside that I constantly face.

And if in these moments, you had to stand all alone,
And not feel the warmth of the place you call home,
And not feel the comfort of the ones that you love,
Neglected, rejected, and made to feel that you are never enough.

If for a moment you had to live the days I have lived,
Where no one reached out to you as you drowned in your grief.
From the time I was a child to this moment today,
I face all my traumas, alone and afraid.

Her screams in the night, on the door's other side,
My brothers and I, too young to fight
The monster in that room with her that filled us with fright.
My house was not a home, but simply a space,
That housed all the terrors that I've had to face.

These are the first tears that I cried,
The ones of neglect and the trauma inside.
I was conditioned to numb myself to this type of pain,
And try as I might again and again,
These sorrows they follow me. They always remain.

If for a moment you could stand in that place
Would you? And could you?
And how long would it take?
To reach for that child who stood alone and afraid?
How would you treat her? What would you say?
What would "you" do, if it were you,
And that little girl alone in a room?
How would you treat her? What would you say?
Would you bring her small comforts, or just walk away?
And leave her again, alone and afraid?

She is her, and I am she, that lost little girl is me.
Neglect was prevalent all of my life,
These are the tears I have buried inside.

If for a moment, you could see the things I have seen,
From the eyes of a child, to the eyes of a teen,
Would you judge me, and snub me, knowing all of these things?
What would you say? What would you do?
If for a moment, you had to live in my shoes?

Where your house was not a home, but simply a space,
That housed all the terrors you had to face,
These things never leave you, they just never do
These are the steps I had to take in my shoes.

So you spend your life trying to find the comfort you crave,
Needing your home to be that safe space.
And what would you do, if in that space you would find
Neglect and rejection all of the time?

How long would you last in that place you call home?
How long would it take, before you just had to go?
And how many nights do you think you could take,
Crying yourself to sleep, alone and afraid?

If for a moment, you had to stand in my shoes,
Which path would you take? Which way would you choose?
Would you stay in that home where you stood all alone?
Where you pursued the love of those all around,
And try as you might, no love did abound?

Would you stay in a place where your voice had no sound?
Neglected, rejected, and put down?
Would you stay in a place where your rights were all bound?
Where everyone else was protected no matter what they would do,
Where all the snickering and bickering were directed at you?

If for a moment, you had to stand in my shoes,
Which path would you take, which way would you choose?

From Broken to Becoming

I was a victim of a childhood I didn't choose,
Why would I volunteer for further abuse?
I've seen enough pain and taken enough blame,
Why would I choose more of the same?
I've cried enough tears all of these years,
I've chased after love but was never enough.

I've spent too many nights diminishing my light,
Until all that remained was the scent of my flame,
I've walked enough miles, carried the burdens of fake smiles,
Dying inside, from all the pain I would hide.

What would you say, what would you do?
If for a moment, you had to live in my shoes?
Which path would you take, which way would you choose?

If for a moment you had to feel the pain of my past,
How long do you think that moment could last?
If for a moment, you had to stand in my place,
How long would you stay, alone and afraid?
Neglected, rejected, and taking the blame?

This house was never my home, but simply a space
That housed all the terrors that I had to face,
Neglected, rejected, alone, and afraid.

Part I
The Story

1

Cracked Walls in a Glass House

With a heavy heart I put the last piece of packing tape across the last box of my ridiculous stuff. I added my new Phoenix address and the label "Box 15" and just stared at what was left of my life here in Oak Harbor. I was taking a new job in Phoenix and leaving my husband behind, still unsure of where this was leading us, but knowing that I was being pushed through it.

We had been fighting for years now, lots of unsettled hurts, and too many things said and unsaid that brought us to this point. We had been struggling through being a blended family, parenting differences, finances, cultural differences, our history, and fighting to find the freedom to love one another without interference or influence.

A month before this day arrived, and two weeks before I made the decision to leave, I found myself curled up on the bed, facing the other side of the room, and crying myself to sleep yet again I was faced with the fact that I was in a stranger's home, alone, and had been for 6 years. He never turned to me in comfort that night. Maybe we were both just beyond that.

At the time, I was a practicing Buddhist, and no amount of chanting nor prayer could comfort me. I couldn't think myself positive through this. I couldn't imagine it better into existence. And so, I laid down my chanting and cried out to God.

I cried for the heartache I was feeling. I cried for the loneliness that was always there. I cried for my husband; for his words that this was all wrong and he didn't care if we even tried anymore. I cried for my stepdaughter whose heart hated me with intention. I cried for every day, every fight, every feeling. I cried for the isolation I felt. I cried for my family so far away. I cried for the job I was just told I was losing because of company cutbacks. I cried for the changes, still uncertain. I cried for the possibility of having to need my husband to support me, and not knowing if he could or would. I cried for everything. I cried, and I prayed, and I prayed some more. Before I knew it, the tears had stopped, and I felt myself falling asleep.

This had not been the first time I cried myself to sleep, but it would be the first time that I stopped crying before my eyes ever closed. At the moment, I didn't associate this with anything that I did differently. Little did I know that I would embark on a journey that would take me places I wish I had never been, emotionally and physically, but it would also take me to places I wish I had been sooner. Perhaps I would not have found myself in the circumstances we were in right now, where love existed, but was held captive to the bonds of our sin.

There has never been any doubt that we loved each other, but there were so many things preventing us from loving freely. Either way, here we were. We had been here before, but nothing with the same permanence that this felt like. I was done. He was done, and then he wasn't, and then I wasn't. But here we were a day late and a dollar short, each dying inside.

We were both deeply grieving the loss of the love we had so desperately been fighting to hold onto all of these years. But we knew that the tensions in the household were at its peak and there were one too many nights of tears cried, backs turned, and a coldness between us that nothing could warm nor console. I suppose the divide was long and wide, beyond our span of reach at the time. Emotions were escalated and unforgiveness was at an all-time high. It went on for so long that all our scattered pieces made no sense together, and even if we tried, there would always be something missing, something off, something lost.

We came together through an affair. An affair that broke two marriages, shattered a family, and caused so much damage to all involved. It felt right but was all wrong at the same time. Never mind that we seemed to think in sync, talk in sync...we had no right, not yet. But that didn't seem to matter. We would pay for that transgression for many, many years following, that eventually led us to box 15.

When we met, he had an 11-year-old daughter, whom he shared a deep bond with. So much so that even though I was there, in her mother's home, she chose to stay. Being childless myself, I had hoped that we could build a bond of acceptance amidst all the pain, and that although I was barren, I could be a mom. And try as I might, we could never bridge that gap. There were high tensions, spoken and unspoken hurts, energy that spoiled the air no matter what we were doing, where we were, or what was happening. It hung above us constantly.

His daughter was rightly hurt by all that had happened to bring us together. How can you explain all that brought us together to an 11-year-old girl who had to watch her mom suffer through this separation, and was forced to accept this new woman and this new life? Though this was not her ideal, she chose to live with her dad, which meant living with me. She had no time to heal from the divorce, accept the changes, nor rebuild her trust with her dad that she desperately needed to do. He knew the hurts we had caused, and this propelled him to overcompensate on everything that had to do with his daughter.

Every birthday and every Christmas, we would try to make it grand and better than the year before, hoping that this would slowly change things. But it didn't. Every party I ever threw for her, I was ostracized and made to feel out of place by her and all her guests. Every Christmas, my husband's stepson and his girlfriend would come over and again, I would be ignored and ostracized by all of them. It didn't matter that I put most everything under the tree. It didn't matter that I sacrificed every holiday to be with them instead of my family. It didn't matter that I put all my energy into making the events everything it could be and more. The fact is that none of this mattered to any of them, and that fact really mattered to me.

The Story

I would take his daughter on trips and try to buy her affections with clothes, phones, gadgets and everything else she would say she wanted, and nothing worked. My husband would buy her things, give her money, overlook her grades, and not hold her accountable for anything she did wrong, unless he was personally hurt by her. Everything else didn't really matter. I was constantly shut out of every conversation between them. I was the only other person in the house, and they would close the door every time. We made no decisions together. They made the decisions together and I would just have to accept whatever decisions were being made, even if they went against everything I believed. If she stole from me, nothing was said. If she ignored me, nothing was said. If she talked bad about me to him or anyone else, nothing was said. If she hurt me, nothing was said.

Guilt can compel you to close your eyes to all else, no matter the additional consequences or casualties along the way. This of course, brought out the worst in me. I would ignore her. Leave the room when she entered. Fight with him about everything. Blame her if I couldn't find something of mine. Stop the trips. Stop contributing to the home. Isolate myself from them, no matter what because I could see the ugliest parts of me coming out into this little world around me. I can be brutal with my glares, unrelenting with my silence, and I know how to emit the type of energy that can change the atmosphere of the room to an unbearable and uncomfortable place to stand in. When the emotions within me are restrained, the ugly comes out in my attitude and actions, and my passive-aggressiveness is anything but passive.

He would be angry at me without understanding why I was the way I became. He would take her side every time and secretly harbored frustration and deep anger against me. We couldn't talk about anything without it erupting into a huge fight. There was so much animosity coming from all of us, all the time. This was the overriding emotion that ran our household for six years, that brought us to this final box, shipped to an unknown future, separated. All of us heartbroken in some way, but desperate to breathe above the heaviness that we had all been living with for so long.

I distinctly remember the weight on my chest, daily. The shivering inside from all the pain I held in, screaming to be seen, screaming to matter; a deep bellow in my belly to be loved enough to see my hurts as well. I was not the lady of the house, though I took care of all the usual stuff a mother would do. I was not accepted, and I knew it, and above all, I understood it. I should have never expected that, nevertheless, I did, and I didn't receive what I needed.

This propelled me to lose the best parts of me, the part of me he fell in love with, the part of me that I loved. I lost who I was and could not find my way home. My depression was so severe that there were moments I just couldn't move, afraid of breaking. It got to a point that I would run and hide in the room whenever we had guests, no matter how long they would stay. I had been through so much in my life before this, but this truly was the hardest thing I had ever had to go through. The war within was made of many sides all battling to dominate. My nature fighting with my environment. My love fighting with my hate. My compassion fighting with my own pains. My kindness fighting with the hurt demon within. My world was falling apart on the outside because the fortress I spent my whole life building was crumbling on the inside. There was no tenderness that could have compensated for the anger, the hurts, the frustration, but most of all, the guilt. The guilt of loving a man that was never mine.

Yet here we were.

There is so much in that.

I was leaving in my car the next morning with my sister as my riding partner, and though I was anxious to leave behind all the hurt, I hurt leaving it all behind. This was my first loss. I grieved over it as I packed. I grieved over it as I signed the contract for my new job. I grieved over it as I signed the lease for my new home. I grieved over it with the grief ever-growing as each day passed and brought us closer to the day I would leave. I grieved over it as I talked with my husband about it. I grieved over it, and though it hurt, I felt it would hurt us all more if I stayed.

And so, the next morning, I would drive away from all that I had known, from all that I had loved, and from all that defined me for so long.

2

Sister, Sister

There is comfort in being with someone who has known you their whole life, who looks up to you, who enjoys being around you – just because you're you. Someone who has loved you no matter what ugliness they have seen in you, no matter what your past looks like. Someone who you could be unapologetically real with about everything and anything. And despite what they may do in the same situation, loves you enough to just listen and want only your happiness. This is my sister. And having her as my riding partner at such a difficult moment in my life was freeing. We didn't have to talk much about what happened that brought us on this road trip, moving me a thousand miles away. We didn't need to. Without being said, I knew she knew I lost myself for a very long time, and without judgment, she just traveled alongside me on my journey to find myself again.

And for the first time in a long time, I could be goofy and laugh from deep within about everything and nothing. The spontaneous girl that buried her identity in the silence of rejection was present in this moment with her. There was no joy in what was happening, but I was praying and hoping that I could find joy again, and because of this, my hope kept my spirits up as we traveled. Her love and her presence were exactly what I needed in that very moment when my world was changing with a sense of uncertainty. She kept me sane at a moment when my sanity was lost. She gave me the sense that I was on the way to becoming whole again, to becoming me again, a woman of strength and positivity, unafraid and full of life.

During our trip, we reflected on a lot of our family memories, on the distance from our native home, our mom and brothers, and all that we were without. We reminisced on everything and longed for some of what we left behind. I was all she really had in Washington, and she was all I really had, and here we were, separating with each mile we traveled. We left that unsaid – but it was there. I could not have done this without her. Little did we know that we would need each other far more than ever before in just a few short days, and that the need would separate us even more than the number of miles between us. We were about to be propelled into our own corners of the world, into a darkness neither of us could share with anyone, not even each other.

Our drive to Arizona was long, but too quick at the same time. She stayed for a few days and helped me find a bed, get some dishes, get necessities, ventured with me around my new town so I could become familiar with my surroundings. It was a godsend having here there with me, and a wonderful distraction to everything I was going through. Though I am the oldest and generally the one to step up for everyone else, it was such a beautiful experience to have someone step up for me, to take care of me, and to make me feel like that was all that mattered. No expectations, no need for compensation, no demands, just love. She reminded me what family looks like, feels like, and is, when family is the bond that keeps you.

She reminded me of the strength I have had throughout our lives and gave me the courage to reach for it again. She helped me see the beauty inside that I had buried beneath trying to be more to others who could not see my worth. She reminded me of the woman I once was, fearless, wise, full of love and laughter, and worthy to receive what I give. On this trip she was the cornerstone that held me up under all that was crumbling around me, and what she gave me would be what I would rebuild upon.

3
Little, Lost, and Led

I had been in Phoenix by myself for about a week and had started my new job, met my team, and was starting to get familiar with my new area and home. I was still very much unsettled in the house with nothing but a new mattress and box spring. The movers had not arrived yet, so my home was as bare as was my heart, a bit dark, a bit empty, and a whole lot lonely. Still, this was my journey to find me again, and to relearn who I lost, discover where I lost her, and work to bringing her back.

I had learned that the empty house made for great acoustics to sing as loudly as I needed to, wanted to, and without shame. And I sang often, which I'm sure annoyed my neighbors, but since no one banged on my door to quiet me down, I sang every day. I sang in the shower, in the living room, in the kitchen, in the car, in the pool. Wherever there was no one, I sang. It was my process for breaking out of the shell I closed myself up in. Even when I didn't feel like singing, I sang louder. Now that I look back on this, I may have been singing to block out the noises in my head and the silence at the same time.

I missed my husband. I missed his smell, and his touch. Even though we spent the last few months together, distant and apart, I still lived with the imagined closeness that had been before it just wasn't anymore. I could still see his eyes clearly as though he were right there with me, hear his voice in the morning and at night. I just missed him, and I had to force myself to remember that I missed me just a little bit more. It is impossible to give someone a part of you that you don't even own for yourself. You can't give someone all of you if there is nothing left of yourself to give. Realizing all of this was breaking my heart but was also the catalyst that pushed me towards change. I needed change. I needed freedom to be myself. I needed so much more that I had been without for so long, that not knowing where I was going, was good enough for me.

We still talked every day and we still argued on each call. We cried each time, and that never stopped. The separation was hard, one of the hardest things that I had ever done, and I am not a fragile, needy person, but I missed him beyond what I thought I would. When we would talk, I would start off by telling him about my day, my team, the job, the house as though we were doing this together. The small talk only led to deeper talks of hurts and heaviness. It probably was not healthy to keep doing this, but we did. Neither of us could stop. And so, we continued talking as though it were normal, and then talking, knowing it was far from normal. It was a continuous cycle that broke us each night. But we would try again the next morning, and on it went.

One morning he called me, but I had been out with some girlfriends at a bachelorette party the night before, and had a few drinks, one to celebrate the bride, one to celebrate my freedom, one to celebrate my new job, and on it went. What would happen on this phone call would change everything, and perhaps the night before was God giving me one more day of bliss before the breaking.

I had been so deep in sleep that he had to call me a few times. When I woke to his voice, he was more broken than usual and somewhat afraid. His next few words would break me more than any others we had ever spoken to each other.

"Honey, are you awake? I need you to sit up and tell me you are listening. Your brother Jerry has died. He committed suicide. We have been calling you all mor……." I don't exactly remember a whole lot of that moment, but I do remember the deep wail that cried out of my mouth. It wasn't my voice, but it was the sound of my soul breaking. And for the first time since I had been there, the empty house swallowed me whole, covered me in blackness, and took every last ounce of joy that I had desperately clung to. I jumped out of bed only to fall to the floor. There was no strength in my legs, everything that held me up, up to this moment, left me, and there I was, on the floor, shattered. He was gone.

My first thought was my mom, then my sister, then his kids, and as the eldest child, I felt the urge to care for everyone else even though I could barely stand by myself. I called my mom. No answer. I called my sister. No answer. I called my husband again. No answer. I was frantic and afraid. I felt so little facing this enormous tragedy by myself. My brother was gone. I was told that he took his own life, but in that moment there was no way that I could believe that. There was more to it, there had to be, and I needed to know what that was. Who did this to my little brother? Who hurt him? I was enraged, and this is where my strength came from. It was temporary, but it was just enough to give me what I needed. I needed it from somewhere.

I was here broken and alone. He left this world broken and alone. All of his life he struggled to survive and here I was trying to live my best life. I felt guilty for going out the night before when I realized that he was hurting so much that he was ready to leave this world at the very same moment I was starting to build mine. My heart was aching and I felt like just closing into myself and never leaving. He left me. He left my mom. He left his babies. He left us all. I left him. I left him there on that island and he needed me. I was so consumed with my life, myself, my job, my dreams, and he was breaking. I left him there. I didn't get to see him. I had been trying to call him for days and his home phone was not working. Each time I would call his home line, it would immediately go to static and click off. Something in me told me I needed to talk to him but I could never reach him, and he needed me.

He died alone with his perceived failures, his real hurts, and his cry for a desperate and imagined peace, a silence, rest. He died alone. He took a piece of me that I will never get back. He took with him the strength we shared as children when we were forced to face the brutal beatings of my mom by my father. He took with him the comfort we provided each other in the moments when we were helpless to help her or our baby brother. He took the laughter we shared to cover the trauma. He took with him the silent words we shared – the knowing we were all we had. I took that from him when I left Guam.

We had been through so much in our lives. So much for the little bodies we were. Our childhood was filled with trauma and sadness from the time we could crawl. The things we had seen had such an impact on me that I remember more than I should have from the age of 2. My dad yelling, and my mom screaming. Those were my first memories. Those sounds continued for years and I will never ever forget them. My brother Jerry was only 11 months younger than me, and he and I always held onto each other when the beatings would start. These were his first memories. By the time I was 3, we had brother Gilbert, newly born, to care for during the screaming, and the three of us just hunkered down, crying for our mommy, waiting until we couldn't hear her anymore, or until we cried ourselves to sleep, hoping to find silence.

At the age of 4, I had an appendix erupt and we had been locked in our home, with chains and bars on the outside of every door and window. I remember laying on the floor in excruciating pain, and my mom and Jerry were breaking through the floorboards of our home. She put his little body through the hole they made, and he ran up and down our village street screaming for anybody to help his sister. His bravery saved me that day. His love saved his sister. I believe it was at that moment that my mom knew she had to leave. To put herself at risk was one thing, but to nearly lose her child and risk the life of another, was more than enough to pull her out. We would finally be free. Or so we thought.

The next relationship my mom entered was with a man that broke down our doors to set us free, stood up to my uncle and walked us out. He became the father of my sister, eight years younger than me. During our time with him, I remember trying to protect my brothers from him all the time. They would get hit or chastised for the littlest things. If they failed to put their bikes away, he would knock them on their heads with a wooden brush, or even worse, dangle them midair from the hair on top of their heads. Jerry and Gilbert never had it easy. Growing up was one struggle after another, and they never really knew the peace of simply being a child. Free to be. Free to laugh, love, and play. They never really knew the carefree happiness that comes with the rights of being a child.

As adults, we were still chasing some kind of peace and struggling to find true happiness, leaving our demons behind. We picked up new demons of drug use and drinking, often done together. It was the wrong path, but still, it was a path we walked through together until the day I decided that my life had to change, and hopefully they would follow in my footsteps too. At that point I left Guam hoping to beat the demons that followed us and held us in its grasp for many, many years.

All of my memories of our childhood flashed before my eyes and I broke, remembering our brokenness. He left this world broken still. Knowing this shattered my whole world, and I laid there on the floor and cried and cried until I fell asleep, hoping to find silence.

When I woke up I was in autopilot mode. I made the phone calls I needed to make and started to make the arrangements to go home. When I accepted this job offer they had given me a sign on bonus of $20,000. Had I not accepted this job, I would not have the funds necessary to get home or get my sister home or handle some of the financial needs for his kids and the family. Little did I know that God had been working in my circumstances before I even searched for Him. He gave me what I needed before I even knew I would need it. Before I even knew that I would need Him. But I was about to find out just how much he carried me through the last 6 years to this moment. The moment this world took my world away and changed me forever.

It would be a few days before I could leave Phoenix and make my way back to Washington to fly out with my sister. So, I would be stuck in the silence of my dark and empty home. I would be alone at a time when I needed someone, anyone, to get me through this. But I had no one there.

I had just started my new job one week prior to Jerry's death. I had a one-year commitment because of the sign-on bonus, which I needed at this moment, but I needed to leave more. But how do you leave a job that you just started, and tell people that still have no real personal investment in you, nor a real relationship with you that you need to leave, right after you got there? I learned of Jerry's death on Sunday and had to go to work the next day. I was faced with the task of wearing the mask of false bravado, standing when I needed to fall, talking when I needed silence, and walking when I was shutting down. There was also the fear of talking to complete strangers and hoping that there would be a way that I could go home to bury my brother and not place my new job in jeopardy and have to give back the money that I spent to get there, and the money I needed to get home and put my brother to rest.

When I got to work Monday morning, I was clearly not altogether there. But it was time to talk to the Director and break the news that I would be leaving. I was filled with fear because of what I knew of my new boss, which was admittedly very little, but enough to make me afraid of being too personal with her. Here is another sign that God had been working in my life before I knew I would need Him.

I walked into the Director's office and asked if I could speak with her, she agreed, and I closed the door. As soon as the door shut, the tears I had been holding in all morning poured out in full force, in front of a perfect stranger. I told her what had happened with my brother and that I would be leaving to Guam for 3 weeks. I offered to submit my resignation and offered to sign a promissory note to pay the company back if I would lose my job because of this. She stood up, took my hands in her hands and looked into me and told me that I could take all the time I needed and that my job would be there when I returned. That is the Grace of God and the provisions that He set aside for me for just a time as this. The right people, in the right place, at the right time. I still did not know God personally yet, nor was I searching for Him. But there He was, working through someone else to give me the comfort and courage I needed to face the most difficult days that I had to live through up until that moment.

The Director took on the burden of working with my team in my absence and made the necessary calls to HR to allow my absence to let me leave. Just like that. She has no idea what that did for me, and how pivotal she was in my search for Christ and in my search for healing. Her kindness, foreign to me, was the first open door that would begin my journey to God.

I headed to my new shell of a home and started to pack. As I was packing, I was overwhelmed with weakness and fell to my knees on my bedroom floor. At that moment, a vision of brother's final moments, crying amidst the branches came to me. I saw his tears. I saw his brokenness. I saw his desperation for peace. I saw him cry out and then I saw an angel bring him comfort. I saw a light in the trees take him from the branches and wipe his tears, and I felt the peace he had been searching for as if I was him in the tree. I know it sounds crazy, but all I can tell you is that I was there when he left this earth. And he left this earth in arms that loved and comforted him. It was at that moment that I knew I needed to find God. There was an urgency deep in my heart that told me I needed to forgive those who took my brother from me. It was that moment that propelled me into his embrace. Every pain, every shattered piece of me was made whole for just that moment and I knew, those weren't my broken pieces, they were Jerry's. And for the first time ever – he found a love unconditional, he found peace.

I can't explain the vision, even to myself sometimes, but I know it was as real as it was to Jerry in his last moments. He let me see. He let me in. And this changed everything I thought I knew.

That night, I was so compelled to find God. I drove around my surrounding area to find a church. I wanted to find a church that I could go to for service and I needed to know how to get there when the courage would come. As I drove by one of the churches, there were people there at 7:00 pm walking in. They were dressed casually and I felt the calling to go in. I parked the car and timidly walked toward the open door. A woman that was walking in greeted me like she had known me forever. She walked in with me, had me sit next to her, and during the bible reading, she guided me through it. Once the reading was over, they asked if there were any visitors and if we would be willing to share what brought us there to their small group meeting. I don't know where my courage came from, but I raised my hand and shared the death of my brother and my need to find God in all of this. She took my hand and told me that I was safe and covered by His wings now, and that He would get me through this, and that this was just the beginning. She told me I was not there by accident, and she was amazed to see the Holy Spirit working in someone's life because she had never really witnessed it before that moment. This was the beginning of my journey home.

When I got back to Washington, I had a couple of days until our trip to Guam would happen so my husband and I went shopping to find Jerry clothes that he would wear during the viewing and last respects during his service. My husband tried on several suits for Jerry. It was a sobering reminder at how precious life was and our petty differences were long forgotten in those moments. He helped me through the necessary stuff. The hard stuff. I was about to clothe my brother in the last thing he would wear on this earth and had my husband not been with me, I could not have done it. I wanted to give Jerry something he would be proud to wear, brand new, without worry about money. If only I gave that to him when he was alive. But he was gone. And this was all I could offer, a day late and a dollar short.

4
Through the Eyes of a Child

My sister and I arrived on Guam to be greeted by my brother Gilbert. It was a bittersweet reunion because I was so happy to see Gil, but one of us was missing. We had such a long embrace filled with love and sorrow, and it lasted long enough for me to feel all the years we missed together. It has always been our thing as a family, to laugh about anything and everything. The four of us together could laugh for hours about everything and nothing all at the same time. We tried to keep that going during our reunion in the time following our arrival, but the heaviness of our missing brother hung over us and changed our laughter to the unseen tears of our silent cries.

When we finally arrived at my mom's house, the house and yard were full of people there to pray for my brother. In my culture, we hold 9 days of public prayer and gathering to allow everyone to come together in mourning for the deceased. There were people we grew up with that I had not seen for years present to pay their respects. I walked numbly through the crowd, extended my thanks for them being there, and gave hugs to all those who needed one from me. But inside, I was screaming "Get out!" I wanted to be alone with my family, to talk with my mom, and my brother, and my sister, and all the kids. It was so hard to be there. I didn't know how to be there. I don't know how I made it through, but I did.

When I saw my mom, I went forward to hug her but just like me, she pulled out her reserves and became a statue of strength for the crowd and for us. There was no breaking through that wall that night, if ever. But I could see the devastation in her eyes and though I wanted desperately to comfort her, I knew there could be none. She was Jerry's rock, and he was hers. And he was now gone. Gone from her sight, gone from her embrace and she would never be the same.

Family on my dad's side was there with my dad, and I could see that he was broken by my brother's death, but we had been estranged for many years, and I didn't really have it in me to comfort him. Looking back on it now, I wish I had, but there were still many unsettled hurts from my childhood that I held onto, and part of my brother's struggle in life, I still held against my father. This was all too much, but I am my mother's daughter, and have the same persona of strength that I can muster when the moment calls for it.

My bravado broke the moment I saw his kids though. I cried as they all surrounded me and held onto me so tightly. I could feel their little hearts breaking and I broke beneath that weight. I knew that I had to hold it together for them. I had to bring the joy to them while I was there. I had to be the light that they needed to get through the first tragedy that they would have to face. From that moment on, throughout the entire trip, they never left my side, no matter what. They must have known that I needed them as much as they needed me. And together, we would make it through the first days of experiencing this painful loss. I am the godmother for all of my brother's children, both brothers. In that, I have a deep connection with them, no matter what. And this was clear to me as all the kids surrounded me, I had to be the strong one again.

As the crowds died down, and just the family remained, I was asked again, what I wanted to be done with my brother Jerry, whether a burial or a cremation should be had. I didn't want the responsibility of that choice, but I had to choose anyway. I went based on something my brother said in passing years before. If ever he died, he didn't want us to make a big deal out of it, and he didn't want to rot in the ground. Though I wanted to have him buried, and my mother wanted to have him buried, I kept hearing his voice and his words, and so I opted for cremation. That was the hardest decision I ever had to make, and because I couldn't make that decision on my own, I fell back on his own words to me years before. I still struggle with that decision, as I still struggle with the story that he took his own life, but something kept pushing me to look beyond that and be the peacemaker amidst the sorrow and make the choices he needed me to make for him.

The emotions were so high on all sides, from the kids to his wife and eldest son, to my mom, to myself. There were arguments, accusations, and competition over everything. It was a whirlwind of escalated emotions, harbored hate, and secret suspicions from us all.

From what I knew, of my brother's death is that he had been arguing with his oldest son, and then his wife, and there were words that were said to him that brought him past the point of even trying anymore. I was told that he went out into the jungle in the middle of the storm and never came home. They got worried and sent out a search party into the jungle hills and that's how they found him, hanging from a tree with his knees to the ground. . How do you hang yourself and fall on your knees? Your body would automatically fight that. I didn't find this part out until after the funeral. Maybe that's why I kept hearing his voice over my own suspicions. I kept feeling the push to do what he wanted me to do. But still, he was on his knees. They said it was suicide.

I just cannot see that. And so, I had always harbored a secret suspicion that there was more to his death than anyone would ever admit. But I kept hearing his voice that all he wanted was peace and forgiveness, and so it took every last ounce of goodness in me to push myself to find forgiveness in myself for anyone I felt responsible for all this. I don't know where the strength, forgiveness, and peace came from, but I know that it was not my own, but even more so, that it was there when I needed it. And as I faced the days leading up to and after the funeral, I needed it more than ever.

We spent the next few days cooking, cleaning, and preparing for the nightly rosary. We stayed busy with everything, and this helped to keep us focused and off the firing range. When we weren't cooking or cleaning, we were out shopping for everything that would be needed for the evening and for the funeral.

I was also asked to prepare the eulogy, and I am so grateful that I would be the one to do this. It was such an honor to relate who my brother really was to those that only knew him on the surface. Though it was a difficult thing to do, I did it from the heart and it was perfect…to me. I also created a slide show of every picture I could get my hands on, from anybody and everybody that had pictures, then put a song list together for the service. Although each picture broke my heart a little more, there was also small healing in each picture, each song, and each word that would be the expression of our love and our loss to those who would gather with us to mourn the death of our beloved brother, son, and father.

The funeral was beautiful. The place was full of people coming to pay their last respects to Jerry. It was so packed that not everybody could make it inside the building, and cars were lined up the roadway as far as the eye could see. There were dignitaries, people from our childhood, family, friends, and people I had never met that came. I never did make it outside though, but I heard that it was an amazing site and during the last prayers, a huge double rainbow appeared above the funeral home. I wish I had seen it that day. It would have been like I was there as he said goodbye.

When the services were over, they needed two people to witness the cremation, and so I went in with his oldest son. I watched them put my brother in the furnace and I felt every memory I had of him go into the fire. The only thing I remember feeling was my heart, squeezing within itself, as the last of my brother went into flames. I will never forget this moment, though I had learned at some point, to bury the memory deep in the recesses of my mind and my heart. Over the years, this memory would creep out and overwhelm me. The memory of holding the hand of his son who stood there stoic and silent and void as we watched my brother burn.

The rest of my trip home was a blur, with the exception of the time I got to spend with all the kids. They ate with me, slept with me, and cuddled up against me. I remember drawing faces on their chins and having them lay upside down as I recorded them talking. This would be the last real laugh that his kids had for many, many years to come. It was the laughter that they needed, that I needed. It was the best moment I had back home, where pieces of me still lay unsettled and broken. Pieces of me went up in flames and became ashes of the strength I once carried, ashes of the joy I once gave out, and ashes of a love that fueled my purpose; Love for family, love for laughter, love for overcoming all that we had overcome together. My reserves burnt in that furnace, and I wasn't sure how I would maintain who I was when so much of who I was had been defined by what we had been through together.

No one will truly understand the traumas of our childhood nor the strength it took for each of us to survive the memories in our adulthood. No one will truly understand the cord that kept us close despite the distance in time and miles, was also the cord that kept us bound in shared sorrow. It was through this bond that my bond with his children was birthed, developed, and cherished above all the forces that wanted to keep me in unforgiveness, bitterness, and anger. It was this bond that built a love within me that extended to his next generation, his legacy, his pride. His children represented the love and connection that I needed as I clung to my brother who was no longer here. "Take care of my babies," was all I could hear from him after he left this earth.

I wanted to take them home with me, protect them, and care for them the way my brother had always wanted to, tried to, and gave every part of himself to do. Their mom would not let them go which was understandable considering the loss they were all facing already. The only way that she would consider it is if I took her eldest son first and once he was settled, we would send for them all. This was my hope anyway. This was all I had to cling to. The promise that I would take care of his kids for him, was the only hope I had to bridge the gap between our worlds now.

5

The In Between

In the year following Jerry's death, I reached for God like never before. I found a little church just down the road from my house that allowed me to just sit there in a corner, cry if I needed to, sing if I wanted to, and hear words of healing that my soul desperately longed for. I found healing in those walls, and I found God on a personal level. My hunger for Him could not be diluted by anything, and this was the start of my journey to the deepest, most meaningful relationship of my life.

During my initial walk with God, I had a deep need to help others and so I brought my little brother to Arizona and brought my brother's oldest son out from Guam as well. It was a struggle with both, but somehow, there was a sense of atonement in taking on the challenge. The challenge in itself kept me focused on helping others, but also kept me neglecting my own hurts, which in the end was detrimental to my healing, but somehow became a blessing to them both as both found their own walk with God, or at least, began their own journeys to finding Him. This was also the catalyst to me finding my purpose; bringing healing to the broken, and helping others find beauty in their own ashes through their own journeys that would transform their entire world.

I did not know, until this very moment, as I write these words out, that this all served a purpose to me finding my purpose. I was able to see the pain in others, look beyond my own, find the compassion needed to reach them, and guide them through to their own relationship with God. This is still a work in progress, but we each walk our own journeys at our own pace, and this too, is a lesson in itself.

While I was still searching, I found it hard to face the real pains within my family and help them through theirs. Though my brother and sister and I had a tight bond, none of us could reach the other. Somehow, without being said, we all chose to struggle with the death of Jerry alone. I wish I were able to see outside my own pain back then and reach out to them, but I didn't. We left everything unsaid. We barely talked after the funeral and when we did, we kept everything above the depth that we were all drowning in. It is strange, how even though we were experiencing the same tragedy, we still could not talk to each other through the sorrows that we all felt. It was as if we were protecting our pain from everyone because it was all that we each had left of our brother. It was our little treasure that none of us were willing to share.

Now that I have gone through the deaths of two brothers, I realize how tragic our silence really was for us all.

Over the course of my year in Arizona following my brother's death, I struggled to maintain the same purpose I left Guam with when he died. I struggled for the strength to help his son through his own darkness. While there, he made connections with people that kept him on a path of drug addiction, and he began to lose more of himself every single day. Because I knew that this behavior was rooted in sorrow, regret, and shame, I did not know how to bring him out of it. I did not know how to love him through it. I did not know how to help him overcome it, and I felt myself failing my brother by failing his son.

Grief compels you to make unhealthy choices to supplement the loss. This was his journey and process, and though I knew that it would only keep him bound to that guilt and shame, I didn't know how to save him. All I could do was pray for him each night, that God would keep him safe, and He did. While he struggled to maintain focus on the reason he was there, I struggled to maintain reason to keep him focused. All I could do was put him in God's hands and pray that he could find himself through all of this. I know that there is a purpose for everything, nothing is random, and all things will come to serve a greater purpose in the end, but boy is it a struggle to believe that when it is happening. And so, I closed my eyes to what was happening, and gave my struggles to God each night and each morning. And somehow through this, He still gave me the ability to love this child no matter what he would do.

God gave me something to focus on while I fought to hold it all together. I made some really good friends, who helped me through the tough times by simply sharing their time with me. I also made my name at work, and quickly became a strong leader amongst all the other leaders in our call center. It gave me a sense of purpose and value and for that I will forever be grateful to those who helped me realize my worth at a time when my failing my brother was all I could really see. Though God was not the center of these relationships, through them, he centered me while I was shattered.

Once I fulfilled my year, I headed back home to Washington, as my husband did not want to leave there for Arizona. He had his family there, his business, his home, and everything that was familiar to him, so off I went, back home. The next year would end up being one of the toughest for us as we battled the banks to keep our home, struggled through the blended family matters, and still had unspoken hurts between us that we never really resolved. I returned back to our normal, but I had changed. Everything in me had changed, and we all still carried the hurts from before. The only difference was that I was now carrying grief like I had never known before. This escalated our tensions in the family. On top of all this, we were facing bankruptcy, repossession of our home and my car, restructuring of his business, and leaving the place we once called home.

We ended up finding a place that seemed to be a godsend. Another event where the right people, at the right time, were present in our hour of need. My husband found a tiny ad in a paper that neither of us barely ever read, that claimed waterfront property. And although it was out of our price range, which in reality was zero, he went to meet the owners anyhow. During his meeting with them, there was a connection and somehow, they struck a deal, owner financing, with time for us to get on our feet first. He had found a beautiful property with old growth, a giant pond, on top of 14 private acres. The owners installed a new well and moved a house onto the property for us. We lived in an RV for the first year while the home was being prepared and this gave us much needed financial relief. All at the right time, for the right reason, with the right people. This was truly God at work for us before we even knew we would need Him.

It wasn't long after we moved into the house, that I received one more dreaded phone call. My aunt called to tell me that my brother Gilbert was found dead on the side of the road, beaten to death.

At that moment, my entire world and everything in it came crashing down around me. I received the call while I was driving home, and I barely made it there. As soon as I walked into the door, I collapsed into my husband's arms, and cried like I have never cried before. No words, just a deep guttural cry that took everything out of me. Somehow or another, I was able to convey what I just heard, and he just held me while I cried. And cried. And cried.

Once I was able to compose myself, I immediately went into autopilot again. I made phone calls to everyone on Guam trying to find out if it was true. I called my mom. No answer. I called my dad. No answer. I called Gilbert's girlfriend. And she didn't even know. I called the mother of Gilbert's daughter and she confirmed it was him. And I cried some more.

Once I had cried all I could cry, I decided that I would drive the hour to my sister's house and tell her in person. She did not need another phone call to hear that Gilbert died. So, I dressed myself, got a bag of clothes to stay the night there, and my husband and I got into the car. We drove there in silence for I had no words to express my pains, and he had no words that could console my heart.

When I arrived there it looked as if they were all preparing to retire for the night, but I knocked on the door anyhow. When she came out, I told her that Gilbert had died, and just like me, there was a moment of unbelief, and when I told her how he died, she screamed out her pain in my arms,

"Nooooo, not again!" She wailed and sobbed, and I held her silently as her tears screamed out my pain. That was the hardest thing I ever had to do. And even now, I am reliving that pain all over again. Our families just sat to the side waiting in silence. What else could they do? No one knew the depth of our grief, and even she and I could not work through it openly, so we just held each other until the silence was all we had left.

From there everything else was a blur. I could not see past my sorrow. I could not talk through my pain. I could barely function enough to talk to my mom, so I didn't. My sister made the phone call and I just sat there.

Because of what the two boys and I lived through together, because we shared deep tragedies at a young age, because I cared for them during the hard times, it was like I was losing my last child to another tragic death. But it was more than that, so much more. No one outside the three of us could really know what it took to survive what we survived, and now they were both gone, and I was left, alone and afraid. Afraid to breathe, afraid to talk, afraid to move, afraid to feel, afraid to think. I didn't know what to do with myself, so I just sat there.

Over the next few days, we had booked our trip home, our family came to see us to support us through another death that stole all that we had left. Nothing helped. Nothing made sense. Nothing consoled me. Nothing. There was simply nothing. The two people in the whole world that knew me best were both gone. The two people who knew my deepest childhood traumas and the person that I became because of it were both gone. The two people who knew how to reach me through thought alone were both gone. My partners in life, my confidants, my ride or die people were both gone. My heart wasn't just broken, it was shattered into a million pieces, brought to dust, and scattered into the raging winds. Gone.

When we arrived on Guam, Gil was not there this time to pick us up, and our rock was now gone away. He held us together when Jerry died. He kept me focused on the here and now, and now he was no longer here, and I could not focus. I felt myself slipping away into the darkness and I just didn't even care. I remember nothing of the flight. I remember nothing of my arrival back on Guam. I remember nothing. It's as if I blocked out everything so I could make myself believe it wasn't happening…again. We were still grieving losing Jerry, and now Gil? What else? Why again? What was happening?

I wasn't the strong one this time around, and I didn't care to be. This was the start of my journey into the darkness that I would fight over the next three years. I stopped praying. I stopped calling to God. I just. Did. Not. Care. Although I sang Amazing Grace at his rosary, that was all I could muster. And I did it for Gilbert. Period.

At the time, the only grace I could see in my life and my circumstances was that I was able to stay with his girlfriend and their new baby. His baby became my focus. She became my rock. She became my comfort and that was all that mattered. She was the spitting image of Gilbert, and I loved her all the more because of it. Even at her age of 4 months old, she had his attitude and his demeanor, and his smile. I needed her more than she will ever know. I just needed to be near her, for I could see him in her, and I needed to see him to get me through his death.

6

The Path to Healing

Over the next three years following Gilbert's death, I struggled with belief, I put down my faith, and fell into depression and allowed grief to consume every part of me. I lost my fight and I didn't care. I had no one to help me out of this darkness and I was surrounded by others that kept me there.

The turmoil in my home just continued to grow. And it was as if they didn't care what I was going through, what I had lost. The demands grew and the coldness in my home enveloped me and stirred up hatred and unrest in my soul. I found the ugly in me, and I just didn't care anymore. Before Gil's death, peace in my home was my purpose and I would do everything and anything to compromise my needs to meet the needs of everyone around me. After Gil's death, I gave up on what others needed, for no one even attempted to give me what I needed at a moment that I needed them most. They never asked, never bothered, made things even harder and colder, until I finally got to the point that I was done.

I was done being forgotten. I was done grieving. I was done being the least in my home. I was done being rejected. I was done with the pain. I was done with the games being played at my expense. I was done being overlooked and mistreated. I was done taking the blame. I was done with them looking past me and my pain and causing me even more. I was done putting myself last. I was done.

My grief had reached its apex and I realized that I had no one. My husband was not there for me like I needed him to be. My stepdaughter was not there for me like I hoped she would be. And my family was going through their own process of grieving, that I found myself alone in this chaotic mess in my mind and the darkness of my brokenness until I just couldn't take it anymore.

I was so lost. I was devastated, not just by the loss of my brothers anymore, but even more so, the realization that I had no one. The two people I dedicated my life to did not care. I was done. I was done pretending like it didn't hurt. I was done hiding my feelings under the rug. I was done putting myself beneath their feet. I was done being disregarded.

What had gotten me to this point was my birthday. My birthday was the catalyst that brought me out and into the need for healing, for love, for hope, and for freedom. A week before my birthday, we celebrated my husband's birthday at our house. I cooked a big meal, we had his kids over, and all seemed perfect for the first time. But the weekend following, brought me back to reality. It was my birthday and not one of them reached out to me. Not one of them texted me. Not one of them thought of me at all. Most of my birthdays in this family have been that way, but this one broke me. And when I told my husband how much it hurt me – again, he said nothing. That is when I knew that I needed to care. I needed to care for myself, my healing, my heart, my life. I needed to love me. I needed to put myself first. I needed more than I would ever get in this home. All these years in this home, every birthday I had been made to feel less than worthy. Every Christmas, I have been made to feel the least of them all. Every gathering I had been made to feel isolated and unwanted. Every. Single. Time. But this time, I was done. Granted, the grief I was already feeling heightened my sensitivity to everything else, but still, I knew I wasn't getting the two things I needed above anything else, kindness and peace.

I finally realized that I wanted peace. I needed peace. I needed healing. I needed joy. I needed happiness. I needed value and worth. I needed more than this family would ever be able to give me. I was done settling for less than I deserved. I was done being the forgotten one. I was done.

No one really knows what it took for me to stay all these years. No one really knows the tears I have cried behind closed doors, in my car, shopping alone, out in the yard, sitting alone on the couch, in the kitchen, at work. No one knows the peace it truly robbed me of every time they would come over and ostracize me in my own home. No one knows the pain in my heart that would grow each year, each event, each moment that he never stood up for me. No one knows the deep grief I had over the loss of my marriage to the childish behaviors I have had to endure in my home just to stay there.

All they see is what I don't do for them. They never see all that I gave to be there. It was a mentally and emotionally exhausting roller coaster that I would endure over petty things, but I was already battling the biggest emotional fight of my life. And I was doing it alone. They just didn't care. It was then that I realized that I didn't need to care either. I was released from that bondage and I chose life, love, hope, joy, recovery, freedom, acceptance, beauty, healing, and wholeness. This place could not take any more of me. I had nothing left to give it.

I had gotten to a point where I needed to be numb to what was happening in my home and in my heart, that I would try to find anything to turn off the emotions. I started gambling, and win or lose, it didn't matter. I wasted countless hours in the casinos, I drank like there was no tomorrow. I sought false validation from anyone that would look my way. My mind was out of control. I had an addiction that kept me numb to what I was really going through. I knew this addiction. I knew this pattern of mine. I knew it from my growing up years where I turned to drugs to block out the pains of my childhood. And now I had turned to gambling and alcohol to block out the pains of my adulthood.

I knew it was happening and I didn't care. I didn't care if I blew my entire paycheck in one hour. I didn't care if I had to struggle without. I didn't care that I had to lie to hide where I was. I didn't care. I was in a tunnel and was willing to keep following that path into the unknown. There was comfort in the dark. There was a relief from my pain in this second life that

I was living. There was nothing there and that was exactly what I needed. I needed nothing. I wanted nothing. I gave nothing. I received nothing.

I was spiraling out of control. I recognized that the girl that stood strong against all the abuse throughout her life had fallen. I recognized that the woman who pulled herself out of drug abuse, mental and emotional abuse, physical abuse, and every other abuse you can imagine, gave up and started to abuse herself. I recognized that the woman who was determined to push against all odds had lost her strength. I recognized that the woman who defied everything that came against her gave up her fight.

And that is when I cried out the cry that would change my life. That is the cry that pushed me out. That was the cry that screamed out "I am tired of hurting!" That was my cry for help. That was the cry that released all the pain I had been carrying. That was the cry that shook me at my core. That was the cry that reminded me what I was worth. That was the cry that validated who I was. That was the cry that told me that I mattered. That was the cry that showed me that this place and its people did not deserve me. That was the cry that said, the petty, every day digs no longer had power to move me deeper into depression and isolation. That was the cry that allowed me to let go and be at peace with letting go. That was the cry that gave me my freedom. That was the cry that God heard. That was the cry that changed my entire world. That was the cry that pushed me into my destiny. That was the cry I needed that would finally lead me onto the path towards healing.

7

The Storm Before the Calm

I moved out of my home and moved into my sister's house. I tasted freedom and had a sense that life was about to change, that healing was closer than it had ever been. I needed to be around her and her family. They provided me with stability as the rest of my world came crashing down. It didn't take long for me to start to find clarity in all that had happened, rediscover my strength, and begin to invest in myself again. I stayed with them for a couple of weeks until I found the perfect little rental. It was a log cabin trailer home in a run down trailer park, but I loved it. It gave me a sense of hope that new beginnings often bring.

Within those two weeks, I had found my humor again, rediscovered my joy, found a sense of purpose, and was optimistic about this new beginning. I slowly started filling my little trailer with furniture and all the necessities that would make it a home. When I left my marriage, I left everything behind except my clothes, pictures and mementos that meant everything to me, one spoon, one fork, one knife, and two plants. Everything else stayed behind. I had very little, but I had everything all at once.

I started accepting invitations to social events, began widening my circle of friends, and living with a sense of adventure that I had not felt in a very long time. I committed to making every day count, and no longer counted the days that were behind me. I began the process of putting my book together and in two months, the first draft was completed. It was during these two months that I realized that God had placed me right where I needed to be. Though the tower fell, His hand was on my life. I woke up between 2:30 AM and 3:00 AM every morning without an alarm clock, and this was my God time. I never missed it, no matter where I was, what day it happened to be, it was the most important time of my day.

I sensed Him with me every waking moment. I felt His strength pushing me through to keep going. I talked to Him, and His Spirit talked back to me in many ways, every day. He blessed me financially, so I had no worries about my new start. He blessed me with friends to keep my spirits lifted. He gave me a reason to wake up each morning. I could feel Him walking me through my journey every step of the way. I discovered my purpose, and it was within these pages that I started finding my healing.

I could feel myself getting stronger and felt the peace around me growing. I started to understand what I had been through and why I had to go through it all. He gave me insights on my struggle, helped me overcome my grief, guided me on my quest to rediscovering self-love. I knew I was on the right path.

Once the book was nearly done, I started spending more time with friends and finding my voice again. Though I had once been this girl before, it all felt brand new and surreal to me. Life was a new adventure, and I intended to live it to its fullest. It wouldn't be until later that I discovered that one of my earlier journal entries would be the prediction and warning about my newfound freedom.

"Remember to focus on why you are on this earth and do not get lost in your freedom, lest your freedom becomes your prison."

The more comfortable I became with my friends, the more open I became with my feelings. This led to an emotional affair with one friend in particular. I felt peace in his presence and could talk about anything without fear of judgment or condemnation. I had never experienced this type of connection where two people could communicate on such a deep level on just about everything. This connection quickly became an addiction and I found myself wanting more.

It seemed to fit the path I was on. I was cautious because of what I had just been through, but somehow, I found myself letting my guard down. I laughed louder, because I could feel it from deep within. I was able to be myself, and this was such a foreign concept to everything I had lived and learned to believe up to this point. It was easy, no demands, no expectations, just easy. I am in no way making excuses for what was about to take place

I felt an instant soul connection and didn't even think about the effect this was really having on me. I recognized synchronicities and little things and found myself really looking at what my inner self was telling me whenever I was around him. None of this was planned but I couldn't deny what was there, what was happening, nor what I began to feel on a much deeper level. At some point, this relationship became physical, though it only happened once at first, it was enough to change my perspective on where it could be headed. New life, new beginnings, new relationship??? Leave it to me to find deeper meaning in everything, but to me everything that happens has a deeper meaning.

The problem – though I was separated and living in my own home, I was still legally married. Never mind that I hadn't really taken the time to heal. Never mind that I had not allowed myself to really look at all that had happened. Never mind that I had not fully processed the emotional baggage that was weighing me down because I wasn't ready to deal with it. Yes, the book provided insight into the events of my life and the impact each one had one me, but I had yet to dive deeper into the whys and whats of my ownership in those events. Yes, I was for the most part, isolated, and learning self-reflection, but I had yet to give myself the necessary time to end the cycles that brought me to where I found myself.

It was about at this point when my husband started really pushing a reconciliation, but I was still steep in bitterness and resentment for all that I lacked in my marriage, all that I felt, and all that I needed that was denied me. I had already resolved in my heart that I was done. I had reached a breaking point and I knew when I left, that for me, it was over.

He started off wanting to talk about the divorce over dinner, then his calls and texts became more frequent. He wasn't ready to let me go, and I didn't know how to handle this. Our talks started turning into crying spells, arguments, and conversations that went on repetitive cycles that just drained me. And still, I would answer the phone, or respond to the text, and it would all begin again.

I knew I was done, but I was also a self-proclaimed martyr who had no boundaries for self-preservation. I was a glutton for punishment if it meant that I was saving someone else from feeling hurt, or lack, or need. This was an internal battle that broke me over and over again. I was fighting for my right to find peace while battling the chaos in this relationship. At many points during this repeating cycle, I found myself flooding emotionally until my emotional responses became full blown mental and physical breakdowns. I didn't know how to stop it without losing my right to choose my own path to healing. I found myself continuing the cycle to prevent an outburst or argument, but every time I answered, it became an outburst of emotions that escalated into an argument anyway. It was more destructive than simply not answering the phone or text or door.

This of course, increased my resentment and I became angry that my emotional needs were still overlooked. That my need for healing was still not a priority if it meant that he didn't get to walk on the journey with me. This propelled me to follow the path to freedom more fiercely, more determined, without shame. I spoke my truth, and at times, spoke it harshly. I told him how I felt, with raw honesty. I told him that I no longer loved him that way and asked him to let me go. I explained my need to find peace and healing, and with bitterness, would spew the reasons I couldn't find it with him. I even encouraged him to see other people. This was a battle between love and hate where there would be no victor, a war of worlds, both a painful past and a hopeful future. This was a war between a heart that felt deeply and a mind that held the memories of heartbreak. To shut the door would be like shutting down who I was, who I strove to be, but not shutting the door was taking away all the love I started finding for who I truly was. Though I knew this, the war continued.

He explained his desire to fix things. He tried to demonstrate his love for me by his expressions of his need for me, and the brokenness he was experiencing because I walked away. He would buy me things and drop them off at my place or do things for me without asking. He put up security cameras on my trailer and would go out of his way to drop off things he thought I would need. I knew what he was trying to do. He was trying to demonstrate what he could do if I were to give him another chance to save our marriage. But I also knew that it only built on my resentment towards him, because I felt cheated knowing it was a day late and a dollar short. He could have saved the marriage before I left. He could have saved the marriage when I came back from Phoenix. He could have saved the marriage before I went to Guam. He could have saved the marriage when my brother Gilbert died. He could have saved the marriage when I read him my journals, showing him how broken I really was. He could have, and he should have, but it was so hard to look past all of this and I found that I no longer wanted any of it anymore.

I hated rejecting him because of the guilt I felt hurting him, but I was hurting. I was rejected. I was pushed aside when I needed him the most, and I refused to give him the comfort that I craved but lacked all those years. I saw his brokenness, but I was angry in an unhealthy way, and at times I was relentless. It was not like me, but I also didn't know who I really was anymore. I just knew that I was done being the me that I was in our marriage. I pushed him harder to find someone else, to go on dates, to open himself up to possibilities aside from me. He did and he started seeing someone. I started feeling a sense of hope when he told me. I had hope that he would find happiness, but even more, selfishly, that it wouldn't be up to me to fix him. I could let go.

During this phase of our separation, my relationship with my friend intensified. It was exactly what I wanted because it had no emotional demands on me. But…I depended on it to be my source of happiness in a very unhappy phase of my life. That wasn't his responsibility, and I should have never expected that of him either. We talked openly about it, and I realized that what would have felt like rejection didn't. And I realized that I liked that part of me, okay with the pace of someone else's journey. He stretched me beyond my limiting beliefs about my needs from others and even more so, my own ability to give myself a stronger, healthier me.

This is where the storm really began. I had fallen in love. And my husband was still in love with me. This began a very destructive pattern that lasted for 15 months and my actions and inability to take the right actions caused damage to us all.

During this time, my husband found out that I had been seeing someone else and confronted me about it. I had wanted to tell him months before that when he was starting to move on with his life, but I didn't. I knew that he would not be able to handle that kind of information, so I kept silent. There are so many reasons I told myself this was the right way to handle it, and that nothing good could come of him knowing. Now that I look back on it all, I wish I did. I wish I was brave enough to be honest. I wish I was strong enough to withstand the storm that would follow. I wish that I was able to close the door sooner and save us all from months of ins and outs, ups and downs, hurt and betrayal. But I wasn't.

I thought I was being strong when I filed for the divorce. I thought I was being strong when I had him served. I thought I was being strong when I stood my ground. But all it took was a little bit of guilt to break down those walls I built. They could not withstand the storms. That guilt grew and grew until I found that I lost my voice again. I lost my spark. I lost reason to get dressed in the morning. I found myself in therapy, on anti-depressants, breaking down in tears for no reason, at any given time, and it didn't matter where I was. I am typically a happy, optimistic, rainbows and unicorns, rose-colored glasses kind of gal, but during this period, I found I hated her.

I hated her weakness. I hated her lies. I hated her inability to stand up for herself. I hated her brokenness. I hated that she found herself on her knees sobbing. I hated that she started to lose her mind. I hated that she allowed herself to keep suffering and struggling. I hated that she didn't know how to say no and mean it. I hated that she lacked integrity. I hated that she felt guilty for needing peace. I hated that she stopped praying. I hated that she was depressed and anxious and afraid. Who was she and where was the girl I met again not long ago?

I found myself putting on a brave face but inside I was terrified, and I didn't tell anybody. I suffered in silence because I was ashamed of where I found myself again. Nobody knew just how bad it really was. I never really let anybody see what was happening. My husband saw me drowning in this turbulent sea of emotions because he was the one there when I would start to flood under the pressure and the pain.

My friend saw the girl I was fighting for because she had no fear with him. My conversations during the day would break me and my conversations at night would build me up. Nearly every day was the same, but at night I could let my imagination soar with possibility.

It wasn't fair to either of them, but every time something would happen that would give me hope for change, the cycle would start again.

It had gotten to the point where I contemplated suicide just to stop the war in my head. I didn't want to look into my distant eyes anymore. I didn't want to hope and then fall and then hope again.

One day I just stopped fighting. I surrendered to the idea that I would lose no matter what. So, I went back. I ended my relationship with the one person that gave me hope, and I hoped that going back would stop the madness. I believed that if it was the guilt that was killing me, then I would take up my old life again and the guilt would cease.

God has a way of taking our destructive actions and making them work for our good. It was in that decision that I realized that surrendering would lead to victory either way. I started to pursue reconciliation with my husband and gave my all to it. I opened myself up to the fights believing that once we got past it, that the second chance would change everything. This was not the case. This was God working to bring out the truth. If it was the guilt that took me away from my path and my calling, then it was the guilt that He would have to kill.

I gave saving my marriage 110% and exposed myself to long conversations and interrogations. I started to reveal truths that were long since hidden, knowing that you cannot build a solid foundation on lies. I strongly believed that the truth would set me free, and it did. As more of my truth came out, I started learning that he had lies and secrets too. He fell in love with someone online and he didn't want to commit to working on the marriage because it would mean hurting her. He was distant and cold but would show enough tenderness to draw me out into a perceived safe space to speak my truth. And then the bricks would come flying. I let them fly and took the blows and truly accepted ownership of my own failures. This wasn't enough. I took the label of a liar and a cheat, apologized for meeting someone and falling in love with them during our separation. I accepted the shame as though I defiled our bed, because I started to understand that in a sense, I did. I let the stones hit me until I realized that no amount of stones thrown would matter.

He pushed and pushed until one day everything changed.

He chose Christmas day to argue with me for twelve hours straight, no mercy. I flooded several times and that didn't stop it. I told him that I didn't want to do this anymore and that coming back was a mistake. He wanted truth and God told me to speak it.

I told him that I felt I had lost my twin flame and that I was ready to walk the rest of my journey alone. I told him how my brokenness gave him power and that I was done being broken. I was ready to take my power back. I told him that I am ready to be the quirky, free spirit that is questionable to him and everyone else, and that I would be her with pride. I told him that I missed that girl who was fearless and free, and that this relationship was taking the best of me from me. I told him I was done grieving. I was done hurting. I was done looking at myself through eyes of defeat. I was done.

I was done losing the best parts of me for the sake of a marriage that didn't support who I really was. I was done apologizing for needing healing and taking action to find it. I was done. And that is the day that God gave me my life back. I spoke my truth and my truth set my heart free.

There were many towers that occurred at this time.

The tower of my hope of saving our marriage fell when I became an option to an online partner on Christmas Eve and I lost that round.

The tower of my desire to keep trying fell when I realized that the brutality of the fights outweighed the desire to heal the wounds inflicted.

The tower of his commitment to saving our marriage fell when my truth was revealed, and he had to pull it out of me instead of me giving it all at once willingly.

The tower of my friendship fell when I felt betrayed by things that were said about me with malice and untruths no matter the additional damage it would cause.

The tower of my indecisions fell when I realized that we all have a choice, and we have a responsibility to make the choice for ourselves while understanding that all of our choices affect the greater good and those who surround us.

All of these tower moments revealed the truth in all that had been happening, and though not easy to see, allowed me to take a good honest look at where I was, where I had been, what was done to me and what I had done to others. It allowed me to look at the destructive cycles that we all contributed to and the person I became along the way. It allowed me to look beyond the illusions of the things in my life that were truly not good for me and allowed me to release the need to hold tightly to the shattered pieces, the half-truths, the fairy tales and all that I thought I "needed" to be. I saw what I became as a result of where I came from. I saw my desperation and I decided I didn't need her anymore. I saw my inner demons and found that life in the light is far better than living in a world of darkness, both internal and the one around me. I found that running harder from God, only brought me to the moment where I stood face to face with him, in all my sin, in all my ugliness, and in all my battered broken pieces, and He loved me anyway.

This chapter and the one following were entered after the book was on its final edit, because God said that if I am to find true healing and walk in His light again, that I must also speak of the darkness inside me. I must open myself up to judgment from others so that others could see the power of redemption. I must tell my story with the hurt that I too have caused others in order to demonstrate His grace. I must tell people about my own shortcomings and failures in order to demonstrate how His power changes us. I must tell people about my own self-loathing to demonstrate how His unconditional love redeems. In order to speak His truth, we must face the truth in ourselves, for He cannot fix what we refuse to acknowledge is broken.

8

Walking the Fire to Become the Flame

I have learned along this journey as pieces of me shattered and fell away that what falls away serves no purpose to building who I am to become. I have learned that just as we shed things that no longer fit us, we must also shed the things that keep us where we are. Whether they be personal beliefs, expectations of and from others, or an old way of being, we outgrow them and must grow from them, or we stay imprisoned by that which no longer serves us. Holding onto the pieces of you and your life that brought you to a place of breaking, will not leave room to grab onto what truly matters. And that no amount of love that you strive to receive from others will fill the empty parts of you when you don't honor and love yourself first.

I prayed for strength when my brother Jerry died, and God placed me in events that would test my strength to the nth degree to show me both my weaknesses and what I was truly made of. He showed me all that I had been through, sometimes in chunks when my mind was too fragile to see it all, and sometimes all at once. I can tell you that every single time broke me, and in the same moment, built me up. I learned to honor my history and where I came from, what I had been through, and what I survived. I learned that a heart that loves deeply breaks deeply, and that I wouldn't have it any other way.

I learned that to truly be valued, I must first see the value in myself, flaws, failures, and all. That what I carry is unique and special, and that one day, if it hasn't already, will make a difference in this world.

If I can reach just one person who still relives the memories of trauma in their childhood by showing them, that in the end, these are things that fill your life with purpose, then I have won. If I can teach them that going deep will reopen those old wounds that we tend to mask or hide, is the only way to find healing and wholeness, and that their darkness can become someone else's light. I have won. If I can show them that once they get past the pain they have been through, they will find the power within to heal another. And in the end, what is meant to break you, God will use in the most amazing way, to build you into what is unbreakable, then I have won.

If I can reach one young girl to show her that her value is not defined by what she can offer, or can be taken without her consent, then I have won. If I can show her that who she is inside is beautiful and worthy of more than anyone could truly know. I have won. If I could teach her through my own story that she doesn't have to deny herself the crown, she is worth so much more than she has accepted, then I have won. I would walk the fire to ignite the flame of her own power and would relive every single moment again to show her what she is really worth. She is a beautiful and creative creature who has lived though some nightmares to become the happily ever after in her own story, and she doesn't need a prince to have it. I have won.

If I could teach someone who is suffering in a world of darkness, struggling under the power of grief, that hearts do heal and the ones we lose never really leave us, then I have won. That when we finally come to a place where we can truly celebrate their life instead of mourning their deaths, we give them the freedom to guide us as we start learning to live again. We have won. If I could show others that because those who have left this earth love us, we have to live like we are worth it, then those who left us have won. You defeat death when you honor the life ahead of you. As God is Spirit, so are we, and so are the ones who no longer walk in the flesh. They are now part of the very air you breathe. Because I understand this, I have won.

If I could reach an addict who has lost their way running from their own reflection, that if they could look deeper into those eyes and find an amazing person worth fighting for, then I have won. If I could teach them that numbing themselves from the things that break them only keep them broken longer, then I have won. If I could show them that the value of the hardest experiences has the power to create an empire, then I have won. The struggle only has as much power as I believe I allow it to have, and I refuse to let any addiction take me under because I am worth more than I am willing to lose to the void. In this truth, I have won.

If I could reach a young wife struggling to be understood and teach her that personal value combined with a true loving heart can change any circumstance, then I have won. If I can teach her that we all have the power to define what happiness means to us, and if we pursue it from a place of self-love first, then we will find and create it in our lives with another, then I have won. We cannot give away what we do not own within ourselves first, and though this was one of the hardest lessons I had to learn, God made a way, and I have won.

Part II
The Prayers

Holy Spirit, reach into me and change my perception that has been clouding my mind and has left me confused. Fall upon me so much so that I can see my healing beyond what my eyes can see. Build me up so much so that my creativity returns that I may fulfill the Will of God.

Take my depression and crush it with truth and lift me out of the darkness that I find myself in. Fill me instead with joy and light that I may fulfill the destiny that has my name on it. Help me to keep my relationship with God my priority, to keep God as my only focus. Let all other parts of my mind and my life that have taken God's place for these seasons, fall away so that it no longer has the power to change my mind. Take it away if it does not serve my calling.

Help me to manifest my true identity in the eyes of God. Help me to let go of the me that I used to be so that I can become the me that God is calling me to be. Help me to restructure my mind so my priorities and beliefs are in full alignment with the Will of God, that I am fully able and capable of harnessing His power in my writing so that all who read it are inspired and know, without a doubt, that my message is God's message for their life, that they will know that they know, that God has never left them, and they learn the value of who they truly are no matter what they have been through.

Help me to fulfill the promises connected to my name. Keep me focused on Him. Open the doors of my heart and my mind to His voice, His guidance, His will, His clear instructions, and give me the will and the passion to fulfill them without question. Let all that held me back die today, so that I cannot continue to reach for it. Help me to trust God when He asks me to let the good things go that have nothing to do with my required growth so that I may find healing, fulfill my destiny and my purpose.

Teach me to act promptly when I am told to act, for I know that some things must go before I can truly grow. Prepare me, my mind, my heart, and my creativity for what is coming next in the kingdom, in my purpose for the kingdom. Prepare me for the part I play in His will for the people. Push me over the edge that I have been teetering on for too long. Radically change my whole life.

Take away the part of me that pushes me down over and over again and makes me forget who I am, who I am called to be. Remind me always that who I am is not a product of what I have been through and that what I have been through does not define me nor my purpose. Remind me that I am not the underdog.

Help me to walk with the confidence of Christ, that my life will make a difference in the life of the masses. Remind me that where I walk, God walks. Remind me that when I enter a room, God enters before me. Remind me that what I put out when my pen meets the paper, that what is written there is God-inspired. Remind me that what I have been through was preparing me to relate to those who are broken, that God can make them whole again.

Help me to break the curse that has followed women in my family from generation to generation. Remind me that this stops with me. Change my belief system that was built from all of this. Don't let my enemies define me and tell me who I am. Remind me that only God's definition of me is who I am. Take away the giants that move against my purpose. Help me to face them and bring them down with God's wisdom. Help me to stand up to those giants that I begin to love myself again with the love of the Lord.

Help me to break down what stands against my anointing for I am anointed. Help me to shake up what needs to be shaken so that what is not of God is sifted out and the only things left are set to serve His purpose, not just in my life, but in the lives of all those that I come to know, and who have come to know me through direct interaction, and through my testimony. Let my testimony be penned by the Power of God so that my own biases and beliefs cannot dilute it.

Help me to answer God's calling on my life. It is time. Remind me that people who love me and know me and will come to know me are waiting on me. Generations are waiting on me to own my identity, the real me. The me who understands the beauty of my process.

Place in me the ability to let go of what must be let go. Bring peace on those ties but let them go. Help me to surrender as God rebuilds what I thought was broken in me. Help me to surrender to the good-byes that must be said before I can take my walk with God.

Help me to surrender to the new level of belief that I have to have. I trust that you will not leave me here, that my brokenness becomes whole again, for I know that my story was written by God for a specific purpose, and I honor Him for all of it. Remind me that there is no chance in my existence, that I was formed with a purpose, and that all that has happened in my life had value, specific to this purpose.

Help me to see that what God placed in me has a place in His plan for those in this world. Place me in the right atmosphere with the right people, that will propel me to fulfill my purpose. Remove all the barriers and let them wash away in the old flow of what is now gone. If it serves no purpose, let it wash away, so that new water can take its rightful place. I am ready.

Cultivate belief in only what God would have me believe. Tear down what is not from God. Help me to believe differently, and in what cannot be shaken nor taken away, for it can only come from the God who loves me, unfailing, unconditional, and without barriers.

Help me to respond to this – always. Help me to move when you say move. Help me to let go when you say let go. Help me to distinguish the difference in your voice against the voice of all others. Help me to look past my experiences. Help me to look past my comforts. Bring me into who I am supposed to be. Help me to surrender who I used to be. Help me to put down what I cannot take with me. Help me to bring only the parts of my life and me that will build who you have called me to be.

Deuteronomy 5:28

The Lord heard the request you made to me, and He said, "I have heard what the people say to you, and they are right. Oh, that they would always have hearts like this, that they might fear me and obey my commands. If they did, they and their descendants would prosper forever. Go and tell them, 'Return to your tents.' But you stand here with me so I can give you all the commands, decrees, and regulations you must teach them to the people so they can obey them in the land I am giving them as their possession.

October 4th

Psalm 71:20-21

You have allowed me to suffer much hardship, but you will rescue me to life again and lift me up from the depths of the earth. You will restore me to even greater honor and comfort me once again.

It was five years ago today that my brother Jerry left this earth, and almost to the hour, I was awakened from my sleep. It is now 3:30 in the morning and I am wide awake. This was the first random verse I flipped open to.

It was five years ago that I accepted Jesus Christ as my Lord and Savior. He was the only one that got me through this storm.

Two years later, brother Gilbert died, and I found myself slowly dying inside. It has been a year now that I have been running from God, hiding in my grief and anger – lost.

Today is the day that I give my life back to Christ, my rock, my comforter, my strength. I am so lost right now and broken. I am desperate for change in me, my life, and the circumstances I find myself in. Oh God! Save me!

Psalm 77:3-6

I think of God and I moan, overwhelmed with longing for his help. You don't let me sleep. I am too distressed even to pray! I think of the good old days, long since ended. I search my soul and ponder the difference now.

October 31st

I woke up this morning @ 4:00 AM, and I laid in bed for 45 minutes trying and hoping to fall back asleep, but here I am 45 minutes later praying for peace in my soul. I can't breathe anymore from this heaviness, anxiety, frustration, sadness, and loneliness. I feel plagued by a thousand disturbing emotions and I just. Want. Peace. When I get this way, I sit quietly and my soul cries, and I pray. Today was no different, except that today I silenced my mind and picked up the bible, held it in my hands, with the simple word – "Help."

When my bible opened and my eyes hit the page, this is where it took me.

Matthew 9:6

Then Jesus turned to the paralyzed man and said, "Stand up, pick up your mat, and go home."

And so, I must. I believe that this will be the beginning of my journey towards healing. I need to be with my family so I am not screaming alone, and they are not screaming alone, and together maybe we can overcome our grief. When you are in the middle of grief, it is easy to rest on the hope and thought that it could be overcome. In reality, it is overwhelming, and you are suffocated with internal screams that no one can hear.

It is hard to be here in Washington, in this home, with people who can never truly understand my torment. It is constant. It doesn't stop. I just learned how to put a smile on my face as I go through it, but even that is harder than before. I need peace and at this point, I am willing to lose everything to find it.

November 1st

The last message I received was to pick up my mat and go home. It couldn't be more clear. I prayed for direction that I didn't have to decipher because I know myself. I can talk myself into anything, but of all the pages, and all the verses, and all the words in the bible, it took me there.

As I start my quest for healing and understanding, I continue my studies and this morning was no different. God gave me a reason.

Matthew 15:3

Jesus replied, "And why do you, by your traditions, violate the direct commandments of God? For instance, God says, honor your father and your mother, and anyone who speaks disrespectfully of father and mother must be put to death. But you say it's alright for people to say to their parents, 'Sorry, I can't help you for I have vowed to give to God what I would have given to you.' In this way, you say they don't need to honor their parents. And so, you cancel the word of God for the sake of your own tradition."

This verse tugged at me hard because it is yet another reminder of how my home is not really my home. When my dad needed me, I had to turn him away. My parents are grieving and just as lost as I am, if not more. To lose not one child, but two, and then have your eldest abandon you, I can't anymore. And I won't.

November 2nd

I was awakened again this morning at 3:55 AM.

Wide awake and prompted to rise. So here I am, on the couch, and ready to receive the word. I randomly flipped through the bible, and these are the verses that came to me.

Philippians 1:30

We are in this struggle together. You have seen my struggle in the past, and you know that I am still in the midst of it.

Timothy 5:8

But those who won't care for their relatives, especially in their own household, have denied the true faith. Such people are worse than unbelievers.

Revelation 3:1

I know all the things you do, and that you have a reputation for being alive, but you are dead. Wake up, strengthen what little remains, for even what is left is almost dead.

I believe with absolute certainty that God is telling me that in order to be healed, I need to help the healing of my parents. In this, I will find my peace. I don't know how to explain this to my husband, but I believe God will make it clear for both of us. And I am reminded again of my journal entry on 10/9/19 – For everything there is a season – and maybe my season here is almost over.

This would explain the distance we can't seem to bridge, the love we don't seem to feel as intensely as we once did, the need for each other that we used to cling to. My only peace with this decision is that I see God working in My husband's life, his business, his relationship with his kids, and it's almost as though God is preparing his life to be lived without me in it. This would have hurt before, but it doesn't. I have a sense of tender peace in my soul seeing his life transform into what it needs to be without me. His daughter is making it possible. That's good. That's God. I didn't know it when it first started happening, but I understand it now.

God pushed me to desperation enough to let go, let God, and to stop fighting and allow his Word to take me where I need to be. Even looking back to when I first started this journal, just a few days ago – I know there has been some healing in these pages.

I have known since Jerry died that God was preparing me for something, and it started in a little church in Arizona, in the farthest, darkest corner where I could cry during services without shame. And when Gilbert died, I knew that God was telling me that I needed to write a book to tell this story, about life, about death, and the lives that shatter, share, and heal together. But I let myself run from God for a while and grieve deeply. I now believe He planned that too so that I would have a greater sense of my tragedy and my healing – enough that my story can help someone else find healing, someone more lost than myself.

November 7th

James 1:21

Accept the word god has planted in your hearts for it has the power to save your soul. But don't just listen to god's word, you must do what it says.

Hebrews 12:12

So take a new grip with your tired hands and strengthen your weak knees. Mark out a straight path for your feet so those who are weak and lame will not fail but become strong.

Ecclesiastes 6:10

Everything has already been decided. It was known long ago what each person would be. So there is no use arguing with God about your destiny.

I asked Jesus what He wants me to know today and the words, "It is permanent," sounded out loud and clear. I can tell I am about to embark on a journey that will be hard, will hurt, but ultimately, hopefully, will bring me to wholeness. I really don't know where this road is taking me and as I face this crossroad. I must admit, I am afraid, but I do know that He will go before me, and I should not fear. I am leaving behind everything that I have known for the last 19 years and headed back to Guam, unsure of what will happen when I get there, but I know that I know, that I know that God is calling me home.

And so, all I can do is walk in faith with a knowing that the plans He has for me are good.

This is hard on my husband, and I pray daily that God brings him the comfort he needs, but it still scares me to think that I am hurting him in my quest for healing. I pray that God gives him joy beyond measure, even amidst the sacrifice and loss we are both facing. This is not easy, but it must be done so that God can use us in His plan for the better of all.

God, give us the strength we need to move beyond what is comfortable, with the knowing that we are moving towards what is right.

November 8th

Micah 6:8

The lord has told you what is good, and this is what he requires of you, to do what is right, to love mercy and to walk humbly with your god.

Micah 5:6

"In that coming day," says the lord, "i will gather together those who are lame, those who have been exiles, and those whom i have filled with grief...for now you must leave this city to live in the open country. You will soon be sent into exile... but the lord will rescue you there.

Galatians 2:2

I went there because god revealed that i should go.

People don't believe in god for many reasons, but i do, because he speaks to me. He speaks to me often. How would i know that i need to go? I am a runner yes, but this time is different. He is calling me home. He is bringing me beyond many words and verses, each one, each day, telling me to go. I think about my husband, but i must go. I think about my sister, but i must go. I think about my job, but i must go.

He has etched the faces of my father and mother in my mind so much so that when my heart waivers, he brings me yet again through many words and many verses directly to his instructions that i must go. I don't know what lies ahead of me, but i must go. I am afraid, but i must go. My heart is breaking at the thought of leaving, but i must go. He will make a way for me because he is telling me that i must go. And because i am listening, obeying, and sacrificing, he will protect me wherever i end up. He has plans and is using me to make them real, so i must go.

James 2:24

So you see, we are shown to be right with god by what we do, not by faith alone.

For some reason, he keeps bringing me back to this verse:

LAMENTATIONS 3

I am the one who has seen the afflictions that come from the rod of the Lord's anger, He has led me into darkness, shutting out all light. He has turned His hand against me again and again and all day long. He has made my skin and flesh grow old. He has broken my bones.

He has besieged and surrounded me with anguish and distress. He has buried me in dark places, like those long dead. He has walled me in, and I cannot escape. He has bound me in heavy chains…He has made my road crooked…leaving me helpless and devastated…He has shot arrows deep into my heart…He has filled me with bitterness and given me a bitter cup of sorrow to drink…

Peace has been stripped away, and I have forgotten what prosperity is… The thought of my suffering and my homelessness is bitter beyond words…I will never forget this awful time, as I grieve over my loss. Yet I still dare to hope when I remember this. The faithful love of the Lord never ends… For no one is abandoned by the Lord forever. Though he brings grief, he also shows compassion because of the greatness of his unfailing love. For he does not enjoy hurting people, causing them sorrow. We are filled with fear for we are trapped, devastated, and ruined. Tears stream from my eyes because of the destruction of my people. My tears flow endlessly; they will not stop, until the Lord looks down from heaven and sees my heart is breaking. But I called on your name Lord, from deep within the pit. You heard me when I cried, "Listen to my pleading." Hear my cry for help. Yes, you came when I called. You told me, "Do not fear."

November 10th

Matthew 16:23

Don't miss the truth of the truth.

Sometimes we choose silence because the truth hurts and as i try to pursue the truth of my life, i cannot speak it with the intent to wound another. But without the truth, we will never know the true condition of our soul. When you put a high value on harmony and repair, above what really is there, you create the dark holes that invade your soul and hidden truths will eat away at everything. Speak the truth in love. Don't pull away from god as he reveals the truth about you, for it is meant to love you and not to harm you. It is meant to love you through it and to who you are meant to be. Are you open to speaking the truth about you? Are you open to Jesus speaking the truth about you? He so desperately wants you to reach your full purpose. Don't create your own alternative but follow his truth for your life. Don't play it safe because it feels like a better option. Do the will of my father.

I need to do what he has asked me to do. Am i willing? Jesus says, "choose me," that is the only way you will truly live. Will you have the courage to lean in even when it is painful? This is the most important time to lean in because it is hard, and you need his power to pull you through with revelation and truth. Do not step away and delay following him. God wants you to do this now.

Wherever you need me to go, i will go. I will listen. I know that although this hurts, it is what you have called me to do. It takes a lot of courage to say "i trust you."

November 11th

Job 36:11

If they listen to god, they will be blessed with prosperity throughout their lives. All their years will be pleasant. But if they refuse to listen to him, they will cross over the river of death, dying from lack of understanding... but by means of their suffering, he rescues those who suffer.

November 14th

Inspired by Pastor Paul Shepard

"When you come face to face with the unknown, you are forced to make a choice…fear or faith."

Live like you have been saved.
Give like you have been blessed.

November 16th

I woke up at 3:05 this morning, and as usual, since i started my journey to healing, i am prompted to rise. I have been feeling out of sorts and out of place again. I told my husband how i felt about him choosing the lunch his daughter made for him at the last minute instead of the one i had already prepared for him, and it was like a switch went off in him and his attitude changed back to the semi-distant, semi-here roommate. Now that i recognize it, it doesn't hurt as much, but it does leave me wondering why i am even trying to come back. It isn't the event that disturbs me but rather that i have never been his choice. I have never been the one to be protected, stood up for, consoled, comforted, nor acknowledged. I am supposed to be his partner, but he would rather listen to a 19-year-old than take my advice on most everything. I know it seems petty, but it is the principle that affects me. I am his wife, but i have no say so in our lives, our finances, our home, our business. It has been this way for years. I feel disregarded half the time and i am just about at the point of giving up hope in this marriage. I am dealing with so much more and it really doesn't seem to matter. So, this morning, i will open the word for guidance.

Luke 1:78

Because of god's tender mercy, the morning light from heaven is about to break upon us, to give light to those who sit in darkness and in the shadow of death, and to guide us to the path of peace.

2 Thessalonians 1:11

So we keep on praying for you, asking god to enable you to live a life worthy of his call. May he give you the power to accomplish all the good things your faith prompts you to do. 2:15 With all these things in mind, stand firm and keep a strong grip on the teaching we passed onto you, both in person and by letter.

1 Timothy 1:5

The purpose of my instructions is that all believers would be filled with love that comes from a pure heart, a clear conscience, and genuine faith. But some people have missed this whole point.

Psalm 37:5

Commit everything you do to the lord. Trust him and he will help you. He will make your innocence radiate like the dawn, and the justice of your cause will shine like the noonday sun.   37:34   Put your hope in the lord. Travel steadily along his path.

November 17th

Inspired by CTK Bellingham: Pastor Grant

"Only god knows what is going to happen in the coming year, because he has a plan, and you are it. There is no greater love than this, to lay down your life for your friends. Jesus enters the space of our regular, everyday lives, in moments unexpected. That's him. Put yourself in that moment where he may ask you, "who do you say i am?" In that room. In that space. In that moment. In every room."

He is the one who changes me, who takes my broken pieces, and works in each moment, to make me whole. He takes me out of places where i am blindly looking for the peace and coming up empty. He is the one that comes to me and allows me to pour out all of my grief, without judgment nor persuasion. Jesus is the friend that i lean on when the rest of the world has forgotten me and overlooked my pain. He is my comfort in the darkness and the cold. He takes me out of my "stuck" places, gently easing me out, one day at a time, one step at a time. He is the one that comes to me and says, "you are never too broken for me." He knows every pain, every emotion, and every action i complete in this world, and in my head. He is the one who can relate to all my dark places and loves me anyway. He is my safe space in my own isolation.

Revelation 21:4

He will bring us all back together.

That's Him. That's the Jesus I know. He is with me always, even when I run from Him. No matter how far I run or how fast I flee. He is beside me, forever waiting to catch me if I fall. He is the one that keeps after me, reminding me a thousand times a day to just choose joy.

§

You're there on purpose. It's not a mistake. You will be home soon. That tension you feel in your heart will be eased away one day at a time, one step at a time. You come with a lot of baggage that you don't know what to do with, that's okay. There is something awesome about being picked by someone who could have picked anyone else, but he chose you. Your friend will never leave you. He will be there to lead you through the tough stuff. Although you are holding on for dear life, He will bring you comfort and console your soul. Jesus is there for you when you hurt. You belong to Him. He wants desperately to heal you. You are doing something really important. You are helping Jesus provide somebody else's miracle. Respond to God, and he will respond to your need. It's not the size of the gift, but rather, the sacrifice to help the hurting and they are hurting. Be there for them, you know why? Because that's Him.

November 21st

It's 2:45 in the morning and I'm awake. Let god take me where he will.

Corinthians 13:5

Examine yourselves to see if your faith is genuine. Test yourselves. Surely you know that Jesus Christ is among you, if not, you have failed the test of genuine faith.

I woke up thinking of a thousand reasons i am awake, reasoning my insomnia by thinking of everything and then coming to the realization that this is the time i can spend with god. When all is quiet enough that i can hear him. So, this verse is again, another indicator that all he has spoken to me so far is real and i will not fear his plans for me, for he is with me still. He never leaves me.

Habakkuk 1:5

Look around at the nations; look and be amazed. For i am doing something in your day, something you won't believe, even if someone told you about it. 2:1 I will climb up to my watchtower and stand at my guard post. There i will wait to see what the lord says and how he will answer my complaint. Then the lord said to me, write my answers plainly on tablets. This vision is for a future time, it describes the end and it will be fulfilled. If it seems slow in coming, wait patiently, for it will surely take place. It will not be delayed.

1 Peter 1:1

I am writing to god's chosen people who are living as foreigners. God the father knew you and chose you long ago, and his spirit has made you holy. As a result, you have obeyed him and been cleansed by the blood of Jesus Christ. May god give you more and more grace and peace... so be truly glad. There is a wonderful joy ahead, even though you must endure many trials for a little while. These trials will show that your faith is genuine. It is being tested as fire tests and purifies gold. Though your faith is more precious than gold. So when your faith remains strong through many trials, it will bring much praise and honor on the day that Jesus Christ is revealed to the whole world. You love him even though you have never seen him. Though you do not see him now, you trust him, and you rejoice with a glorious, inexpressible joy. The reward for trusting him will be the salvation of your souls. This salvation was something even the prophets wanted to know more about when they prophesied about this great salvation prepared for you…they were told their messages were not for themselves, but for you. And now this good news has been announced to you by those who preached in the power of the holy spirit sent from heaven. It is all so wonderful that even the angels are eagerly watching these things happen.

1 Peter 5:12

My purpose in writing is to encourage you and assure you that what you are experiencing is truly part of God's grace for you.

I have never read this chapter of the bible before, but it spoke volumes to me this morning that I just couldn't stop. I read it all the way through and could see the messages for my mom and just knew the verses that were specifically to me. What amazes me most this morning is that the term "genuine faith" came to me from two totally different books in the bible. It amazes me because as I have been waiting for enough money to buy my ticket to Guam, I started questioning whether I should still go or not.

My relationship with my husband has changed so dramatically since that day in the counselor's office where he was faced with the reality that he was never truly there for me when I needed him most, and even more so since he was able to witness this grief I have been carrying for five years, in its rawest form.

Anyhow, this change between us has made me question my decision. But this morning, again, I am reminded that it is not my own decision being made, but rather, the decision of God, to rescue someone who has been more broken than myself.

These past couple of weeks and this waiting period seems to me like God is working at strengthening our bond so that our love and friendship stands against the storms of separation. God has been working in mine and my husband's life separately while giving us each, together, an unspoken peace that is strangely united. I could be wrong, but that's just the way God intends for me to see it right now.

November 22nd

Romans 15:21

Those who have never been told about him will see, and those who have never heard of him will understand. 15:23 But now i have finished my work in these regions and after all these long years of waiting, i am eager to visit you… and i am sure that when i come, Christ will richly bless our time together…then, by the will of god, i will be able to come to you with a joyful heart, and we will be an encouragement to each other.

1 Corinthians 2:1

When i first came to you, i didn't use lofty words and impressive wisdom to tell you god's secret plan. For i decided while i was with you, i would forget everything except Jesus Christ. I came to you in weakness, timid and trembling, and my message and my preaching were very plain. Rather than using clever and persuasive speeches, i relied only on the power of the holy spirit. I did this so you would trust, not in human spirit, but in the power of god. But it was to us that god revealed these things by his spirit. For his spirit searches out everything and shows us god's deep secrets.

Our dedication to Christ makes us look like fools even now…we bless those that curse us. We are patient with those who abuse us. We appeal gently when evil things are said about us. Yet we are treated like the world's garbage, like everybody's trash, right up to the present moment…i am not writing these things to shame you, but to warn you…some of you have become arrogant, thinking i will not visit you again. But i will come, and soon, if the lord lets me. Even though i am not with you in person, i am with you in spirit…god has called you to live in peace.

November 23rd

I woke up at 1:30 this morning and felt the prompting that it was time to buy my ticket. And try as i might, to fall asleep again, the prompting would not leave me, so I laid there, phone in hand, with my husband snoring beside me, and purchased my ticket. I don't know why I feel a deep sense of loss and fear right now, but it is there and so here I am two hours later, pen in hand, seeking his guidance to remove my fears and remind me again.

It seems silly to need a daily reminder and I pray that God looks past my faithlessness and continues to gently guide me, no matter how many times I need to hear it, to overcome my sadness and fears, to build in me the courage i need as I travel into unknown waters. I know that I know that I know god is calling me to something bigger than myself, but still, I tip-toe lightly. Oh God! Build in me the courage I need to do what is right, the wisdom to understand, and the faith to go all the way. This is where he brought me today.

Proverbs 3:1

My child, never forget the things that I have taught you. Store my commands in your heart. If you do this, you will live many years and your life will be satisfying. Never let loyalty and kindness leave you. Tie them around your neck as a reminder. Write them deep within your heart. Then you will find favor with God and people and you will earn a good reputation. Trust in the lord with all your heart. Do not depend on your own understanding. Seek His will in all you do, and he will show you which path to take.

§

My child, don't lose sight of common sense and discernment. Hang onto them, for they will refresh your soul. They keep you safe on your way and your feet will not stumble. Do not withhold good from those that deserve it when it is in your power to help them. If you can help your neighbor now, don't say, "come back tomorrow and then I'll help you." Pay attention and learn good judgments for I am giving you good guidance. Take hold of my instructions, don't let them go. Guard them for they are the key to life.

My child, pay attention to what I say. Listen carefully to my words. Don't lose sight of them. Let them penetrate deep into your heart, for they bring life to those who find them, and healing to their whole body. Guard your heart above all else, for it determines the course of your life. Avoid all perverse talk; stay away from corrupt speech. Look straight ahead and fix your eyes on what lies before you. Mark out a straight path for your feet. Stay on the safe path. Don't get sidetracked.

November 24th

I don't know what it is today, but I have a deep sense of foreboding and anxiety. My depression is kicking in high gear right now. I'm nervous and uneasy and I can't shake this feeling. I opened my bible and this is where he took me.

Isaiah 40:1-2

"Comfort, comfort my people," says your god. Speak tenderly...tell her that her sad days are gone, and her sins are pardoned. You will open the eyes of the blind. You will free the captives from prison, releasing those who sit in dark dungeons. "Do not be afraid for I have ransomed you. I have called you by name, you are mine. When you go through deep waters, i will be with you. When you go through rivers of difficulty, you will not drown. When you walk through the fires of oppression, you will not be burned up, the flames will not consume you.

Jeremiah 29:11

"For I know the plans i have for you says the lord. The plans are for good and not for disaster, to give you a future and a hope. In those days, when you pray, i will listen. If you look for me wholeheartedly, you will find me. I will be found by you," says the lord. "I will end your captivity and restore your fortunes. I will gather you out of the nations where i sent you and will bring you home again to your own land."

November 27th

It's 3:03 in the morning and I am wide awake. I woke to a dream. In the dream, my husband and I were hosting a party and prior to the party, we promised to escape for a bit to meet for alone time and then return to our guests. During the party, for the entire dream, I was trying to get his attention to make good on his promise to me, but he never did. He spent the whole party with his ex-wife, his daughter, and others in their group, looking at pictures on his ex-wife's phone. They were doing that for so long that it ended up just being the two of them. When he finally came to me, he was on the verge of breaking down, so we went to our room and as soon as the door shut, he started crying. He was telling me that he feels so terrible because she had it really hard after he left her, and he felt so bad for putting her through it all.

I remember feeling and thinking, "You don't feel that way about everything I have been through. Why?" But I never voiced it. I just woke up feeling dejected and forgotten again. This of course led me down a rabbit hole of rolling thoughts on his current demeanor of distance and small remarks and digs. I feel like we are back to pretending and his affections are not sincere. There is coldness about him right now, not cruel, nor mean, just distant. So here I am seeking God's guidance because I am just tired of feeling this way and need answers. This is where He took me.

Psalm 77:1

I cry out to god. Yes, i shout. Oh that god would listen to me! When i was in deep trouble i searched for the lord. All night long i prayed, with hands lifted toward heaven, but my soul was not comforted. I think of god and moan, overwhelmed with longing for his help. O, my people, listen to my instructions. Open your ears to what i am saying, for i will speak in parables. I will teach you hidden lessons from your past.

JAMES 1:21

Humbly accept the word God has planted in your hearts for it has the power to save your souls. But don't just listen to God's word. You must do what it says, otherwise you are only fooling yourselves.

And now I am prompted to listen to the first message that pops up on my phone.

TRIUMPH OVER OPPOSITION - JOYCE MEYER

"Raise your voice in prayer. Father we are so sorry that we stood back passively and let things drift so far down hill from where you had originally brought us to. We must do our part and take our responsibility. I pray that you urge us to do everything that you ask us to do.

Anytime that you take a step to build your life, to build your faith, you will get opposition.

God help me do this right.

God has already given you what you need, but you need to believe it. You are only uncomfortable because there is a spiritual battle that is forcing the changes that will finally lead you to peace. Be encouraged."

November 28th

In desperate need for the Word of God. A deep hunger that satisfies my grief, not only the loss of my brothers, but also the loss of myself. I have felt discounted for so long that I feel a fresh burst of hope that God is using me to reach others. I know that my healing can only come through all this. Sometimes God's best miracles come through deep suffering. It is in those storms that we begin to recognize God in the small places.

The blessing is in the breaking. Some of the most blessed people you will ever meet have known a brokenness so deep that faith was all they could hang onto.

The greatest blessings come out of the hardest breakings. All it takes is a small ounce of faith. You cannot feed other people the bread of life without knowing the depths of sorrow that only come from death. Be it spiritual, physical, or mental, death can crush the spirit beyond your own strength, but faith. That small ounce of faith can show you a strength that you never knew you had. Through that personal breaking, you learn how to be a blessing to someone who is broken.

December 9th

I am headed to church in Bellingham with my sister and cousin, and I am filled with a deep gratitude as I recognize the people God has placed in my life that love me despite and beyond who I am and what I have done. With eyes wide open, I can see love from every angle and in all the faces that have been so common to me. That's the thing about it all. When we are willing to look beyond our daily circumstances and see the people within them, we can see the Hand of God gently nudging us to recognize His love. I see it in the face of my husband, who through his pain and fears of me leaving, has practiced patience and a need for understanding to support me through this very challenging part of my life. I see it in the face of my sister as she cries at the thought of my leaving, with a fear and uncertainty at what is happening with my mom at home.

I see Him in the love and generosity that my coworkers have shown me in their donations and acts of kindness. I see His love in my family that has traveled far to see me before I leave. It's in the small moments with everyone that surrounds me that I see Him.

For the past five years, I became so lost in my grief that my vision has been clouded in my darkness, but since I opened my heart to God again, I have seen him gently moving the gray out and bringing me into His light, His love, and His comfort that I and my family have so desperately needed.

May my renewed faith be the instrument that God uses to demonstrate His love for them. He is sending me back for my mom, and a few days ago He reminded me of my experience on the operating table as a child. He told me then, just as He is telling me now, go to your mom, she needs you. That is His love, and it has been there all these years.

In a midst of crises, we compartmentalize every fear we have that we can get lost in that muck. And for just one second everything is calm, and everything is silent, and it is in that moment that we can begin to recognize His peace and the courage we need to move beyond our crises.

Two contrasting pictures of our grief, and how we choose to experience it. Do I open my eyes to the comfort that is waiting for me? Do I close my eyes and stay in silent yet screaming darkness? It is all I have to hold onto with my brothers. But are their prayers making a way for my peace?

What do they see and feel about me and for me as they witness what their deaths have done in me? What happens when I realize that they too, loved me this way so my sorrow is now their sorrow, and does this mean that their peace is as shattered as mine? No, their prayers are to bring me the peace they now experience. His love has taken them in and removed all their pain and inner anguish, and it could be that this is the first time that they have ever known true love and peace without question.

This will be the first Christmas that I will be spending at home in 20 years. I am hearing the message to make the most of it. This is a moment that His love is being demonstrated to us all. I feel this so deep right now.

As I sit here in the church, writing in my journal, I can hear Pastor Grant's message, and know that God meant for me to hear this today as I have been struggling with my decision to go back to Guam right now. I am hearing the message to take the nature of a servant to those who have not found this peace yet, to service the people that God loves and wants to bring comfort to. Pastor Grant is saying that if I want to make this Christmas season great and not just good, to travel far to share this love, His love for those whose tears he has seen and whose gut cries he has heard.

§

He is calling you there. It is time. Service to the people is not about convenience, but rather, your calling. Show them in the most tangible ways that they are worthy of your love, your time, and your commitment to their healing. There may be times you will be uncomfortable, but do not fear. He goes before you.

His goal is not your own healing, but the healing of your mother. In serving her, you will find peace. Honor her. She needs you and the light that you carry within you. This is why you carry it. This was preordained the day you died on that operating table. This was His message to you then, and this is His message to you now. He has never forgotten her desperate cries. They ring in His ears every moment of every day. It is time. This is and has been your calling. You mom is your charge. She is the reason you lived. She is the reason you have been called. Stay present with her for she needs to be heard. She has suffered for so long. It is time to bring her peace and joy and love, unconditional, and without personal agenda. It is her time. She has been held hostage for too long.

He is giving you His power to help the helpless so that they are lifted from dark places so they can find their way home. You can have a good Christmas and do it your way, or you can have a great Christmas and do it His way. Choose humility. Choose service. Choose generosity. Choose sacrifice to light the way for a people who are lost in darkness.

December 12th

I arrived on Guam safe last night and was absolutely exhausted. I can normally sleep on the plane but sleep just wouldn't come. Ugh! It was a long trip, and i was rushed all the way through with an added tension in my belly the whole way.

It was nice to see everyone when i arrived. As is our tradition, we went to the Chinese restaurant that we always go to and i was able to have my honey walnut shrimp that i had been craving for so long. I can see everyone tip-toeing around me not sure what i am going through and what brought me home again, but still i am welcomed. It is a familiar hug in my soul, and there is nothing in the world like it. I am home and free to be me.

After dinner, i was spent. I was done. Sleep was deep and much needed. The tension in my belly is still here and it feels as though something big in my life just ended. Although my trip is scheduled for 3 months, the feeling i got from my husband was this was more permanent than i expected.

December 14th

It's been a bit uncomfortable here. It seems as though my mom feels my visit is an imposition. I suppose it is, and i probably should find other places to stay too. I believe that my husband, in his desperation to make me stay, reached out to her and caused this inner chaos i now feel. It takes a lot to shed off the years that have tormented my mind, taken my spirit, and hurt my soul, and it is still going to be a long road ahead of me. I pray for the strength and the staying power to get through all of this and move beyond what i have left behind.

We went to bingo the other night and we didn't really talk much. We spent the whole day yesterday at mom's house and still, we didn't really talk much. I know that she knows the main reason i came to Guam is because i am worried about her health. She said as much in the car and did not appreciate it. She feels as though a greater use of my thoughts would be in prayer instead of worry. Encouragement and belief instead of fear and doubt. I can understand that. But how do we get past this now that my husband has put in her mind that i gave up my life to come home for her. What she doesn't understand is that i also gave up my life to find me.

I flipped open a random page in the bible and this is where it took me.

John 2:4

Dear woman, that's not our problem," Jesus replied. "My time has not yet come."

And that's that. It amazes me each time. Out of all the pages, all the verses, all the words…it simply amazes me. I thank god for giving me the peace i needed right now. I knew it would be hard. Okay. And that's that.

December 16th

I just finished taking my hand-written journal and typing it up and realized that God gave me messages about my last entry long before the day arrived. He also gave me new insight today from my past writings about what I am currently experiencing now.

I am worried about mom. She is obviously very depressed, and this explains a lot of what I have been feeling. I should know. Conversation is hard when you are going through what she is going through, and her grief is 100 times greater than mine. We are often going through the same experiences even though we live miles apart and it is almost as if we are tethered to each other through our own personal struggles, yet we never really talk about them fully. I pray that we can get past the "middle" and move towards the bridge to healing and wholeness since we are together now.

She has been going through a few things on her own lately. She was recently told that there was a lump in her breast, but she refuses to go back for a biopsy. I understand this as she has already been faced with so much tragedy. The only thing I can do is pray for her and love her through any and everything. We also have not discussed a more personal issue that she let out to my sister that is definitely high on the scale of sorrow. She will tell me when she is ready. I cannot rush things just because I know in my heart why I am here. I cannot expect her to know what I know. Even if she read my entire journal right now, she could not truly know everything that is in my heart that I have yet to put on paper.

I just hope a breakthrough comes before Christmas, so we can experience the best the season has to offer and find healing in the meaning of the day.

Isaiah 38:4

Then this message came to Isaiah from the lord...this is what the lord, the god of your ancestors (David) says: "i have heard your prayer and seen your tears. I will add fifteen years to your life and i will rescue you."

December 17th

My husband has not called me once since I have been back on Guam. I asked him why that was, and he said he wanted to give me space. The sad thing is that I asked him for his support, not space. But I suppose it is easier to give someone space than it is to support them through some challenging times. I had been battling this emotionally since last night, and this is the verse the Holy Spirit brought to me.

> Galatians 4:27
>
> Rejoice, o childless woman.
>
> You who have never given birth.
>
> Break into a joyful shout,
>
> You who have never been in labor.
>
> For the desolate woman now has more children
>
> Than the woman who lives with her husband

What i got from this verse was that i am currently free to focus on my family and all those my brothers left behind. I am grateful for the opportunity and the time, but the sting is still there about my husband specifically. I supported him through all his family problems, his struggling business, and mortgage trials we faced. I was his cheerleader, his confidant, his emotional soundboard and that took a lot out of me. I have never really received that same kind of emotional support from him. This was the thing that drove me to Arizona, drove us to marriage counseling years later. I drowned in my grief, alone. What was the point in being married to him if the support has always, and still, only goes one way?

Marriage is supposed to be a partnership through life. I don't feel that partnership and i suppose, never really have been on the receiving end of having my emotional needs cared for and provided for. I believe i really need to ask god for a deeper understanding here because my heart, my mind, and my gut says that staying together is wrong. It is not god's plan for me. This marriage has brought me much hardship, much hurt, and much loneliness and god is trying to bring me out of all that.

I am hurt by my husband. He knows that and still responds short and distant. I told him to let me go when i was there so that i could move and secure everything before i left. He didn't. But he sure is showing me now that all that really matters is what he needs, feels, and he will protect that to the bitter end.

Corinthians 4:16

That is why we never give up. Though our bodies are dying, our spirits are being renewed every day. For our current troubles are small and won't last very long. Yet they produce for us a glory that vastly outweighs them and will last forever. So, we don't look at the troubles we can see now, but rather, we fix our gaze on things that cannot be seen. For the things we see now will soon be gone, but the things we cannot see will last forever.

Isaiah 52:11

Get out, get out and leave your captivity, where everything you touch is unclean. Get out of there and purify yourselves, you who carry home the sacred objects of the lord. You will not leave in a hurry, running for your lives. For the lord will go ahead of you, yes, the god of Israel will protect you from behind.

I was listening to dynamics of a blended family with Jimmy Evans this morning, as i was writing this entry, and this is what i heard once i was focused on the sermon again.

"I am not going back there. I am not going to let you (the devil) torment me with those thoughts. I take that captive. I thank god for this right now. The second thing is, i forgive everyone in my past, regardless of what they did or did not do. You see unforgiveness is an invisible umbilical cord that connects us with our past. It feeds our spirit from the past."

"You haven't forgiven. That is feeding your spirit. It's still feeding your disposition. Clip the cord. The devil is no longer feeding my spirit from my past. I forgive that person, and i bless them, and i move on."

December 18th

My last entry was about my husband and his silence during the time when I needed his support. It has been eating away at me for days, and I finally went to God in prayer. "I need clear direction," I said. And today, he brought me to a Joyce Meyer sermon online called, Don't Rush Anything, When the Time's Right, It Will Happen. In her sermon, she said God would shake things up to get what is not good for me out and that I need to let go of what he is shaking out to make room for all he is ready to bless me with. This also means letting go of people that are not good for me, to stick it out, press on, and trust God and continue to be a blessing to other people as I go through my own storm.

It isn't easy to face the fact that we are nearing an ending and I am beyond hurt that I couldn't trust my husband to support me through the hardest time of my life, but I know in my gut that this is the right thing. Although I love him, I believe I love the idea of him, and I love the him that he shows his daughter. I love the him that I didn't and don't have. We have been hurting each other for years now and it's time for healing for both of us. I am not sure what will happen with my stuff. I'm okay losing most everything I own, except for the stuff I have left of my brothers like pictures, Jerry's Kamyu (coconut grader) and Gilbert's pot. I would also like to ensure that all my pictures of my wedding and our time together are preserved and given to my sister, so I still have those mementos of a time in our life that was good. I hope he gives the same consideration and respect to my things as he did for his ex-wife's things when they separated. Either way, I will trust God and do good.

The next sermon that came up was also by Joyce Meyer titled Don't Be Afraid of Losing Someone Who Doesn't Feel Lucky to Have You. She started with the following verse.

2 Timothy 3

But understand this, that in the last days, will come and set in perilous times of great stress and trouble, hard to deal with, and hard to bear. For people will be lovers of self and utterly self-centered. They are lovers of money aroused by an inordinate desire for money and wealth… They will be without natural human affection, callous and inhuman…

She said that *"When people are callous, they can look at needs of others and not try to be the one to do anything about it. Somebody else should do something, but somehow or another, it's never them."*

This sermon is reminding me of my loneliness in his home for 6 years, and my loneliness for the past 14 years. It is reminding me of his not being there for me when Jerry died, or when Gilbert died. He never offered to help me at all. He never went to either of my brother's funerals, and he could have. Had I been a priority, he would have. He would have done it for his daughter no matter what. This is the basis of our relationship failures and troubles. He never sees the need to meet my needs. I am not bitter about it right now, but I am being reminded of this truth.

Joyce continued, *"For although they hold a form of religion, they deny the power of it."* This struck a chord with me because I have read my journal to my husband, told him about what I believe God is calling me to do, and demonstrated the faithfulness to answer that calling, he clearly believed that this trip was self-centered and a strike against him. No matter what my family is going through, he remains focused on the fact that I chose not to stay instead of why I was going. Healing for myself. Healing for my mom. Healing for my dad. Despite the fact that I bought a round-trip ticket, secured my job, and have a return date, he still treats me as though we have already ended our marriage. He never calls. Never messages me. Never bothers. Again, at a time when I need him most.

I have been struggling with this because I just don't understand his lack of care or concern. He says that I am leaving him with financial burdens, and this is his priority, and not the fact that I have reached my apex of grief. I needed him for 5 years and he was not there. I need him now, and he is nowhere to be found. I just don't get it. So, I will trust God and continue to do good. But the facts remain, and the Holy Spirit is really bringing them to light tonight. Reminding me, guiding me, instructing me, and releasing me from the bondage and captivity that I placed myself in.

"If everyone who considers themselves a part of Christ, were walking in love, we would not have the mess in our society that we have today. We

should be getting out in society and representing Christ, with the character of God, walking in love. But it has to be real love. True love. There are opposites to those as well. The kind of love that is no good is the kind we talk about, there is that which has no action to it at all. But when it comes down to really putting it to work in our daily lives, then we back off from that. It really is pitiful how much we talk about love but how little of it there actually is. Where were you when I needed someone? Where were you when they were talking about me? Where were you when I needed help?"

JOYCE MEYER

These are the questions I am faced with today that drove me away years ago and continues to drive a wedge between us.

"We need to start a war against selfishness and say, I am not going to live a life when I am the only person in it. God has a formula for solving our problems and that requires us helping someone else. This is a planted seed that allows us to reap the same and more blessings in the future. It all starts at home. Why is it that we are willing to do more for strangers than we are for the one we profess to love? He will sacrifice his time and money to help others, but never me. It's a sad reminder of what we lack.

Are we able and willing to even ask God to teach us how to love the way that he loves? That means that we are going to love when there is nothing in it for us? When it is just an all giving out instead of trying to do something to stay mad at somebody, it is the absolute worst thing that we can do for our own selves. It poisons our lives and is all based on feelings that are self-centered. I feel, I feel, I feel. Whether you feel someone has done something wrong to you, you need to give without expectation. One of the main reasons people don't walk in love is because love is an effort. And it will always cost you something. Time, effort, and pride. Swallow your pride. It doesn't mean that you let people walk all over you. It means that you wait on God, trust in Him, and do good."

JOYCE MEYER

In my sorrow, I needed my husband to show me love without expectation. I was going through the grief at my lowest. He could not understand my distance and lack of interest in everything. Grief robbed me of it all. I held back the power of it for a long time. I went through many stages before I got to this one. Instead of loving me enough to try to understand it and try to feel what I could possibly be feeling, he shut me out. It was easier for him to withhold emotional support instead of helping me fight the war that was going on inside me. Perhaps he knew he wasn't giving me what I needed and should have had from him.

This message opened my eyes and reminded me of what I have lacked, what I needed and need now, what I don't have, never have had, and what I should have had, and why I am where I am right now. I am looking for healing somewhere else besides my home, needing the love of my family as I am estranged from that kind of love in my marriage. I no longer need to understand it. I no longer have the need to pacify him while I am experiencing the worst I have ever gone through in my lifetime, and I have gone through a lot. I no longer feel that I need to do what he wants me to because it has been a detriment to my soul at a time when I could not afford to lose anymore of myself. I no longer need to search deep for the "added value" he brings into my life because I am reminded that we have both stopped adding value to each other long ago. Little does he realize that his love and tenderness would have been returned tenfold had he given it when I needed it the most. That act of kindness would have been the best thing he could have ever done in our time together.

I have been hurting and received no comfort. I have been depressed and tired and received no relief. I have been hopeless and received no joy. It is time to let go and let God give me what I have needed and did not receive. It is time for God to shake things up in my life and make room for the healing. That means I have to let go of all that is hurting me. This is something that I have to do on purpose whether I feel like doing it yet or not.

I am trusting God through this – everything in my life is shaking right now, and it is not easy to remember this in every moment. My study time right now has provided me with the insight that I needed to remind me – that I am trusting God through this – and to keep on trusting God.

December 19th

I am re-listening to the first message. Let Go of the Unstable Things In Our Life, and sometimes that means letting go of the people that you put your confidence in that need to be removed from your life. It is not easy when I am not ready. Though I am disappointed, I am not broken by this anymore. Though I was hurt by it, I am finding healing from it.

For a long time, God has been revealing the weaknesses in my marriage and showing me that this no longer has a place in my life if I am to do what I am being called to do at my next destination. I cannot do what I need to do while I am devastated and heartbroken. It isn't that he intended to hurt me this much, but he just doesn't have the capacity right now to help me while my world is shaking. There are people that I need to let go of before I can let God. I need to trust that God is working this for my good. Many of those things that are shaking are things that I don't need in my life. The less of the bitterness I have in my life, the more room there is for God to build a relationship with me.

I cannot focus on my lackings and still rejoice in the blessings. I cannot live under heaviness and still raise others up. I cannot be consumed with the ashes. He is burning up everything in my life that is useless, all my misconceptions, lack of trust, anger, resentment, jealousy, hurt and pain, and making room for that which is good for me. I cannot demonstrate the light of God while being drowned in these emotions. He is sending his fire and shaking everything in my life that can be shaken to remove what needs to be removed and getting me out of the cycle of going around the same mountain over and over again.

I need to allow God to do what he wants to do in my life – even if I think I don't want to. His message to me is that I can rebuild, but not under bondage to devastation. Life is not over. Life is just beginning a new chapter and no matter how devastated I am, He is loving me back into wholeness if I can just trust him. He knows where I am at and He will go to any length to help me and find somebody that He can love me through. He will meet my needs if I trust Him.

Isaiah 40:29-31

He gives power to the faint, and the weary, and to him who has no might, he increases strength causing it to multiply and making it abound...but they that wait upon the Lord, who expect, look for, and hope in Him shall change and renew their strength.

I can rebuild.

December 23rd

I had been going through some questioning emotions regarding my husband. As soon as i wrote my last entry, almost minutes after, he called. But our conversation was strained and stressful. Almost as though he were intentionally draining me of any potential peace, healing, and joy my trip could be bringing me. And there I was, crying in Kmart, in the middle of the Christmas shopping crowd.

I understand that the separation is hard on him at Christmas, as this will be the first one we have ever spent apart, but can he just, for once, think about me, and my needs, above his own?

We got through that weird and tough conversation. It went from me telling him i was shopping for Christmas to him accusing me of having intimate attraction to one of my coworkers who commented on one of my posts, to him saying it would be understandable considering he has not been there for me. This of course is not true. Not that i haven't thought that he didn't deserve me and that there are others that would care for me, but it is still far from the truth. I needed the support of my husband and family more than anything during these dark years. Needless to say, each call after that over the last few days has been normal and friendly, as it should be. During the Kmart conversation, i told him that i do want to talk to him, but not if each talk would end up with me crying again. I have had one too many years of that and enough is enough.

So, I have been praying about it because, to be honest, I have thought about just staying on Guam and starting anew. At least that has been the message I have been receiving each day. So, I prayed last night and this is where it brought me @ 3:40 this morning.

Lamentations 1 (every other line)

Deserted – now sits alone like a widow – she is now a slave. Tears stream down her cheeks – there is no one left to comfort her. Oppressed with cruel slavery – and has no place of rest – and she has nowhere to turn. Her oppressors become her masters – how bitter is her fate – taken away to distant lands. (7) In the midst of her sadness and wandering -there is no one to help her. Her enemy struck her down and laughed as she fell. All she can do is groan and hide her face – with no one to lift her out. "Lord, see my misery," she cries. (16) For all these things i weep, tears flow down my cheeks. No one is here to comfort me, and those who might encourage me are far away.

This scripture was a clear reminder of what brought me here – to my native land, far from my home. I was devastated and grieving – alone. I cried out, and god sent me on a journey to find him and to find peace and healing. The next scripture i flipped open was:

Galatians **4:8**

So now that you know god, or should i say, now that god knows you, why do you want to go back again? (17) They are trying to shut you off from me so that you will pay attention only to them. If someone is eager to do good things for you, that's all right, but let them do it all the time, not just when I'm with you.

I am still battling letting go. I am still battling wanting to be home again. I am still battling the directive to stay where i am right now. But i am still listening and seeking and praying.

December 27th

I woke up this morning at 3:09 AM, startled from a bad dream. In that dream, I had a conversation with my husband one evening about not having any friends, a few nights later, at my new job, there were 11 women who asked me to join them for dinner after work. I did, thinking "This would be great! I would be able to make some new friends." But as it turned out, on our way to dinner, I realized that I forgot my phone at home and was worried about not letting him know where I was the whole time, even though it had only been minutes after work. I remember being filled with so much anxiety that I left just after the drinks arrived, and before dinner because I didn't want to argue with him. When I got home, he was already angry, one, because I forgot my phone at home, and two, because for the first time in months, he was waiting for me to spend the evening with him. We went through a short argument of me trying to explain myself, to him throwing me out of our house and calling it quits.

I woke up realizing that I actually do go through these emotions on a regular basis with him. I am filled with anxiety and worry about his reaction often, especially if I am enjoying my time doing something without him. But when it comes to his time, I see him when I see him. I also realized that I am obviously worried that if I go home to him again, I am at the mercy of HIS emotions.

We have been talking about separation over the last few days, talking openly at first. He was nonchalant and mature in his approach. He wanted me to think about what I really wanted, and he would do the same and then we would make a decision together whether it was best to stay together or separate. Then he was texting me asking if I was ready to continue the conversation and if I thought about it yet. Almost as though he is forcing me to make the decision to divorce. So yesterday, I told him, that I would not be the one to make the decision this time, and it needed to be him. He started crying and telling me that he was so lonely and constantly doing things alone and that he didn't like it. I have only been gone for two weeks, and he has had his daughter there a few nights, had his granddaughter there another night, had the kids over one night, been to his brother's another, so really, there is probably a total of one week that he really has had to wake up alone and go to sleep without anyone home. The point is, I am on Guam because I need healing, my mom needs healing, and my mom is going through a health crisis that she refuses to talk or do anything about. I thought that if I came home that she would go to the doctor, but that conversation only brings up an angry response from her, so I really don't know what to say or do next.

Even here, I find that I am at the mercy of volatile emotions of somebody else.

I prayed that I would make the right decision regarding my husband last night before I fell asleep, because all day yesterday after our emotional phone call, I had been thinking about him and his needs and my love for him the whole time I was helping my mom. My mind was elsewhere again. So, before I fell asleep, I texted him the following message, "I love you and I miss you more than you know. I know I need you in my life because you are my best friend and I have never loved anyone more. Despite all that we have been through, I know that you have my heart and I don't want anyone else. Even if you decide that you need something more than I am capable of being right now, just know that I will always want you." He never responded. I can see that he is online now, and I know he has a routine of responding to every message first thing in the morning before he even turns to me. He has a sense of urgency to respond to everyone that sent him a message or commented on his posts. He feels the need to reply immediately. I have not received a response to my message yet, and it has been a while that he has been up. It is 3:53 AM for me, so it is now 9:53 AM for him. I don't understand why I am always last.

I fell asleep full of love for him and the need to let him know. Then I woke to this dream reminding me of my anxiety to please him and not upset him. Um, I am going through a lot right now and needed him to be the one to provide ME with the emotional support, but instead he is making me think that I am on the verge of divorce since I am here. Same old, same old. I hate this feeling and can see that I have been living with this fear of upsetting him for years that I never really enjoy anything I am doing at any moment that I am not with him, and I am afraid to enjoy myself when he isn't there. Even though I feel I am following God's calling not only for my mom, but my own healing as well, he just isn't there for me the way that I need him to be, the way he would be for his daughter, and the way I have asked him to be for me.

It is now 10:11 AM and still no answer.

JEREMIAH 5:1 - 5

"Run up and down every street in Jerusalem," says the lord. "Look high and low, search throughout the city! If you can find even one just and honest person, i will not destroy the city. But even when they are under oath saying, 'as surely as the lord lives,' they are still telling lies. Lord, you are searching for honesty. You struck your people, but they paid no attention. You crushed them, but they refused to be corrected. They are determined, with faces set like stone, they have refused to repent. Then i said, "but what can we expect from the poor? They are ignorant. They don't know the ways of the lord. They don't understand god's laws." But the leader too, as one man, had thrown off god's yoke and broken his chains.

JEREMIAH 5:23

But my people have stubborn and rebellious hearts. They have turned away and abandoned me.

ACTS 28:26 – 27

"Go and say to this people: when you hear what i say, you will not understand. When you see what i do, you will not comprehend. For the hearts of these people are hardened and their ears cannot hear, and they have closed their eyes – so their eyes cannot see, and their ears cannot hear, and their hearts cannot understand, and they cannot turn to me and let me heal them."

I opened up youtube and the first thing that popped up on my screen was a message from joyce meyer, titled "to be happy, we must not be too concerned with others." She started out the message like this:

> *"We are actually going to use the s word today, sacrifice. We act like it's a dirty word these days. Everybody always wants to know what they can get, not what they can give. Invest in yourself. Invest in your health. We need to live a life where we are not always trying to please ourselves, but please god."*
>
> JOYCE MEYER

January 10th

My last entry was 2 days after Christmas, and i have neglected my writing because i let my frustrations get the best of me. I allowed myself to sit on a roller-coaster of emotions, stopped reading my bible, and started to get lost in self-pity again. Although i have heard several sermons online, i did not record the messages in my journal and found myself getting lost again. Why do i allow these emotions to hold me in bondage? Because i love my husband. But what is love really? What does it look like, sound like, live like?

Yesterday, i heard a message by Joyce Meyer about love. Here is what I received from it:

> *"Love is in the fruit of the spirit. Love is seen in our behavior. Love is seen in how we treat people. Love is not theory, it is not talk, it is not in a sermon we preach. It is not a word we use. Because to be honest, that can just become something we say. But really, what i want to know is, are you going to be there when i need you? How are you going to treat me when i make a mistake? How are you going to be when i need mercy? When i need understanding? Are you going to just be with me only when i am a rising star, or are you going to be with me if i am ever going down? People can forget about you really quick. You could be the most important person in their life, but they can forget about you overnight."*

She quoted the following scripture:

1 Corinthians 13: 4-8

Behaviors of love – Love is patient and kind. Love is not jealous or boastful or proud or rude. It does not demand its own way. It is not irritable, and it keeps no record of being wronged.

> *"Love acts right. It is not conceited or arrogant with pride. Love is not rude. I wonder what would happen in marriages if we begin to practice better manners? It's amazing how we will act with somebody we want to impress, somebody we want to do us a favor; a boss that we want to get a*

good raise from. Compared to the way we treat our spouse behind closed doors at home. You know how I know you can control yourself? Because you don't act like that in front of people you want to impress...because I think with certain people, I can get by with it."

Joyce Meyer

This message really hit me yesterday because it made me take a long hard look at what we don't have in our marriage – on both sides. We have reached a point in our relationship where almost every conversation turns into something hard and hurtful, or has underlying messages that are full of hurts, both past and present. I am grieving and desperate for healing because I cannot give what I am empty of. I need his empathy and love and compassion right now, but he keeps bringing up that he is the sole person responsible for coming up with so much money. There are business taxes, employee taxes that are past due, the mortgage, property taxes, his truck, and everything else. While I agree that these are stressful, I have followed him through all this for years, and he promised that we would try it one more time for two years only, and that if it caused strife in our marriage, he would stop because he learned it wasn't worth it. We are going on year 4. But my empathy has faded. He has not followed me through the death of my brothers at all. So when is it my turn for his compassion, empathy and support? I am not holding a record of his wrongs, but I am reminded each time he does this knowing what brought me here to Guam, what he seen of my grief before I left, and knowing what I have been faced with coming here. He has quickly forgotten all of this. Or was it ever a true revelation into what has been happening inside me, as he said he finally understood before I left?

How can I focus on healing and truly facing my grief if I am constantly forced to focus on him?

I woke up last night at 1:00 AM and lay there trying to fall back asleep. Nothing really disturbed my sleep, but I was wide awake. Minutes later, my husband called me and told me that we needed to talk and come to a decision. I had no idea that we were still there. I thought that we had come to an understanding that I needed to be here, and above all, that he understood and would support me through it.

Our conversation quickly turned to an argument because I had asked if he was saying all this because his life and business were going smoothly, both financially, and with his daughter's help (which he brought up earlier by telling me how much help she was giving him, and that he didn't have to stress about much anymore,) but blamed me for bringing her name into our conversation. I really did not ask this with any malice nor ill-intent, I really was just curious if this is the reason he needed an answer and a final decision on our marriage.

Up until this moment, our conversations were civil, even friendly. It was almost as if he was worried that if I came home, I would interrupt or ruin his successes. He accused me of bringing her up in every conversation and blaming our problems on her. In every conversation prior, I had always made it clear that it was never about his daughter, but rather about what I lacked from him, as his wife and partner, and above all, the woman that he professed to love.

In any case, the conversation ended, and I ended up crying – again. I suppose I needed this, because this brought me back to seeking God. I kept getting the message that I needed to read my entire journal again to remember God's promises and guidance and that these entries would be my reminder to His purpose in my life. I didn't do this right away, instead, I listened to a message that popped up on my YouTube screen. Joyce Meyer's sermon popped up, oddly titled, "Disconnecting from Toxic People." The title really did not match the sermon, at least to me.

She quoted the following verse:

2 Corinthians 10: 4-5

We use God's mighty weapons, not worldly weapons, to knock down the strongholds of human reasoning and to destroy false arguments. We destroy every proud obstacle that keeps people from knowing God. We capture their rebellious thoughts and teach them to obey Christ.

"You have to learn how to talk back to the devil. You don't hear him in words. He affects your thinking or your emotions, or how you feel." Joyce Meyer

I was able to sleep after this.

When I woke up, I started my day with the following sermon by Jentzen Franklin, titled the Power of a Personal Prophecy.

"The enemy would love for you to discredit all prophesy and say, 'There's nothing to that,' but the word of God is a prophetic book, and God has a prophecy for your life today, and it's personal. Prophecy is God coming to you with a word about your future. God will always keep his promises, but he is not obligated to keep your potential. You are obligated once God speaks prophecy over your life, to hold onto that prophecy, to war with that prophecy, to fight the forces that come against that prophecy with the word of God that will take you to your highest potential." Jentzen Franklin

Again, I find God rescuing me, but swifter each time I begin to stray or lose hope, and before I can lose myself again entirely. I am reminded that I have an identity in Christ, it is not earned, it has nothing to do with me earning it, but it is who I am, and whose I am. It is my responsibility to steward the word of God that he has spoken over my family and my life. This is why He has called me to read my journal all over again. To remember what He has told me. To remind me why I am here. And to remind me that any sacrifice I make is done for Him and no one else.

I am called, and no one can take that away from me.

And so, I will battle these difficult conversations with the knowing that God brought me here for a reason, and whether I understand it or not, or whether others understand and accept it or not, it is my responsibility to follow where He leads me to, and do what He has called me to do. I am reminded that my time with God is important and necessary to remain strong and faithful to His calling. Although I cannot earn his favor, my heart is reminded that I want to and choose to and need to follow Him. Thank God for His Grace and His Presence in my life! Without all of this, I would remain lost and broken and desperate. I call out, and He answers, no matter how far I think I have run. Thank you, Jesus, for loving me through the tough stuff, and reminding me of your love, unearned and undeserved, but loved anyway.

January 10th

After reading through my journal again, I was reminded of how close I am to God. How near He has brought me to Him. He often speaks to me, and I could say that I don't understand why, but I do. I called out for Him. I cried out to Him with a heart full of faith, knowing that He will hear me, and He will answer me. Although I may get lost, He does not let me remain there in my own darkness and my own wilderness. He rescues me from myself often. Needing Him this way does not make me less of a believer, nor less deserving of His love, as a matter of a fact, just knowing that I need Him this way, draws Him nearer. I am on a journey to finding peace, and to sharing that peace with others who are lost in their own darkness and chaos. He answered me when I cried out and promised me peace, and no matter what I do, as undeserving as I or my actions may be, He reaches in, pulls me up, and saves me from myself – every time.

Although he sees me as I am, it wasn't until the moment that I chose to open myself up to him, in all my bitterness, in all my anger, in all my hurt, in all my ugliness, to see me as I am, that he began to work in me. In the moment that I showed myself to Him, He revealed His love to me. He chose me as His own and gave me a purpose and a hope when I couldn't see beyond my hopelessness. There are times that holding onto this is difficult as I can get lost in much of the circumstances around me, and the feelings that they bring, but He is always there, ready to rescue me. This is the love that I have longed for all my life. I may still be immature in my walk with God, but that doesn't matter. He loves me anyhow because I call to Him, because I believe in Him, because I know that He loves me more than my circumstances can tell me otherwise.

We often fight for this type of love from others, become bitter and resentful when we don't get it from them, and carry that hurt while displaying those open wounds in our actions and emotions and responses. But we are all human, and all on our own journeys, so I need to remember that I cannot expect it from anyone, but knowing that I already have it in me, should be, and is enough. This is where my foundation of peace will be. And so, going forward, I will read and reread my journal until it is so embedded in my soul that nothing can shake me in this area. My walk will become more purposeful, and my faith will become stronger. Defeat will be harder, and my personal prophecy will become my path that leads me to His strength, for it was a promise directly from God at a moment that I needed just a little hope.

I am not ashamed that I believe in God. I am not ashamed that I know He speaks to me. After all, how many people seek answers from someone or something else and never receive a firm knowing in their hearts that it is truth. I know my truth. It is alive inside of me. Many of these words in this book are not my own, or they are, but they are not self-conceived. How in my desperation could I find hope on my own? How in my self-deception, could I find truth about who I am, and who He says I am while lost with eyes that refuse to see my own reflection? How could I know love that is unconditional if I am filled with bitterness and anger? These gifts were not my own before God gave them to me. I didn't need to change. He is changing me. I didn't need to be pure and without guilt, He drew me to Him in all my ugliness, and told me that I am worth more than I believe I am.

Growing up, I had often heard, "Jesus loves you," and it never really had an impact on me, and to be honest, it bothered me that this was all they had to offer me during all my troubles. I never understood the power of that statement until this very moment. Somehow, because I lacked this unconditional and gentle love all of my life and had seen the ugliest parts of the people that I loved and craved a protecting love from others that I never really received, I realize – right now – that His love was all I really needed. Jesus loves ME! There is nothing more powerful while you are developing an intimate relationship with God in this way, than the moment you see the power of the words, "Jesus loves you," and all that didn't make sense before, doesn't even matter.

February 12th

It's been a long while since I have written in my journal, and even more so, that I rarely have touched my bible. I have been on Guam for 2 months now and every day has been a very busy one. I have let my need to DO for others be a priority over my dedicated time to God, and he to me. I have not had time for myself, and I find that I am heading back into depression. The days have been a blur. There is always something to do, to work on, to clean out, to sell, someone to take somewhere, to help, to support, and so on. My mission coming here was to help my family heal. There has been so much tension between me and mom and most days I feel that silence is better than any verbal war we could get into. I am her mini me and our personalities blend so much that it's often hard to tell who the tension is coming from. Our car rides are filled with uncomfortable silence, and that invisible wall feels like it is constantly closing in on me. Her words can be harsh, and she can be quick to criticize. I am probably overly sensitive considering all that brought me home, and I suppose I allow myself to wallow in disappointment because I had hope that home would be the comfort I needed to make it through the craziness of my own emotions. It's all too much. It brings back so many memories from my growing up years that I am shocked, now 47 years old, and I still have an inner fear that I am doing something wrong or just not right. I am a grown woman who has overcome a lot, started over with nothing several times in my life, led and inspired people to grow, to develop, to laugh, to love, and to live. I have been recognized by others for my uplifting, kind, generous, joyful disposition, by others for my skill, problem-solving abilities, analytical intelligence, leadership, and team building expertise...but around my mom – I feel like an idiot. I suppose, in order to find healing, you have to identify all hurts that you have carried throughout your life. Healing is a process, and certainly, not an easy one, but we must all have to face our own inner demons and our own misconceptions of the reality we told ourselves we lived in order to appreciate where we really come from.

My healing journey must also be a true reflection of my pain in order to move past it. To recognize my blessings, I must see the sorrows I carry. To be salt and light, I must also taste it without. I love my mom, and I know what she has been through, but we all must choose how we live and love those around us, as the people around us are part of our journey towards healing. But if we choose to push people away, we walk alone. If we choose to be bitter to those who love us, we will push them all away until all we are left with is a superficial world.

I am angry right now. I can see that. I don't want to hide this from myself as it is starting to turn into a deep hurt, and quickly building to a wall of resentment again. And I am on a journey to find the love inside myself so that I can love those around me with the love of Christ. I feel like I am going crazy in my own mind sometimes, and there is a constant gut ache. I am uncomfortable and walking on eggshells around here and I don't fully understand this part of my trip. But I must move past it. I am almost 50 years old right now, and I am reliving the feelings I had as a child and a teenager. It is unsettling to say the least and has triggered deep sadness that I thought had long been buried. But it has also shown me parts of myself that need changing, including my perception on the realties and struggles we all had to face to get to where we are. I honestly cannot even fathom the pain she has carried from what she has been through. At this realization, my heart becomes tender towards her. And no matter what, and no matter how old I get, she will always be my safe space.

So, I am opening a random message this morning, after a prayer for forgiveness. Forgive me for my thoughts and unforgiveness. Help me to find healing that I might be who and do what God has called me to be and do. Help me to overcome the anger and replace it with love. Help me to replace my hurt with peace and understanding. Help me to have compassion. Help me to move beyond my past childhood traumas so that I can be the leader you have called me to be, so I can love as you have called me to love, so I can heal others from my own healed soul. Help me to move past my flesh reactions so that I can show the compassion of Christ. Help me to stand against personal oppression so that I can help others grow out of their circumstances that kept them internally oppressed.

Here is the random message I received today right after I wrote the last word above. Of all the messages that could come up – this one! This one! Now, that is the Power of God working in my life.

John Hagee – Never Fear the Harsh Words Spoken by Those Around You

The Prayers

"Why should you be concerned about holiness? Because the bible says, without holiness, no man shall see the Lord. The Word rules our hearts, it guides our thoughts, it controls our speech. You don't read this book. This book reads you. To bring life, to bring love, to bring joy, to bring peace, to bring hope to every troubled heart that would read it. – This book is a chain breaker. It breaks the fetters of sin. It takes the pain out of death and dying; it takes the gloom from the grave and it gives a hope that is steadfast and sure. The Power of the Word is greater than the storms of life. Fight the good fight. Endure hardness as a soldier. And when you battle, put on the whole armor, and fight to win. Let us quit walking around in timidity. We must return to the book. God's compass will point you to peace. God's compass points us to love. God says, 'If your father and your mother forsake you. I will lift you up.' You wanna read something that's hopeful, read this. Are you looking for joy unspeakable? This book says the joy of the Lord maketh rich and has no sorrow. In his presence is the fullness of joy. Weeping may endure for the night, but joy cometh in the morning. Are you looking for health and healing? It's in this book. The bible cannot help you if you don't read it. Jesus described the bible as spiritual food, but when you refuse to read it, you are starving yourself to death. It's spiritual suicide. First you get weak, then you get depressed and sick in the soul and sick in spirit. And then you spiritually die because you refuse to feast on this food. Victory that is greater than your trial, greater than your giants, greater than the problems of your life, greater than the mountains you're climbing, greater than the burdens you are carrying, hope in the midst of the storm. The bible is confidence that God is on his throne and everything's gonna be alright. It's here in this book. Saul said the second sign of spiritual starvation is joylessness. The bible says the joy of the Lord is your strength. If there is no joy, there is no strength. You need to have a joy explosion. God's joy leaps from the pages of this book into your soul, and you become a happy warrior. This book is the answer."

JOHN HAGEE

June 29th

It has been over 3 months since I have been home, and I have neglected my time with God yet again. I had been so focused on repairing my marriage that I had nothing left in me to give to God. Perhaps I have been hiding my face from God because I came back, even though He kept telling me to go. But in the same sense, I had the urge to come back to Washington. Could it be my idea that I HAD TO make my marriage work no matter what? No matter what I heard, no matter what I felt, no matter what I knew? Since I have been home, I have seen God reminding me of all the reasons He had me leave to begin with. It's just sad that I have to wait until my sorrows bring me here, to a place of surrender.

When I was preparing for my flight, I had already sensed the distance and the reservations my husband had for my return. Although I could tell he was hoping I would just stay where I was, I also knew that he missed me. But he had learned to steel himself against the sadness and the fear of being alone, and this was his strength that he did not want to give up. When I arrived back in Washington, it was awkward. Our embrace was awkward, our time at home together was awkward, our conversations were awkward and uncomfortable, and I knew that there were underlying hurts in us both that neither of us wanted to confront.

During this time, it seemed as though we had only pushed each other further and further away. The fights were harder, the silences were longer, and the distance was wider than ever before. He still held the fact that I left to Guam against me. He still held it over my head and provided himself this as his reason for his bad behavior. If only he could see himself through my eyes. If only he could know the damage he was doing to my ability and desire to stay in this marriage at all.

Because of my obedience to God when he called me to Guam, I believed that I would not have to face challenges that disturbed my mind and my heart, that I would find the bright side of things beyond the dark, but I have continued to face battles that have become more fierce than the ones that I have fought before starting my journey to healing. I continue to face battles that break me. There are things that come against me, but I need to remember that the closer I get to fully committing to my purpose, the bigger the battles may be, but one thing that stands true, is that my God fights for me. There is power in my very presence, that is not mine, but is His.

I have found myself defeated more days than not, but there is something different in my defeat, it is not long-lasting and fades as quickly as I begin to feel it. The connections I have in my life have influenced me instead of me influencing them, and although I am a good person, I allowed others to pull me down, and found myself facing giants and battles that were not mine to face. When God opened the door for me to go, with a sound of permanence, I allowed myself to return to the places which break me. However, even this has been a blessing, for it has opened up my eyes fully to my pain and allowed me to defeat those giants in prayer.

My cries are powerful. He hears me even when I make certain decisions that do not align with His plan for me. Even when I am wrong, He hears me, and His hand continues to make a way for me out of the dark. There was a time that I was losing my mind. Nobody would help me, and I didn't know how to ask for help, until I cried out. And even though I still find myself in the middle of the battles that hurt me and push me towards depression, He hears me, and I recognize how powerful my cries truly are.

I need to trust God in the midst of all this chaos. I find myself questioning why this is happening to me and I realize that I have been breaking the giants down, and I don't always see the full battlefield clearly as I stand in the midst of it. Though I feel like I am doing everything right, and following His promptings in full faith, I find myself in battle again. I felt as though I was losing my mind, being beaten down on the inside, every time I would try to rise above it. I didn't understand why I was under attack and why no one would protect me. Who was I becoming as a result of all of this? That's what God has been showing me. I had been praying the right things and asking Him to show me. Show me what is not good for my growth. Show me how and why I let others break me. Show me what I need to remove from my life so I can finally break free and become the me that I am called to be. Unshakable, unbreakable, and whole

Part III
The Revelations

§

I AM NOT GOD, separate from a source, I am Source.

I AM Spirit.

I AM Reason.

I AM Movement.

I AM Meaning.

I AM Creator and Creation.

I AM Essence and Existence.

I AM Life and I AM Living.

I AM All and I AM One.

I AM the Great Mystery, and I AM The Answer.

I AM All that I am, and I AM All that you need me to be.

I AM.

§

July 1st

Deuteronomy 10:14

Look, the highest heavens and earth and everything in it all belongs to the Lord your God. Yet the Lord chose your ancestors as the object of His love. And He chose you, their descendants above all other nations as is evident today. Therefore, change your hearts and stop being stubborn.

> "The more that I have chosen to not settle for stuff, the more I have seen God just show me who I am. And I really begin to understand that everything God desires for us is outside our comfort zone."
>
> — Sarah Jakes Robert

He places us right on the edge, so we have the need to reach for Him. I struggle with it a little bit because I know that I am bypassing people that have been waiting on God, but I realize that's all that they are doing, waiting on God. I have to actively pursue God no matter who is around me and what their personal journey looks like. I have to actively pursue God to discover your own personal journey, no matter how uncomfortable it is. I realize that I have to be willing to get uncomfortable.

§

God is leading you to the place you need to be. Not everyone will accept this, because what you are doing will separate you from people that don't understand. Do not allow what seems to be working for you to blind you from what you need to see, because sometimes we allow what is working for us to cause us to rest in what seems to be working. You can get too focused on what is working for you that you stop paying attention to and focusing on what God needs you to see. God is exposing you for a reason, no matter what you have to go through to get healing for your family.

Pay attention, this is a clue to what God wants you to be. It is a sign to what's down on the inside of you. What have you seen in your life, and are you daring to believe that God exposed you to all of it so that you can grow into who you really are?

Life has changed your disposition. It has changed your heart. You keep coming up short, while everyone else can see it, but you. You do not fit in where you are because that is not where God needs you to be. Be aggressive in pursuing this. You don't have to accept the environment you are in. Destiny needs to be manifested in your life and your situation is not the answer. Know that you know that God has already told you how to see the proper perspective. You have to be willing to allow God to take you out of some places so He can show you your growth.

You have to be willing to be uncomfortable and relocate outside of the distractions and obstructions and be grateful that they are letting you go, and that you aren't good enough for some people. Thank them for making you an outcast because there is something more that God needs you to see and become. There was something about that isolation that has allowed you to move outside of what is uncomfortable.

Find your way, look up. God has chosen you. God has been searching for you. He needed you in isolation to reach you. You have been desperately searching to see God working in your circumstances, not realizing that the isolation they put you in was where God was waiting. Thank them for rejecting you. Thank them for judging you less than what they wanted. Thank them that you were not perfectly enough for the crowd, for their culture, for their needs. God found you there. He is calling you out now.

Because you were an outcast, because you did not fit in, because you found yourself without a friend, He found you. He found you because you didn't truly have anyone. You became a fixture and not the friend they would fight for and defend. You became something less than who you truly are. Do not be angry about it anymore. Thank them that you were rejected.

They always have a problem when they see the favor of God in your life because it is exposing what they lacked to provide you. But Jesus has seen you in your isolation. He has seen you. They will never truly see you the way God sees you because they can only see you the way they have always seen you. This is a word for you because you seem to need someone else's approval before you come out of isolation, and they will not understand that God is calling you closer so He can change you. There have been some things on your life that have prevented you from being who you are because you have only been shown what you are not.

Make some decisions about your life. Remember what hurt you, but do not live there. You need to know what hurt you in order to write your testimony. Everything must come from the depths of your heart, your sorrows, your grief, your neglect, your insecurities. You need to remember what caused that pain, so you know how to get out of it. The next few days will be teachings that will remind you of what broke you. In this brokenness, you will find the beauty God intends for you to see so you will always remember what He brought you out of.

> *"There are a lot of us who are struggling in life simply because we have allowed the wrong people into our lives. And some of us are absolutely, totally, and completely devastated because we continue to allow the wrong people into our lives, and it becomes a habit that we don't know how to break."*
>
> RC BLAKES – *NARCISSISM*

§

When you experience emotional trauma from relationships that are dysfunctional because you fail to relate to one another away from self-focus, you begin to breed narcissism within the relationship. There are wounds in your hearts because you keep fighting for the attention that your spirit needs, but you fight with the flesh, battles that cannot be won when each of you perceive and require the world to revolve around you, what you want, and what you need, without a clear commitment to the whole of the relationship.

There are issues buried underneath the façade that nothing is wrong and underneath bravado when insecurities and fears permeate the environment you are in. You silence conversations that are necessary to grow beyond the real pains that are overlooked by committing one selfish act after another, until one day you wake up and realize that there is no substance to the union that should feed your soul. You continue to get caught up in situations that further push you to become numb to the very thing you need. Because you are prone to give and provide and serve, while you may be entangled with those who seek only their own satisfaction and are self-serving, then the foundation of that union begins to crumble. You become bruised on the inside and all that you are left with is confusion, doubt, and hurts that cannot be comforted by the façade that has been created out of deep needs that are never met.

You are left in the hands of trial and error until your heart becomes broken and all you have is anger and resentment and bitterness from trying. You keep falling for the same stuff because you continue to try to appease others while denying yourself what is vital for your heart to survive the hurts. They don't look at the space in your heart as a sacred space that they have been privileged to occupy and their very presence makes you anxious and uneasy and uncomfortable because it has consumed you for so long. You allow the thing that breaks you to break you beyond the need to repair it. You are consistently faced with this reality and yet you close your eyes consistently to the things you lack and the things that produce deep hurts.

Though you know what you are feeling is valid, you continue to invite that same behavior to destroy what is sacred in your heart. It breaks your heart, one to be right, and two because it has been your reality. These are just a few of the things that you need to pay attention to.

When the soul of a narcissist is broken and the heart is empty, it is impossible to celebrate much of anything or anyone because they are not whole enough to understand. They are so self-consumed that there is no room inside to accommodate others. You are all broken little children fighting for the attention of others. Your broken soul has prevented you from truly loving.

Until one day, you wake up, shed the skin that was never yours, find who you are again, and see the ugly that you have become. You begin to question the value of these relationships and what they bring to your life. You question what holds you there. You see that you have become like your surroundings because you have been fighting for your place in your own sacred space. You struggle with this because narcissism is not part of who you have been before, and who you strive to be now. You have adopted a spirit of narcissism because you have been fighting for acceptance, acknowledgment, and a sincere appreciation for who you thought you were in their lives.

You are a serving spirit. You give even what you do not have. You drop everything to rescue others, but you have been subjugated for too long. There is a need for genuine love and acceptance, and you realize that you never receive it. This has injured your soul.

This is no longer your battle. Let it go so you can find true healing and wholeness and return to the you that I have created you to be. I know you recognize how these relationships have changed you at your core, but you need to release all of it. This is not you and you do not need to establish yourself there any longer. It has damaged your spirit and love cannot flow out of the place where nothing of true substance flows in.

You cannot change others, but you can change your acceptance of them and get out of the way. Leave them in the my hands and move on with your life while you still have it. Let me work in their hearts like I am working in yours right now. You cannot change this situation in your own power and the longer you hold on, the deeper that spirit will dwell, and you will repeat the same experience of emotional trauma and self-isolation that broke you to begin with. You will do no good when you lose control in your mind and in your heart. You have seen this pattern consistently. Once the dust settles, the patterns will begin again.

You have been socially isolated through guilt. You have been kept silent, afraid of rocking the boat, but the right you inside knows it isn't right. When you needed someone to defend you, these people defended those who were hurting you. They participated in the conversations that tore you down and minimized your personal value. When you were on a path to healing and finding your strength again, they found ways to break you down, made you feel bad for your need to find healing, for finding strength that they did not give you, until you found yourself trapped in depression and desperation all over again.

This is not the life Christ died for you to live. What are you doing this for? You have been humiliated and disregarded. You have been condemned into submission through their silence and have been made to accept your place beneath those who continue to hurt you. How are you going to help other women find their strength if you continue to allow others to keep you in this spirit of defeat?

You have been drained of your confidence and your joy. You have become bitter and angry and cannot even hide it anymore. You just don't have the strength to hide it because all of this was intended to break your spirit and force you to internalize the pain. They have constantly contradicted your view of reality even though your pain was real to you. They made you question your own moral fiber by making you think less of yourself as though you are just petty and overreact. They refused to see your pain because it gave them ownership of how you got there. This has happened on many occasions, about the smallest of things as though something was wrong with your memory or your perception on what has been happening.

This was intended to make you feel crazy and as if you needed serious help instead of lovingly opening up the space to help you through it. There is a spiritual and psychological game being played. This is a hard message, and it is shaking you to the core, but it is necessary. They have made you not trust your truth.

What is the intent of that? The rejection of it and the abandonment created within you a soul tie so much so that you need the approval of the very person that has rejected you. Your self-esteem has been broken by all of this and they do not have the power or the need to restore you because it isn't about you. It never was. You do not need their approval anymore. You will never receive it.

Anybody that you have to run behind does not mean you well. This is a life lesson. Do not allow them to continue to break your soul. Pick up what you have left so I can rebuild it from that tiny seed that still exists within you. You have moved in and out of their life, trying to hold onto that seed, one too many times. That's not fair to you nor them. I cannot work through each of you with all this controlling your hearts and your home.

Do not love anybody so much that you fail to love yourself. Do not let your love for anybody make you hate yourself. Your soul is sick and that is not the my will for you, nor them. You need the light of wisdom to come into this situation. I have exposed you to this part of people and yourself for a reason. You do not have a destiny of coming up short to people's expectations, and especially coming up short in your own eyes.

July 2nd

Leviticus 5:1

If you are called to testify about something you have seen or that you know about, it is sinful to refuse to testify.

§

Look at your life with honest eyes so you can recognize your insecurities and how your experiences and your broken heart have given you a strength from above and it is time to draw it out of you. You have more now than you had before you were broken, rather, before you realized that you were broken. You have received grace, so you can give grace. I have done something inside of you and your life so you can reproduce from what I have done inside of you. At the end of the day, this will be all that remains.

You went through everything you went through so you can help somebody else come out of that same thing. They need to see how I can transform their lives, starting on the inside and that everything else is temporary. I will carry them through what is temporary, to a permanence beyond all that they can imagine. Do not look at your own strength, this must come from me, because at the end of the day, this is all that remains, and this is what they must learn to see.

Miracles still occur every day, and the fact that you made it through all that you have gone through in life, that in itself is a miracle. This is what you need to share. Activate your light so that others are curious again about what makes that light grow beyond your brokenness. Let your soul shine from your eyes. You were a wretch, but I have saved you for my own. Never forget that miracle, because at the end of the day, this will be all that remains.

Keep your mind clear and your circle tight and release all that is toxic to who you are becoming. Remove yourself from all that would continue to drag you back down into that brokenness. I have unleashed my anointing on you because your need for my power was great. Darkness is running out of time because I have established myself in your situation the moment that you cried out, the moment that you exposed how broken your soul was. Your need was heard in the heavens, and I recognize that you are ready to strike.

Now is the time to release the fullness of who you are. Bust down the doors open in the culture because I am ordering your steps now. Your power cannot be released in just any environment, it needs to be released in an environment that recognizes who you are and what you carry. You do not need anyone else's help to do it because you have already lived it. Your testimony is your strength, and at the end of the day, this will be all that remains.

You don't have to pretend to be anybody else. The doors have swung open so you can share who you really are. Your light has been activated in your darkness so you can lead the way for others to follow that light. Protect your flame. Because at the end of the day, this will be all that remains, and it cannot be replaced. This is your resource. Whatever I say, do it.

Be willing to draw it out and I will turn it into a miracle. You are connected to my power and the miracle already exists in you. Your testimony is your miracle. You may not think you have what I am asking of you, but you do. It is time. You did not start ready, but you have been refined and polished in the fire of your experiences and you are ready. Trust that I will do what I have told you will happen and that I gave it all to you in the midst of your struggle. I have anointed you and I will create situations and scenarios that demand that fire burning inside of you, so that I can show you that with me, all things are possible. Trust in me because at the end of the day, this will be all that remains.

Give me what you have now, in all its brokenness, discombobulation, and inorganization, broken and shattered, because this will be the miracle of transformation and transfiguration. I will take your "not enough" and turn it into more than enough. What you feel you have lacked in the past has been removed and replaced with so much more than even you realize right now. What you once needed from others, is in you. What you once cried for, hoped for, strove for is already in you now. Take hold of who you are, because at the end of the day, this will be all that remains. Your miracle is ready.

You may think that what I am asking of you is more than you have to give, but if you surrender to who I have called you to be and trust my transformation of your life, overnight, your heart will be changed. Your mind will see things clearly and in full definition. You will see beyond your past, your past pains, and flourish in who you are becoming. And at the end of the day, this will be all that remains.

It is time to deal with breaking ungodly soul ties because it is time to deal with what is entangled up in your soul. There are soul ties, both godly and ungodly, and you need to break the ones that keep you in a perpetual pattern that breaks you. It is time to stop following these patterns. It is time to celebrate the gift of life, and your words have life. And at the end of the day, this will be all that remains.

My love is transitioning you, transforming you, and taking you out of the you that allowed others to break you. I am breaking your dependence on what you thought was safe and what is familiar, to bring you into a fullness of life that you never imagined. Today you are dealing with all of this because of the wrong relationships that have tugged at you and taken you under. Your need for them reduced your own power and increased their ability to control your soul. These relationships can ultimately break you, and the ones that you just left nearly did. But I am giving you your power back and reminding you that you are more than what you allowed in, and at the end of the day, this will be all that remains.

Do not be attached to the past, for the past no longer feeds you. You love me, and your attachments have clouded the part of you that knew where your power came from and is coming from. They were a driving force that forced you into darkness to delay your destiny. You idolized people and depended on these relationships for what your spirit needed, and you found that you always came up short because they cannot and will not produce what your spirit truly needs.

Do not deny your destiny. You are destined for more and are being held captive by that which you idolize, and it will keep you far from doing what you need to and are called to do. Protect your path. Protect your destiny, for at the end of the day, this will be all that remains.

You have been pursuing personal value and validation from people that cannot and do not produce value in your life, not in the way that your true spirit needs value. This does not come from them, and their validation is false and self-serving. I have seen you overlooked, unloved, and positioned less than you deserve. I have seen you left empty time and time again. I have seen you allow what does not satisfy your heart to break you down at the core of who you are, who you know you are, and who you allowed yourself to become, overpowered by those who break your heart. You have remained unsatisfied because you have wanted from them only what you can get from me. You have placed too much importance on who you wanted them to be for you that you have forgotten who you were already. You created an idol in these relationships because of your need to be valued and validated. But they cannot validate who you are for you are more than they can even see or want to see. There is no power for them in you finding your power. It robs them of control, and they are consumed with that control. It is time to tear down the idols that you have allowed to dominate your world, your heart, your mind, and show them the power that you already hold, because at the end of the day, this will be all that remains.

Do not give your strength to anything that does not add value to who you are becoming. Do not be so consumed with what others think of you, for you are more than their minds can even imagine. Make yourself a priority for your life is made for more than that which you have given priority to. This is a crucial part of your journey where your commitment to my guidance is necessary. You have given priority to others that have distracted you and when that happened, your writing stopped, but your writing has purpose, and that purpose must be pursued with everything that you are. This is your connection to your destiny and your calling. Do not allow unfulfilled needs to derail your destiny for it is in your destiny that all your needs will be met. Do not allow others to pull you into a different direction. Stay focused on what lies ahead of you. Do not get lost in emotional tug of war for your heart will provide direction to others along your path. And at the end of the day, this will be all that remains.

You have found yourself in unsafe and unreliable environments that have changed the way you believe because you have depended on others to provide needs that have always remained unmet. You have done some desperate things to have those needs met and have come up short every time. This has driven you to places inside yourself that has derailed you from following the plan that I have for your life, the path that I have laid out for you to follow, and you must follow the path, for at the end of the day, this will be all that remains.

You were told to go to Guam at a time when I was speaking truth to your soul. You allowed others to change your heart and your mind. You have spent your life trying to impress them, trying to win their love, affection, and attention more than you wanted to follow the path I have set for you. This is where you created the ungodly soul ties that continued to break you. They are not capable of giving you what you need the most, and their opinions and perceptions of you do not determine your value. Remember this. For at the end of the day, your value in my eyes will be all that remains.

I am your source, and any relationship that interferes with your connection to me needs to be examined closely to ensure it adds into your spirit that which will lead you to recognize that you carry my love that you may be a blessing to others through that love. Any ties that bind you to a lesser version of who you are now called to be through a healthy place of love needs to be left behind lest it deplete your spirit of the love that must flourish to feed others.

Do not yield yourself to what entangles you in other people's emotional ups and downs, because you have enough to carry on your own. And you have already carried yourself out of that dark place with my love and grace. You needed others to contribute to your strength to make it through the dark places, but they cannot give you that strength, and their strength does not measure up to what you already carry within you. You have found yourself defending what others have perceived as your weakness, not realizing, that was your strength. You needed unconditional support to make it through and instead found yourself crying to be understood. It brought about a whirlwind of confusion, but remember, you are not what you went through. You are more than all this, and at the end of the day, this will be all that remains.

You tried to prove yourself and came up empty and bitter once again. So, step back, take an honest look at who and what you were trying to prove yourself to, and recognize that there is no value in the thing you placed the most value on. Nothing can become a priority over your calling again. It won't be easy to change that mindset and the habit of needing to be validated and understood, but it needs to change. And if you find yourself striving for this again, know that you will come up empty again. Remember that how you prioritize people and your relationship to them will determine which of the two soul ties that they become.

Your relationships have to have a foundation of my love. It must mimic that sacrifice. It must pursue your happiness and provide you peace. It must contribute to your growth and healing. It must demonstrate faith in you and your calling. It must take your burdens on as their own. It cannot be pride-filled and self-centered. It must pursue common peace, and love above all. It cannot survive on hidden emotions and bottled-up thoughts. It must be formed of a mutual respect and reverence for the blessing it is, or it is not a blessing to either of you. Your relationships must be able to cultivate trust and recognize each other's moments of vulnerability and step back until peace and strength return. If you cannot achieve this, then it is better to be alone in the wilderness than in a crowd at war. For at the end of the day, this will be all that remains.

You will encounter different connections in life. If it is part of your destiny, it cannot leave you. If you are glued to someone emotionally, you must learn to recognize how that attachment occurred and what it brings to your life, and how your purpose serves that connection in the kingdom. Do you recognize my hand in your connection, and was it there from the start? Are there influences in your history that work against that connection? No matter how you came together, when you formed that connection, you formed it before me, for I am determining what can and cannot be connected to you now. And how you treat each other in those connections will determine whether I bless that relationship for your life or whether that relationship becomes an ungodly soul tie. The choice is yours on what you do with that blessing, and it is important to know and fully understand that your connection in the life of another is a blessing to them. And at the end of the day, this will be all that remains.

Do your connections provide each other with the unconditional love and support necessary to build the bridge that will allow you to pass over the hard times, for this is the blessing of every connection that is blessed by me. Your connections must contribute to wholeness, one for the other. It cannot be the thing that breaks you. It cannot restrain you from independence, but rather it should provide you both the freedom to live to your fullest potential. It cannot constrain you by authority or obligation, but rather give you the true sense of living beyond all that can restrain you from living. There are lives attached to your name, and you must nurture this idea for it is your truth. And at the end of the day, this will be all that remains.

Your love and your life must provide a healthy place of nurturing where love can flow in all directions. That is my intention, to provide you with a healthy place where you are free to be you and they are free to be them, and if it does not provide this freedom, then it is not of me. There should be a mutual exchange and a mutual benefit that takes you both to a better place, where the fundamentals of your union are a blessing that comes naturally and brings you closer to your purpose in this life.

Do not allow yourself to become trapped in a place of conflict, darkness, and disorder, for it will affect who you are on the inside and pollute what has been blessed. Become the living demonstration of my love to everyone you meet, this will propel you both to be better than when you first came together. Because at the end of the day, this will be all that remains.

I love you more than you will ever comprehend. I am challenging the things in your life, both good and bad, so that you can see what needs to be sifted from your life until you understand that it all has to do with your heart. I do not want what you are giving up for me, I want you. Because you have obeyed my voice, I will bless you. Continue to seek me in prayer, my guidance for your life, the decisions you will be faced with, and I will answer. You need to ask me sincerely, "Lord, is there anything that I need to lay down?" My answer to you will be very specific and will be absolute and will bring you to the places and the people that will bless your life. For I only want what is best for you.

I will require a personal surrender and full obedience to do what I am saying, without delay. Do it now. I am speaking to you directly without condemnation. Do everything I tell you to do. I am a good god and though I require your surrender and your sacrifice, it is all for your good. Put it all in my hands. Put your future in the hands that love you best. I will resurrect what is good for you. Lay everything down and I will provide every blessing that you are looking for in life. You will not lose something good for something less. That is not the way I work.

> *"You have to be sensitive to when God lays somebody on your heart. They serve even when disappointed. They serve even when they are confused. You would never know it because they are still in their routine and rhythm. Everything looks like it is functioning on the outside, but on the inside, they are wondering how they are going to make it to the end of the day."*
>
> SARAH JAKES ROBERTS

People become familiar with serving while disappointed and doing it in excellence, no matter what is happening on the inside. They are still righteous before God, pursuing Him morning and night, praying through the disappointment, praying through the pain. This is when they are most powerful. They are pursuing God while crushed underneath unbearable pain. This is the heart God pursues. They have had to hang onto their faith when faith was a small flickering light, barely seen. It wasn't easy for them to stay and keep their head held high through all their losses. They surrendered to that ounce of faith and pressed on. They were not perfect, but they pressed on, and they served others because their desire was to be a reflection of how God served them. You know them, but you do not know them. You see their sadness, but you do not know their pain. You love them, but you do not know the depths that their heart had to swim through to hold onto that small flicker of faith and hope and love. That was all they had left. But you did not know that.

She fights for reconciliation with God though she is bitter. She pursues Him even though she is lost. Her hope is in Him even though she feels disappointed by Him. She seeks His truth for her life even though she feels that He led her the wrong way. She trusts that He loves her even though she still feels broken. She believes in His promises even though she feels let down. Still, she connects with God on a personal and real level. He speaks to her no matter where she thinks her heart is or is not.

She is being forced to grow though she feels inadequate. She is being forced to create even though she feels she has lost her spark. She is being forced to stand and walk even though she is burdened by a heavy load. She is being forced to support others even though she gets no help from anyone. She is being forced into the arms of God because that is where she will finally find comfort.

The pull is so strong that the line cannot be broken. She knows her greatest blessing is her relationship and friendship with God. He speaks to her even when she shuts her ears. He shows her things even when she closes her eyes shut. He places His Spirit deep in her heart even though she thinks she carries a hollow soul. This is the heart God is pursuing. She is not perfect, but she is perfectly His.

She pressed in even when she felt like giving up and because of this, He is pulling her up now. He has been watching her heart even when she tried to bury it. She is not perfect, but she is perfectly His.

She carries wisdom even though she is constantly overlooked. She loves deeply even though she has never received the kind of love that kept her whole. She is finally being allowed to know God intimately, in all her flaws, she knows she is not perfect, but she knows she is perfectly His.

She buried her prayers, but He is pulling them back up to remind her that no matter what happened the last time she tried to fulfill God's purpose, He has preserved her prayers for such a time as this, where she knows that she is not perfect, but now, even greater is her knowledge that she is perfectly His. God is reaching down for her buried prayers and is pulling it out to resurrect and reconcile her to God, to His purpose, to her destiny.

§

Don't be afraid. Pursue this prayer. This is what your soul is made of. This is what your experience has been creating. This is your testimony that will glorify my power and my love that carried you through. You had this prayer since you were a child. You lived with this purpose for your mom. Don't forget that. The power is in the prayers that come out of your mouth. Everyone has told you that your prayers are powerful. It is time to own that. Your prayers can change hearts and circumstances. Your prayers touch the depths of my heart. It is time for you to recognize that your connection to me is where that prayer comes from and no matter what anyone thinks, this is truth. This is your truth. This is the truth that I have placed in your heart since you were a child. I have been with you though you are not perfect. You have always been perfectly mine.

This is why children are drawn to you. This is why people seek you in the midst of their chaos. They see that flickering light in you that is powered by my love. It is time. Stand up and produce. You cannot produce it in your current mindset and situation. Let go of your condition. Give it to me for I am waiting for you to lay it all at the foot of the cross. This is where your comfort lives. This is your blessing. Hold onto it with all that you have. This is the heart that I am pursuing.

July 3rd

"The argument that broke you was anointed to separate you from them so that you could move forward in the direction of your destiny."

Sarah Jakes Roberts

§

I have been with your wherever you have gone. You are the one that has been appointed to lead your people. Though you question who you are, it has already been decided. Receive the word in your heart, your spirit, and your soul. Do not be intimidated.

There comes a point in your life where you have to stop and recognize what kills you on the inside and what builds you up. Stop being addicted to the fight. The fight is not yours anymore. I have laid out a place for you and a plan for your life where your purpose will flourish so you can inspire someone else and someone else and someone else. Get out of your comfort zone. You survived heartbreak. There is something about you that attracts others to you. It is your anointing. It is your spirit. You have experienced much and survived much and still kept your joy. This is your anointing. You carry the name for a reason. That is not just a coincidence. There is an anointing on your life because of what you carry.

When you look back on your life, you realize that you should have lost your mind, given up on all that is good, and you nearly did. But something inside of you continued to look for the good in others and recognize that their blessing may not include you, but still respect their blessing with joy that is sincere.

The fights you have had to endure pulled something out of you. You may not have close friendships, but that is because not just anyone is allowed to follow you to your destiny. There are higher qualifications that those who surround you have to meet. You need to realize that you are anointed because of what you had to overcome. Truly step back and look at what you have overcome, what strength it took to overcome, and what you have gained as a result of overcoming it all. Look at your heart now compared to where it was the day you cried out.

A few weeks ago, you were defeated and dejected. You were weakened from your fight. You lost your mind and your joy until it was barely a whisper of who you really are. Take a moment to reflect on the transformation that I have brought you to. I am pulling people out of your life that which doesn't belong there, because they would have killed that last flicker of love and of hope and of faith that you held onto. I am still working in your circumstances. Take a minute to reflect on this.

From the depths of who you are, you will light the way for others. You cannot go another round waiting for a reason to have to defend yourself against others that should no longer have the power to hurt you. They are already behind you. I have made it so and am producing so much inside of you right now to heal those feelings of despair and rejection. This is your time to reflect on the events I have planned that shook your circle to sift out what no longer belongs. Take a moment to reflect on the transformation I have brought you to. That is no longer your pain to bear. This was meant to break you, but I have made it into something that has blessed you. I made it work for your good.

I know where you come from. Everyone else sees you as strong, but I know where you came from and the battles you had to face to overcome all that came against you. I know the brokenness you had. I knew you when you were invisible. I knew you when your voice didn't matter. I know your hurt, but you can no longer live there. It is part of your history, but it no longer has the power to break you. I am your power, and I am not weakened by your enemies nor the attacks you have had to endure. I am your strength and your comforter. Take a moment to reflect on the transformation I have brought you to.

Seek me with every fiber of your being. When you are at peace, seek me, just as you did when you reached the breaking point. Seek me with the same hunger you had when you didn't know if you were going to make it. Seek me in your strength. Seek me in your joy. Seek me in your new identity. Take a moment to reflect on what I have brought you through and what I have brought you to. This will be your resource for your anointing.

I am speaking a word to what I have called you to do. Be still. Take a moment. Reflect. Do this often so you do not forget. The blessings are becoming a reality. And as you experience the blessings, you must always make time to sit for a moment. Be still. Reflect on the transformation within you, of your life, of the people that will come into your life, and the connection you have made with me. People strive to hear from me. People strive to feel my presence and you have been given so much of me.

> Remember the change at this moment.
> Remember the chains breaking.
> Remember the grief lifting.
> Remember the sorrow turning to joy.
> Remember the inadequacy turning into power.
> Remember the rejection turning into anointed acceptance.
> Remember your shame turning into grace.

Take a moment to reflect on the transformation I have brought you to. This is how you will handle the blessings I am about to pour into your life. This is how you will keep them. Be still. Take a moment. Reflect on the my power.. Reflect on how I love you. Reflect on how I have seen you. Reflect. This is your anointing.

You think you are doing something for me, but I am doing something for you. Never lose sight of that lest you become arrogant and entitled. Remember always, this moment and where you came from. My love is changing you. My love is lifting you up. My love is comforting your wounded soul. My love is shifting things in your life. It is my power, not yours. It is my will, not yours. It is my love that will react to the broken ones you encounter, not yours.

You are the messenger, but the power of the message will always be mine. For I so loved the world that I gave my only begotten son. Be still. Take a moment. Reflect on this. I chose you because I loves you. I did not choose you above others. I chose you amongst others.

§

You are going to have to give up your normal to give birth to what I have on the inside of you. You're going to have to give up what is easily accessible to be accessible to me. I listened to your prayers. This is the confirmation that you're not in it by yourself. Take the first step and let go of what your idea of normal is. You're ready to no longer be normal. This is the moment to activate the faith you prayed for. You have heard my voice and I have heard your prayers. You are a survivor, and you will survive this.

God, I hear your voice, and I don't know what's going to happen to me next but because of what exists inside of me, I have to do what I am called to do because this world needs it.

.

July 5th

§

I have been revealing things to you that show you what your brokenness gave birth to. It gave you the strength to survive and be able to tell your story with the purpose of helping someone else survive. You know what it means to have survived everything and still find joy in the little things, still look for the good in all things, still seek me in everything. Because you have survived with hope still in your heart, you have a responsibility to demonstrate how that looks, what that means, and how you have learned to thrive in environments that have hurt you. You have been preserved for a reason. It is time to begin again.

I am calling you higher to meet me where I sit, and deeper to know me where I live. I live in you and that requires you to go deeper into your life, the events that brought you here, and the blessings that were derived out of the pain. You have survived much and have survived for a reason. You must determine what your life must look like now that you have survived and what you will give into the lives of others that are barely surviving.

You are not the same person who has lived through the pain. You have evolved from the pain, and it is time for the world to see what my grace has done within you that brought you up and out of survival mode. You cannot go back to the broken girl. She is no longer you. You now recognize that the spirit of that girl has changed, and although you carry what you went through, it no longer breaks you. You have found grace in my eyes and that grace covers you always.

There is a call and a purpose on your life because you held onto that small flicker of hope and gave everything you had in the cry to me to save you. That desperate prayer was grace. That need for comfort was grace. You could have gone in a completely different direction, but you chose to press into me instead, that spirit is grace. I pushed you there to help you see that it was time to begin again. To shed the old skin of sorrow and put on a new skin of hope and faith and belief in something more, something better, something that would feed your soul into wholeness.

You heard me and pressed in beyond your fears, beyond your doubt, beyond your anger. You pressed in. That was grace. It is grace that pulled you in to develop an intimate relationship with me that has shown you that in all your flaws and failures, in all your shortcomings and sins, I chose you. This is the core of who you are, full of faith when nothing is alright. Full of joy when your world shatters. Full of hope when you are abandoned. There is a strength in you that cannot be denied. It stirs your soul to survive. It stirs your spirit to seek me. It stirs your mind to think beyond your circumstances and see a future that sings to your heart. This is the light that others see. It is time for you to see this within yourself and honor that part of you. Dare to allow your love, your light, your life to be the change you want to see in this world. Share your testimony. It will help someone else who is suffering. The thing that will lead others to their healing lives inside of you. It is time to believe it.

Be careful at how much you allow the people connected to the old you to continue a codependency, because you need to protect the you that you are becoming from old patterns and old ways and old relationships that keep you in that identity. There is too much riding on your comeback. There is too much at stake for you to step back into the thing that I took you out of. Do not be ashamed of what you went through, and do not feel guilty that you have survived it. There is beauty in both.

As you start walking your path towards peace, be mindful of the relationships that you allow into your life, whether they be old relationships or new ones. You are required to separate yourself from the places where your pain left you, but you must still honor those places and the people in them for they were part of your journey that brought you here. Walk away with the knowledge that in order for them to be who I am calling them to be, you cannot stay connected. Separate well, out of a place of love.

You have to be willing to need something different. Be real about this. Be filled with more than anything the world can give you or take away from you. Take authority of your life but demonstrate humility as you do.

July 8th

Yesterday was one of the hardest days of my life. It broke me the same way I broke when they told me that my brother Jerry died, alone in the jungle, hanging from a tree. It broke me the same way I broke when they told me my brother Gilbert died, beaten to death by two strangers he gave a ride to. They beat him to death and left him in a ditch on the side of the road. Yesterday broke me that way.

I had been fighting depression all of these years, and never has my husband taken a step back to recognize that his words and his actions could either keep me in depression or help me out of it. Yesterday, I was at my most vulnerable because I had opened up old wounds by writing a poem to his daughter so she could know who I was and where I come from, hoping that this would be the catalyst to repair my marriage. The tensions between us over the years caused so much damage in my marriage that in order to fix it, I had to start there.

Over the last two weeks, God has been pouring His word over my life, specific to what I have been going through in this home, and through His word, I was becoming stronger, finding purpose, finding peace in my soul. But yesterday, my husband's words broke me. He broke me all over again, knowing all this, words were spoken from his mouth that made me out to be crazy, obsessed with God, mentally incapable of becoming healed without psychiatric intervention. His words spoken made me believe that my sadness was unbearable for him, even though I carry it, and have carried it alone all of these years. I still work, though my bones are tired. I still cook, though I hunger. I still provide all our food, though I have nothing left to offer. I still provide all his clothes, though I lie alone naked. I still throw big family functions – single handedly, though I have no one to comfort me. I still help others, though I cry out to no one. I am still standing, though I want to fall. I am still functioning, though I am broken. And I am doing all these things with excellence, consistently, though I feel inadequate and unappreciated.

For the first time in years, I was finding purpose, peace, and happiness. I was finding strength and becoming the woman I need to be for me. For the first time in my life, my happiness mattered to me. I deserved happiness.

For the first time in my life, I was learning to love myself and appreciate my past and reconcile with what hurt me. And yesterday, his words nearly took all that I had been working towards away from me. It brought me to that place of brokenness all over again. But I realized something in the middle of all that; I don't belong there anymore.

I don't belong in that broken place anymore. I had been there long enough. I had been hurting long enough. I had seen things that tortured me in my childhood that I carried with me long enough. I let others define me long enough. I chased after their love and validation long enough. I could not live in that place inside of me anymore, and I wasn't going to let anyone tell me that's all I am nor all I have. I have done that long enough.

In order to become whole, I have to release the things that break me. I have to be able to walk away from what drives me deeper into that brokenness rather than helping me up and out of it. I don't feel a sense of home here, not in the way home should be. I have never known home, not in the way home should be a place of safety and security, a place of love and comfort and warmth from a cold world. I have never known home, not in the way it provides me rest and strength when I am weary, a place that shields me from the world and people that hurt me. I need to find home. I have been homeless long enough. I have been without a safe space long enough. I have been searching long enough to recognize that I have not found home here.

July 9th

God keeps nudging me and telling me that it is time to leave the place I have called home because I have not found it here. He has been showing me day after day, message after message (no matter who is speaking) event after event, incident after incident, dream after dream, that my home is not where I have been craving to belong. I have fought year after year to just belong here, to belong in this family, to belong with my husband, to belong in our home, to simply belong.

I realize that I have never truly been accepted, therefore have never truly belonged. And every time we get somewhat close to that sense of home, something happens. Something small and meaningless becomes a huge mess that disrupts the comforts of home. And in an instant, without notice, I am forced to feel out of place. I am snubbed and rejected, and I don't even know why. No one says anything about it to me, only amongst themselves. But I notice. I see the little looks they share when I enter the room. I feel the cold shoulder my husband gives me when he has yet to build up the courage to say something.

This goes on for weeks, months, and years. All this is happening during the hardest years of my life. I am judged without a fair trial, and I am the least and the last protected from it all. I have tried to feel like I had value in this place. I did. I realized I was the least valued, and that hurt more than all the cold and empty nights. I fought to be seen. I fought to be heard. I fought to belong. I fought to be valued. I fought to be loved the way love should love, the way home should love. I shouldn't have to fight in my home for the one thing home represents – love.

The deeper God takes me into my past in order to heal my present, He keeps showing me all that I have lacked here, all that has been deprived to me. At a time when I needed the safety and security of home, I found myself defending myself inside those very walls from the very people that could have been the ones to help carry me through the tragedies I had to face. But I found myself alone all the time. I had to love myself through my grief. I had to search for comfort elsewhere and I found my comfort in God.

It has been a long, hard, and lonely road until I put my trust in God. He has been the one constant for my cries. The one constant for my comfort. The one constant to help me make it through another day, another moment, another memory that was breaking me. He gave me what I lacked here. He is the only one that has given me a purpose to find my joy again and the safety to do it. I have been needing this kind of love from my husband, but it has been a struggle to receive it from him. Perhaps he never really believed I deserved it. But I do.

I deserve to be happy. I deserve to be secure. I deserve to be loved. I deserve understanding. I deserve healing. I deserve peace. I am a child of God and I have been treated like less for too long.

If others get mad because I am finally crying out, so be it. I am speaking truth. This has been the truth and the life I have had to live for too long. I opened myself up to the wrong people long enough. I have allowed others to determine my value long enough. God is moving on my behalf right now because I found myself so desperate that I finally found myself broken at His feet. Broken enough for Him to show me all the shattered pieces of me and show me the beauty that each piece made me into. And I am beautiful. I am becoming the me that God sees.

I needed that kind of love. The kind of love that gently held me in my brokenness. The kind of love that knew when I was hurting and loved me through my ugliness with an absolute acceptance, without judgment, and gave me the security I needed to be vulnerable enough to cry out.

I cried out in anger, and He let me. I cried out in pain, and He held me. I cried out about everything I carried, the good, the bad, the ugly and He loved me anyway, without condemnation, without judgment. He saw beyond my anger. He saw beyond my actions. He saw beyond my response to grief, and gently loved me though each one, every time. That's what home means to me.

God gave me the Word when I needed to hear it. He gave me the Word when I was ready to hear it. He showed me things about myself and my surroundings when I was ready to see it. He gave me the faith I needed to believe it. He gave me the strength to get through it. He gave me the hope to move towards something more. He gave me love when I felt all alone.

He gave me comfort when I didn't find it where I was looking for it. He showed me what love looks like when I stopped believing in it.

When I ran from Him, He ran beside me. When I hid from Him, He came to me in those dark places and waited with me. When my mind was in chaos, He gave me peace. When my world was falling apart, He started building me up. When I lost faith in the goodness of others, He showed me the good inside of me. When I started giving up, He gave me purpose. That's what home means to me.

He showed me what home should look like. He showed me what home should feel like. He showed me what home sounds like. He showed me love. In the gentle whispers of comfort, He showed me love. In the stirring warmth in my broken soul, He showed me love. In the silence of my chaotic mind, He showed me love. He gave me strength when I was at my weakest. He showed me love. When others came up against me, He showed me why the world needed me. He showed me love. He defended me, protected me, supported me, consoled me, provided for me, raised me up, dried my tears. He showed me love. This is what home means to me.

July 10th

There are different types of people in our lives that help fulfill part of our destiny; those who make something out of nothing and those who hold onto just what has been given to them. Be careful who you allow to hold things and who you allow to make things in your life because you may find yourself at the mercy of those people who hold onto parts of you that they should have never had in the first place.

If you give the wrong ingredients to the wrong people, they will start making up ideas and beliefs about you that you should have never started to believe in the first place. Take inventory of who's holding you down and who's putting you together, and ask yourself, can you trust them? You have kept them close enough to run around free when God is trying to make something new in you and you end up making friends with those who can harm you just to get along, because you don't want to shake things up. Do not allow their opinions or actions to shape your life or you find yourself in a prison of those thoughts, opinions and ideas. This will stagnate your destiny until you find you have lost your voice. Because they have been talking so much over you that you don't even know who you are anymore, and you find yourself confined in a season when God wants you to be free. You may find yourself in a position of submission to what has not been ordained for your life. Some of these moments are ordained to your call, it is your process, but it is not your place to remain there.

There is a calling on your life, and you cannot allow yourself to remain stuck in the idea of the you that others have made you believe that you are. You are more than you have been made to believe. God is waiting to see if you can tap into your purpose while feeling stuck in that prison. Can you make the best out of a bad situation? Can you turn your prison into a palace, recognizing that it became a palace because you walked into it? Do you know who you are and who God has called you to be? Because when He calls you, everything that is inside you will come out to remind you that you are above your circumstances no matter what it looks like to you or others.

It may make you look foolish or crazy to others because they don't understand who you are to God and what He has called you to become. You need to recognize that you don't have limitations based on what others believe you have. Live for the moment when God manifests what's inside of you. Tap into your gift, this is all that matters. Do what God has called you to do.

Have you ever wondered how you were able to make the best out of many situations that could have broke you? How you were able to lift the spirits of those who were in their own breaking seasons? How you were who they sought? If they could just talk to you, be near you, it helped them through their moments? You have helped others through some very trying times without realizing that your very presence eased the blows life was throwing at them.

§

Open your eyes and remember who you are to the people who love you. The ones who seek you for the simple joy that you bring just because you're there. When you begin to forget, remember those kids during the time when they lost their father, they clung to you because you were the only one that helped them laugh while they were crying inside, who felt safe with you when their world was falling apart. They know who you really are. Gravitate to the people who strive to be like you because they have seen you building even while you were breaking. You have inspired this in others that have always seen your worth. There is more inside of you that you have forgotten exists because you have been rejected for too long by people that didn't deserve you.

There are lives connected to your purpose because of what you inspire in them. This is your gift. Protect that part of you always because there are people that need you. They need you to believe again. They need you to smile again, really smile from the inside. You have inspired the broken just by being there. You carry a light within you that they need. You always have. Do not forget who you are and who I have called you to be for the souls that are still searching for their place. It is time.

July 10th - The Breakthrough

I am at a point in my life where growth is absolutely necessary. There is no other choice than to be stretched beyond my comfort zone because there have been only rare moments of real comfort. There is a deep longing down in my heart, aching my belly, building up so much that I can barely breathe. It's as if what is inside of me is growing beyond what my body can hold. I have to break out of what's boiling over and out of me. I cannot stay trapped by what no longer fits my identity.

I have to let go of the hurt that I have been carrying on this journey because it no longer fits who I am becoming more and more every day. God is pulling me out and every day I am more amazed than the day before at the word He keeps bringing me, especially at moments that I find myself trying to rebuild what no longer fits me. God is breaking beliefs, processes, patterns, and people off of me and making a way for me to "reorganize the way I have people in my life," and I need to truly reorganize what I have allowed others to pour into me, adding to my brokenness and putting nothing good back in. That change has to have a permanence that helps me to become whole again. Those who don't have the capacity to meet me where I am, nor see the me I am re-becoming are being repositioned in my life, and in my need for them in my life, not because they have no value, but because I do. They only see me in darkness, and try to keep me there, because that is where I am most vulnerable and available to them. They try to keep me in the dark because they cannot see my light.

Not everyone is called to handle who God is calling me to be. Not everyone is ready for that. They still doubt the possibility that God works in today's world, that He speaks, and guides, and instructs people. They still struggle to believe that my becoming is because I have been faithful in my heart to God when the world should have broken all my ties to faith. In an instant, I have changed. They struggle to believe that I am chosen and that I carry a divine light inside of me because they have only known me in my darkness. They struggle to believe that there is an overflow anointing taking place, and it is real, and it is God moving in my life.

A time is coming where what they don't understand will make sense later, because what they will see will be undeniable. Something is taking place here and I find that I am no longer afraid to speak up and I am no longer afraid to break old patterns. I cannot force old patterns into new situations because those patterns no longer have the power to keep me down at a level I have grown out of. This is how I have to live because the way I was living was not really living at all.

God is redirecting me, removing my insecurities, restructuring my beliefs about who I am. He is reorganizing people in my life that don't support this necessary change. He is reestablishing His presence in my life, my thought patterns, my behaviors, my beliefs. He is destroying the things inside that destroyed me. He is moving in "my" life.

I am no longer afraid of being rejected, for their rejection of me will only hurt them in the long run. This has taught me self-love because I had to dig deep to see what I really lacked and what I truly held. I realize that the hurt of rejection served a purpose in allowing me to really begin to know and love me. Rejection told me what others believed I wasn't, self-acceptance told me what I knew I already was.

I am finding that I no longer need to be validated by anyone, because other's validation of me is fickle and temperamental. I am finding that my value no longer depends on how they see me because I know who I am and what I bring. I am no longer afraid of being defined by my past and my past patterns, they were simply lessons that created who I am becoming.

God is doing something new in me and I cannot believe them and God at the same time. I cannot believe their doubts about me and still have faith in who I am. It was part of my process to becoming what my testimony carries; the power that built it, the faith that saw it through, the trust that withstood everything that was trying to keep me in doubt.

I have been flip-flopping on what I know I have heard and seen and experienced in the middle of my grief. This is not me being lost anymore. This is not desperation anymore. God has graced me with His presence and has been pulling me out. He is resurrecting me from my own death, and that death was necessary so I can know and pursue with my whole heart, the life He is leading me into; A life destined to pull others out of the same sea I was once drowning in.

July 11th

Galatians 1:11

But I make known to you brethren that the gospel which was preached by me is not according to man. For I neither received it from man, nor was I taught it, but it came through the revelation of Jesus Christ.

There is something that has been set in motion through my transformation the moment that I opened myself up to God, to His will, and to His presence. He came here, into this home, and started moving in my heart, creating the necessary environment needed for a radical change that is leading me beyond my own expectations. He has calmed the minds in this home to hear truth without bitterness and anger. There is something that has been set in motion. I cannot fail this time. I will not fail this time. I am called to be more, to do more than I have allowed myself to become and do. But God!

God is moving because I opened myself up to Him, begging Him to show me the way out of this chaos in my mind and in my home. I opened myself up to the truth about the way I was living, thinking, being. I didn't care how ugly the truth was, as long as it radically changed me and my life, because I was not living anymore.

I need to keep focused and stay in the movement that is happening and I cannot waste my time. It is time to be selfish and protect my momentum because of the promise of change that God has made for me and everyone connected to me. I need to reorganize that which makes me weak and unfocused, that which interferes with what God is doing right here, right now. There is no room for sadness and depression. I cannot settle into distractions and circumstances that prevent me from doing what I am called to do. I have to release bitterness so I can see the beauty in my ashes that will propel this movement with the power it really has.

§

Do not allow anything to dilute your momentum. Do not allow anything to influence you right now. You must see this all the way through, and you cannot be distracted. There is more depending on you completing this than your own healing. There is healing needed for others through what is happening to you.

Stay focused. Cling to what is happening inside you. Cling to the words I am bringing you. They will be your strength. I will remind you about what happened to bring you here, so you never make the same mistakes again. You will win this war because I am fighting on your behalf and I put part of that fighting spirit in your heart. You have to go head to head with those influences because it will break your momentum, but you cannot allow it to happen. There is more depending on you winning this war. Don't be fooled. It is a war.

They will know. You will become stronger when you recognize what influences make you weaker. Do not allow yourself to be hit in that same spot again. It is time to grow out of that which brings you down.

Remember this. Do not be persuaded to believe what isn't true. Do not be persuaded to accept what is only half true. Do not be persuaded by that which is hidden. Do not be persuaded. There are still forces working against you but what they don't realize is exactly how much of my power is working on your behalf. You can see something working, but even you do not know just how much of my power is working in your circumstances to change your life so you can finally move towards your calling and fulfill your purpose. Stay plugged into my power. Keep your prayer time. Keep hold of your separation from everything and everyone so that strength can become so deeply embedded in who you are becoming that it is no longer a question of becoming, but rather, being exactly who you really are.

Where you are going will require a strength and a faithfulness to your calling that cannot be persuaded by those who are easily influenced by others. You are too valuable to the kingdom and what I am about to do in the lives that have been calling on me to allow anything and anyone to keep you where you were.

The Revelations

Your journey will require stamina and commitment to the calling. You can no longer be tied to emotions that do not serve a purpose in your purpose. That time is over. That season is finished. I am moving. There is something that has been set in motion and it starts with your transformation. You have no idea what is coming, but your faith to follow it, wherever it leads, will be the cord that binds you to me and will be unbreakable.

Keep watch on what you are allowing to influence you and stop it in its tracks. There is no room for error. There is no time for delay. There is no allowance for compromise any longer. Remember this.

Go back to the moment this revelation occurred, the day your brokenness forced you to see. Remember this.

Go back to the memories of what was happening that caused you to pray with radical expectations and a deep desperation to change which brought you this revelation. It no longer has the power to persuade you because you are not allowed to allow what beat you down before to beat you down again. That no longer has power to move your heart. Do not go back to that corner. Do not go back to what broke you. Move these things out of your way and create the environment needed now. Remember this.

You are growing and there is no more space for that which has a negative influence on your mind and heart. It no longer deserves your attention. Those who lost you, lost you for their own reasons. Let them go for your own reasons. I started this and you are required to follow me all the way through to that destination. Those things were only part of your journey and it brought you to this moment. It caused you to cry out with a bitter honesty. It caused you to cry out from deep sorrow of rejection. It caused you to lean into me like never before. It caused you to see your true worth. That was its only purpose in your life, and it is now time to lock the door on that which influenced you before, that which broke you has no place in your life anymore. Remember this.

When you lose sight of everything, go back to this revelation because the momentum is connected to the revelation. The vision is connected to the revelation. The breakthrough is connected to the revelation. The strength to walk away is connected to the revelation. Remember this.

Your gift is too big for this room, this space, and the people that are not ready to believe. Remember this.

This is why you find yourself reading your journal over and over again. You are seeing the connection on what started this revelation and watching where it has taken you because you realize that you cannot go back to that place ever again. You realize that the brokenness started this. Those who mistreated you started this. Thank them and move on. That is where you will shed your bitterness. Remember this.

They served a purpose to bring you to this moment. What you experienced served a purpose to bring you to this moment. Your pain served a purpose to bring you to this moment, but there isn't any room for any of that now that your heart is taking hold of your purpose. I am filling you up, which means that you have to let some things on the inside of you go to make room for what I am bringing you into. Remember this.

Don't allow yourself to be influenced again. Your revelation is more powerful than any of your old influences. You had an encounter that cannot be disputed. That revelation is more powerful than any of these influences. Remember this.

I set you in that family because there was a revelation that I had about who you are and I have been waiting for you to live your life by that revelation to change the culture around you so others can see who I am and what I can do. Your strength must be found in me. Remove the influences that are in you that prevent the momentum from flowing through you and in you. Be connected to who and what will inspire and add to your momentum and not take away from it. This must be your priority. Protect your heart from outside influences that try to take you back to the old you with the old hurts that keep you down.

You can no longer allow disappointment to break you any more than you have already been broken. Your change and your transformation will be an influence for others whose brokenness has overwhelmed their souls and who live with that death in their souls every day. You are the catalyst because you reached out of the darkness towards the only light that could save you. Remember this.

July 13th

§

In order to take the next step, there are some things you will need to sacrifice, and going through the motions is no longer an option. The shift has been made and a change has occurred, and you no longer fit into the circles that once were yours.

You have received too much knowledge about the old you to fit in as the you that you are becoming. Pray that you do not enter into temptation because you long for the old times. Sometimes you have to teach others to live without you. You are not their resource and the longer you stay, the easier it is to depend on you and not seek me during their own transition. Your gain is not their gain, and their gain will not be yours. Your destinies have shifted in different directions, and you need to accept that and acknowledge that it is time for action.

The way that you find me will change and you will need to discover new ways to find me because your pain will not be the force that drives you to seek me. You have elevated beyond that and your hunger for my presence will now have to come out of the peace you have found in the knowing you have been given in the destiny you will now pursue. Your hunger must be built on the relationship you have developed with me. And just as you have fought to be loved by others in your past, you must recognize that dependence on your need for my unfailing love must be that constant in your life. This will be your source for acceptance and belonging. This will be your source of comfort. This will be your source. Remember this.

I have moved from the place that you have always found me. You now have a direct connection with me, and you must protect that at all costs. Though you are still familiar to those who have known you all of these years, you have changed and evolved beyond what you used to indulge. Those attitudes and behaviors are no longer acceptable to who you are becoming. You are not better than them, you are just traveling on your journey at a different pace than everyone else because I need you to move ahead of them. Because at some point later you will be the one I use to guide them. But for now, you must leave them in my hands so I can continue this work in you so when the day comes that you are needed, you will be a ready and peaceful spirit, free from all the hurt that made you bitter so you can help others shed that same bitterness at a crucial point in their journeys.

I am calling you out of these circumstances and surroundings to a place where you can connect with me without distractions. I will isolate you for a time and then slowly add people in your life that will push you to the next level until you are where you are needed for the moment others need you, solely for the purpose you were created.

And if you remain too close, they will become bitter at this, and it will be too easy for them to stew in that bitterness rather than recognize their own need for me. You are not helping them reach me by remaining so close and available. Not now, not yet.

Were they loyal to you when you were broken and hurt on the inside? Were they a loving support system that saw your brokenness and did everything to shield you from further pain? Or when you became dysfunctional and lost, did they cease to provide for you the love they said they had? You must recognize this because this is your discernment on the people who are allowed to travel with you on the rest of your journey. Do not be tied to what you wished could have happened when you were breaking. Do not be tied to what you had hoped would have been given to you while you were broken. Do not be tied to what you wish was, but never truly was. Do not be tied to a false love or you will miss what love truly is, my way.

Do not remain tied to the people who were not loyal to your cross because the road ahead of you will be even harder for them, for they will not understand your journey nor your purpose. Do not remain tied to the people who failed to remain loyal to you when your life turned upside down and your pain overwhelmed you, and you found them talking about you rather than to you, judging you rather than seeing the weight of the cross you were carrying. They further beat you down, rather than helped you up. They made mountains out of molehills about the little things rather than have to see the real things that you were breaking under. That is not love.

Although you have forgiven this of them, you cannot forget the pain that it caused you when you thought you couldn't bear any more than you were already feeling, for this pain is the catalyst to serving others. Remember the pain, but do not live there in the pain. This will be your reminder of the strength you really have on the inside of you. This will be your connection to me. Remember the pain, but only for the strength that it showed you that you possess. You have already evolved out of that pain, and you will now connect with me through your purpose that evolved from that pain. Your pain was only a small piece of what shaped you for who you will become. It was only your experience, not your existence.

Remember this.

Do not remain loyal to having company when what you need are genuine relationships. Company serves no real purpose to your soul growth and can serve to shatter your peace depending on the company you keep, or the company they keep that influences them. Just as your very presence can change the atmosphere of a room, these other influences can change the atmosphere of your space. It has always had that power because your foundation in your home was never fully planted in me. It did not operate solely based on what is right, what is of me, what is love. It did not correct that which needed correction. It did not comfort that which needed comfort. That is not love, not in the way I love.

You have been given too much knowledge and awareness to go back to that. You have grown out of it and it is time to move on.

July 14th

That which once hurt you no longer has the power to hurt you.

Mark 11:22

Then Jesus said to his disciples, "Have faith in God. I tell you the truth. If you say to this mountain, 'May you be lifted up and thrown into the sea,' and it will happen. But you must really believe it will happen and have no doubt in your heart. I tell you, you can pray for anything, and if you believe that you've received it, it will be yours. But when you are praying, first forgive anyone you are holding a grudge against, so that your father in heaven will forgive your sins too."

You prayed and I answered you because you prayed for the right things. You no longer prayed to be saved from your oppression, you prayed to see it for what it is. You no longer prayed to be loved, but prayed to know what love looks like, feels like, and acts like. You stopped running from, but rather ran back to that place that hurt you, with fresh eyes to see what has been forced into hiding for so long. And once you saw it, you had an appreciation for the pain. This allowed you to move past it for you saw that it was no longer good for you and no longer fit who you are becoming.

It's okay to say to a thing, "This no longer works for my spirit," as long as you can appreciate that it too has a place in my heart. Hate for a thing cannot fill the heart where love needs to grow. You cannot carry it with you and expect love to flow through you. You had to go back to forgive so you could release what caused you to hate. I have shown you the things that have hurt you, but have also shown you your own ugly responses to others that hurt them so you could see with the eyes of truth and be ready to release what has bound you to that pain. Unhealed pain is the catalyst for damage to another, and you cannot carry that pain with you while hoping to lead others on the path to healing.

I know you have longed for that place and the promise it could have, but it is no longer a place for you. This is where you bury your pain and move on. I know you longed to stay and be normal, but you are not normal, and you need to see beyond your vision of what you should be and accept who

I have called you to be. You needed to return to the place that broke you to make peace with your pain, to make peace with the people, to understand the dynamics there and to forgive so that you do not harbor bitterness in your soul, for you cannot carry that with you.

You cannot leave the same way as you have before, running from someplace, while still carrying the pain of that place. You needed to face it, see it, and set it down, for you cannot carry those hurts and pains and burdens with you any longer, and still be filled with the Holy Spirit at the same time. You needed a way of revelation so that when you leave, you leave better, knowing who you are. You are not the same person that was buried with the pains of loss, rejection, and fear. You are more because you survived that loss. You have survived that rejection. You survived the fear of not being enough. You found out that you are more than all of that. It was only your experience, not your existence. Remember this.

This time you are leaving with clarity. This time you are leaving understanding your pain, your connections, that place, and its blessings. This time you are leaving, not from a sense of rejection, but a true personal acceptance of who you really are, and an understanding that there is no more room for the pain because your heart is finally healing. This time you are leaving with grace, and my blessing. This time you made peace with your pain. This time you made peace with the truth of your pain. You could not leave until you understood what oppressed you. It is no longer yours to carry. You faced it. You saw it. You accepted its value, and now it is time to set it down and let it go.

You went back broken and came out believing again. But this time you have made room for me to work miracles in your heart so my love and spirit can flow freely through you. I have made it so. That is my grace. You used to be someone else, but I have brought you full circle, and you can leave the heartbreak in that circle. Take only what you learned about yourself and what you really need so that when you go, you never have to go back to that person you left behind; That version of you that wasn't working, that version of you that only saw brokenness. You have broken the patterns when you opened up your heart to me, for I led you through your oppression so you could leave healed and with grace.

You are not the same as you were before. My hand has moved in your life and my spirit has moved in your soul like never before, showing you things about your oppression that did not define you. I wanted you to see your worth, and you have. Hold her and protect her for she has been chosen to lead others out of personal bondage.

You are not perfect, but you are perfectly mine. Now that you know this, you can move on. You're going to be the bridge. You can leave now. Leave well.

July 15th

It is easy to do what is expected of you but what do you do when something completely unexpected starts happening inside you that changes your perspective on who you really are, and what life and love should look and feel like? What do you do when God starts showing you truth about your situations and people in your environment that influence your spirit?

§

You need to measure everyone against the standards that I have set for you, for your healing, for your purpose, and for living the life Christ died for you to live. You are no longer in a position that allows you to settle because your destiny requires you to have strength and light and joy. Remember, you cannot effectively give what you do not have, and those in your environment either need to participate in building that up in you or they are not serving my purpose for which I have designed for your life. Your mission is too important to settle.

You are called to lift the spirits of others and because of that, your spirit needs to be lifted above where you were. Your environment needs to contribute to and refresh your spirit for the greater purpose. You are no longer bound to the thoughts others choose to remember about you if they refuse to see who you are becoming. Your environment needs to nurture that growth, or they are only harming and preventing the restoration that I have called you into for your own healing, and what you will to bring to others.

Do not let their doubts about your calling make you question your relationship with me. I have been speaking to you, building you up, and reminding you of your value. I have used different people and different messages to speak the same thing to you so that you adopt that belief deep down in your soul and begin moving out that which has damaged you for so long. You cannot afford to settle for the things that hurt you because you are being called to heal others and you cannot effectively give what you, yourself, do not possess. Your belief about yourself must be set in your own personal strength and value, if that is what you hope to instill in others. You cannot give what you, yourself, do not possess. If you deny yourself value, how can you teach others of their own value and worth?

This is how you need to qualify every decision you make going forward and weigh it against everything I have already told you. You cannot allow yourself to be persuaded by the thoughts that bring you back to the pain I have been working to heal. If you find yourself aching in your gut at the thought or idea of certain choices or paths, then that is not from me. I bring you peace in your choices because you recognize my presence in those plans and a hope for your future. Do you not recognize what I am doing inside you and in your life? It is essential at this moment that you stop your thoughts and remember what I have shown you and remember what I told you.

Matthew 13:16

But blessed are your eyes because they see, and your ears because they hear. I tell you the truth, many prophets and righteous people longed to see what you see, but they didn't see it. And they longed to hear what you hear, but they didn't hear it.

July 17th

Isaiah 65:6
Look, my decree is written out in front of me. I will not stand silent.

§

I have created boundaries for a reason. Even seasons start and stop at certain points, and the atmosphere changes instantly. There is a certain level of freedom that occurs when these changes come about, but you will also need to establish new boundaries. Learn how to manage yourself in this freedom and teach others. You will come across people that need to learn to respect your boundaries for those boundaries have been set to protect you from what you have left behind. Those boundaries are set to serve my purpose and you cannot allow those lines to be crossed. You will also come across people that will need to learn how to break through those boundaries for they also bear a greater responsibility in fulfilling my purpose, and you must gently teach them how to break through the boundaries that are not set for them.

Remember to focus on why you are on this earth and do not get lost in your freedom, lest your freedom becomes your prison. Realize that although you have been filled with my word, not every situation will give you the freedom to express that word in the way that you feel it and know it. You have a tendency to speak your mind about your truth, but don't always recognize the truth in someone else's journey. Respect the boundaries other people have set for themselves. You have a kind of love inside that can be overwhelming to people that don't understand that kind of love, and you cannot freely give that kind of love to a people that are still learning to discover theirs.

You have been struggling with the patterns of abuse for so long because you never let yourself create the boundaries for you. Everyone else around you had boundaries that you had to respect and work around, but you failed to create ones for yourself, your own sanity, and your own freedom. You have done this until you resented it because you became boxed in by the boundaries that others had for themselves, that when you needed boundaries for yourself there was no room for those boundaries in the patterns you allowed. It is time to break through that box you found yourself in.

July 19th

Daniel 4:36

When my sanity returned to me, so did my honor and glory and kingdom. My advisors and nobles sought me out, and I was restored as head of my kingdom with even greater honor than before.

There was a time in my life when my brokenness nearly brought me to an uncontrollable insanity, inconsolable and self-rejected. This time was not that far back, and in an instant, I was propelled on a journey where God began pulling me out and giving me purpose by exposing everything that I had been going through, everything I allowed myself to become, and everything I desperately clung to no matter what it was doing to me.

I had reached a desperation that was enough to drop my walls, secrets, and self at the foot of the cross. I cried out and He helped me through it all. It has been a process, that at times, brought me to my knees in exhaustion. I started seeing things about myself that I closed my mind off to, things inside me that were too ugly and shameful to accept, but with His consistent and gentle promptings, He led me through those realizations until I started to see the beauty in all of it.

July 25th

Because I had reached a point in my life where God no longer walked with me through my sin and suffering, my desperation for change made me cry out. And when I did, He answered me immediately. Something amazing started taking place on the inside. Although the process of change has been challenging, it has been necessary. I still battle the need to please others and occasionally find myself being drawn back to that desperation. It is in those moments that the Spirit of Christ comes to me to strengthen my bones so I can continue my walk with Him.

He knows my pain for He took a lashing for it and carried it away before I even knew I would experience it. When my distractions overwhelm me, He finds me and straightens my path. As I continue my walk with Him, I can see the changes in myself, but this is a process of releasing and removing my guilt to need this change, above everything. Nothing can take priority right now. God reminds me every day that I do not belong in the dark to be swallowed up by the dark, for I am His light that will change the dark I stand in, for He is in me, and I am in Him.

His nature lives in me and I must remember this always. Daily, He dusts me off and daily, I am a little better than I was the day before. He wants me to recognize how far I have come. The darkness is not my home anymore and is no longer my identity. It was my experience, not my existence.

He has shown me how my experiences started changing my identity, and daily he brings be back to who I really am. He shows me the ugly parts of myself so that I adopt the desire in my heart to change those things forever. It is not always easy, but it is necessary. He shows me my failures so I can move beyond them and forgive myself. I recognize the miracles daily and even when I think I am still in the darkness, it is a daily fight to recognize the power He has given me, but I need to. Every day it gets a little easier.

I also have to remember that my change is a process. This is a peeling off of each layer of protection that I built against everything with each sorrow I felt and each injustice I have lived through. I have to peel back those layers, discard them, replace them with purpose, adopt a new skin, and then move on. Some days this process is quick and instant, and some days it is harder and requires more faith to let these things go.

For every moment that I am set back into what I was, He comes to me and brings me revelations on who and what I have become. For every instance that I find myself questioning what is happening and why I am doing what I am doing, He comes to me and shows me how the path He has set me on is better for all. For every time that I am faced with the pain of these changes, He gives me insight and shows me the beauty that I have become from that pain and reveals purpose in what and why my life is becoming.

When I am teetering on the decision to go back just to keep the peace, He reminds me of the peace I did not have and reveals what the past has robbed me of. This is not to keep me in unforgiveness, but to provide me direction on why I need to keep going. He shows me the years that I have lived in that darkness. He shows me the ways that I have become that darkness in my heart. He shows me how I allowed myself to become less than what I am called to be. He reminds me each time of what I need to do, where I need to go, and does not let me fall back into who I was before all this.

When my faith is shaken, He reveals how His hand has been moving in my life. When my sadness is overwhelming, He lightens my spirit through others, to remind me that sadness is no longer my cross to carry. When I feel that I have nothing, He shows me everything He has been preparing for me. When I feel lost and alone, He lights my path. All of this comes through interactions with others or a message that is tailor-made for the moment I am experiencing, to show me that all is well, and all is right. He lifts me up and allows my spirit to soar in those moments that I feel most defeated. When I begin to doubt the path that I am on, He causes things in the moment to change my doubt into faith again. He does not let me fall back into the trappings of my own mind. He does not let me fall back into the sorrows that I once felt. He does not let me fall.

When I consider going back, He causes events to happen to show me what I would really be heading back to so that I can see beyond the empty promises. When I consider going back, He shows me where I am currently standing and the love that He has brought back to me, so my steps do not falter back to the familiar. I cannot explain these moments, but they occur when I feel my vulnerability is leading me back to the things that broke me. When my mind wanders back, He pulls me in closer and shows me where I am, and it is good.

§

I know you. I know where you are weakened. I know what strengths to pull out of you to move you beyond your weakness. You must become whole in the beauty that I see in you before you can share that with the world to inspire it in others. You have to peel back what is not of me in order to replace it with what I have for your becoming. You will be an influence for those that you know and will come to know. That influence must be purified by me, for the effect you will have can make or break a person's connection to their own walk with me, even for a moment. A moment can change someone's path for a long time. My love and my light must be your foundation, or it is something other than me.

You must qualify parts of yourself and attitudes towards people and things of this world before allowing that thing to enter the spaces between you and others. You must discern each connection and what is creating that connection. Does that connection add to each of you, or detract from one another? By applying discernment in your connections, you will learn where to apply light and when to leave that connection in the dark, for it no longer belongs to the you that you are required to be. Every relationship has the power to move you in one way or another, so be wary and guard yourself, for you must protect who you are and what you offer to the world because it can be poisoned by connections in your life.

You will always be growing and becoming, so be careful of what you allow to be added to yourself, always. You are not needy, you are needed, but do not allow yourself to be consumed by your connections. Remember to discern each one. Does it add to or take away from who you are called to be? Not everyone bears this responsibility. You have been chosen to demonstrate to a broken people what true wholeness in Christ looks and lives like. You are called to demonstrate your broken pieces that I have carefully put back together into beauty.

Your pain of change is necessary because this is you recognizing what does not fit into being who you are required to become. Others may not understand it, but they don't need to yet, and you must remove the need to be understood at this time so you can focus on what He is doing inside you. I am reshaping your beliefs about yourself, your experiences, your tragedies, your past, to show you the person you have become from it all. You have allowed yourself to believe things about yourself that have no place in your consciousness where my light must live. It is time to shed all these things. It is time to become whole in my hands so I can do through you all that needs to be done, and there can be no attachment to the you that can be allowed to distract you from your calling. You are not needy. You are needed by me to do good works for my people.

I am bringing about a change in my people. I am restoring my people back to their kingdom walk, to change the world and the hearts within them. It is time to align yourself with this purpose. Your spirit needs to change from the mindset of loss and defeat to one of power in what I have placed down inside of you for a purpose that belongs to no other.

When you begin to recognize this, you will have moved out of an old layer and into a new you. You have a divine purpose. It is time to own it. Those years no longer have the power to persuade your calling. Your current process of change is me restoring the you whom you have always been before life, people, and circumstances began to change your perspective on who you are. You are now under my protection and covering, and what used to affect you and hit you can no longer reach you long enough to make a difference. Continue to do good and love others through this process but understand that your love cannot change who you are becoming. You cannot allow yourself to be influenced, you must influence others and inspire them to recognize their own truths for I am calling my people back to me. For my people have been living in fear from the follies of this world and there is a spiritual battle that has been overwhelming them. It is time to remind them who they are, who they represent, and what they stand for. You must inspire them to see truth in their circumstances so they begin to open themselves up to my light, where I can begin to reach them again.

You have been favored beyond your own earnings for a purpose, and my mercies cover you daily. Remain connected to this truth. There are instructions you have already been given and you must remain connected to these instructions. If that requires you to go back into your journal often, then do it. These are your instructions from me. This is my word to you. This is my word for your life. In those pages, you will remember your calling. When you start to feel disconnected, go back to the beginning again. You have been given what you need to move into what you need to become and into your connection with me. My light is your light, and my guidance for your life is already written in these pages. Do not keep looking for answers, but seek confirmation in all things and all connections, and be sure they align with what you already know of your truth, for I have already revealed it to you.

Do not want what does not serve my purpose in your life for these things can tarnish the mirror that reflects to you my hand on you, in your life, and over your purpose. Do not forget. Don't let yourself be distracted and divided from my Spirit, for I will be your guide through all things that threaten to invade your environment.

July 26th

§

Though you see the troubles of this world, remain faithful to my cause, changing one heart at a time. Worry not and pray about everything. There are many wounded souls that need just a flicker of light to begin their own journeys to healing in the same way you have, and your responsibility is to help guide them through the process, for as you know, it is difficult, challenging, and can often feel like defeat. The ultimate goal is to guide them through to the path of peace. Remember not to judge their journey for these are the steps that I have ordained and planned for them to take, and each person's journey is valuable.

Honor their journey and always keep in mind that their process is their own. This will test your ability to tap directly into the love, understanding, and truth of Christ's heart. Be mindful of how you approach each person and their situation, remember that they are in my hands and that what you learned from your own personal journey is only a small portion of wisdom for their personal journey. My Spirit will guide you if you remain connected and always pursue my Spirit in all your interactions. Remember that every interaction will present an opportunity for you to bring my Spirit into it by allowing my Spirit to tame your thoughts and your tongue.

People will forget the words you say but will never forget how you made them feel. If you allow only my Spirit to penetrate your soul, you will emit my Spirit into your meetings and interactions, and this is what they will remember, my touch, my Spirit, my presence. This is the ultimate goal, that they too will come to know me with a deep intimacy that I speak to them, and they too see me in all things.

All open and old wounds can be healed through their personal relationship with me. They will find their peace, wholeness, understanding and healing. My touch, my word, my presence, when received, even through a small sliver of hope, will change hearts and minds and lives instantly. That small flicker of hope is key to finding me. Refrain from speaking about other's situations with judgment and condemnation and remember that every wound is precious in my eyes. Every wound requires a gentle touch and reverence for the opportunity it brings to lead others to the Hope of Christ. Offer only the wisdom of hope and what blessings even their wounds will bring. For every wound is important to me and I see them all and feel them all, as my own. That small flicker of hope will be the salve and medication for their wounds.

With hope, speak faith, for faith will be their strength during the healing process and will be required when their wounds are exposed. Faith will be what carries them through each step in their process even if it just a tiny flicker of faith, this will grow through their process. Guide them into faith, speak of its power always. Demonstrate faith in your speech, in your actions, in your view of every situation. Every situation will present an opportunity to speak faith. This will be a spark that will ultimately create a fire that cannot be put out. So always speak hope and speak faith in all things.

July 28th

§

Guidance is found in me. Inspiration is found in me. Healing is found in me. Breaking strongholds of depression, worry, and anxiety is found in me. You will not find this in another, until you first find yourself in me. You have a direct connection to true peace, true love, and true strength, with Him. When you seek me, I will show you what all of this has been about. When you dedicate yourself and your time to seek me, in all things, then open up your heart and shut out the rest of the world, I will light the way to true change.

The world can love you, they can support you, but they cannot give you the self-love you seek until you are equally whole in my love. I want you to see yourself from my eyes, but you must go deeper. I see the you that is evolved from the trappings of your circumstances. I see the you that dances through the storm. I see the you that overcomes adversity and comes out stronger than before. I see the you that you do not see in the mirror. I see beyond your own limited beliefs about who you are, for I see you in your fullest.

I know when your prayers are sincere and not just a show for recognition or religious obligation. I hear the moaning in your heart when you are too afraid to speak your truth to me. I see beyond the failures that you feel inside yourself. I see you rising above it all. I know when trusting me is difficult, and when the difficulties destroy your trust in me. I run beside you when you run from me, knowing that I need to be present the moment you can no longer run. My mercy and love for you are greater than your self-inflicted judgment. I see you through eyes of unconditional love, for I know your true self, and gently guide you to who you really are.

I wait for you to seek me so I can transform the pain inside you, for this is where your healing is waiting. I will work until you find wholeness, so that you too will learn to love yourself from a place that is free.

Stop looking for immediate answers. Healing is a process, and the process is divine, and only happens when you fully invest in the process.

Do not rush it, for there is beauty in the rebuilding of who you are. Even opening yourself up entirely to me can be a process.

If you want to see your strength, you must first face your weakness. If you want wholeness, you must first admit your brokenness, for you cannot pick up all the pieces in the dark. If you want joy, you must first face your sorrows and release them, for you cannot live in the fullness of either while keeping tethered to the other. If you want love then you must also face the hidden hate that lives within the depth of your heart, for love cannot survive what hate consumes. If you want trust then you must first face your own failures towards another and learn to see them with the same grace you feel you deserve. When you go through transformation, all that was difficult to do and be are buried, and you learn that peace was produced from the lessons of your own chaos.

Everyone has their own journey to revelation because it is their journeys that make them who they are. It is their journeys that make their own purposes unique to them, but it is their own choice on how far they will go. It is the universal desire to know why one has been born to this life, but few will look beyond the impossible answer, to find that the answer was within them all along.

Pause long enough to hear my voice in your decisions. Move in my power, and never forget that my power is something you already possess. Where there is great power, greater is the responsibility to others who have yet to begin their journeys.

You must become whole to lead others to wholeness. This is also the same lesson in letting go.

You must recognize what builds you up, and what breaks you down, in order to build others. This is the same lesson as self-control.

You must learn to love yourself in all your flaws and failures in order to instill self-love in others. This is the same lesson as forgiveness and acceptance.

You must recognize what disturbs your peace, and what causes disappointment, in order to teach others that relationships cannot work when expectations are unreal. This is the same lesson as truth and understanding.

You must learn the value of wisdom and understand that it can be destroyed by intellect. Wisdom is attained through a hearts personal experience and what you gain through intellect is learned from another. In order to teach another value of perception, you will need to learn the difference between the two. This is the same lesson as compassion.

You cannot give what you do not have for yourself first. Lest you become depleted and resentful towards those you vow to help. Then your help becomes the thing that breaks another down. This is the same lesson as strength.

Do not become selfish with the gifts you have been given, lest you become distracted from the light you have found. You cannot teach others that the power exists within them if you are busy competing for some place perceived to be above them. This is the same lesson as true love.

I will give you what you need, what is good for you. I have shown you this many times, even in times that you did not recognize my hand in it. Stop striving for recognition of self-power. This is not persuasive. You have found yourself asking "What am I doing this for," and expect an answer to come from others, but you must first find the answer within yourself. You will know the real answer when it is not tarnished by self-seeking gratification, everything besides this will leave you empty.

How are all your relationships? Are they fulfilling? Do they all add to your wholeness? Do they each bring you joy that cannot be shaken? Or do you find yourself empty deep inside, still? That emptiness is my voice to the true you, not about others nor your circumstances. Self-reflection is powerful, ownership of your failures and successes even more.

The power of fulfillment does not appear from your circumstances, nor your achievements, nor the people in your life. The power comes from me. Never stop seeking me, lest you find yourself lost in the need to prove your worth and your value to those who don't know who you truly are.

Nothing will fulfill you until you accept this fully. Your experience with me cannot be based solely in what you need in the moment. Your moments must be based entirely on your experience with me. Your experience with me can no longer be based on me meeting your temporary needs, for all things are temporary. It needs to be based on a permanence, a relationship with me where you seek me in all things first.

Though you have prayed to me, and I have answered you, you need to go deeper. When your prayers become shallow and self-serving, pray to serve and all will be given to you to do what needs to be done. If your prayers only serve yourself, you will always come up empty.

Do not allow circumstances in your life to shake you but follow the path in full faith that I have guided you there for a purpose. Do not give too much power to your circumstances lest you take the my power out of them and come up empty. Always lead with the belief that all things will work for your good when you follow the path laid before you.

Never stop believing. Never stop seeking me. Never stop listening for my voice. Always remember that no turn is the end of your story, but rather a chosen path to a new lesson, new beginnings, and new experiences that will continue building you into who you are meant to be. Rely only on me and I will lead you there.

The season is now. Reach for me with the same drive and desperation that you have reached for everything else. This is where your power will come from. Things are happening around you that you do not understand. You think you do, but you do not because understanding comes from me. I have moved everything in your circumstances so that you find yourself alone with me. What are you going to do with it? The season is now.

August 1st

Last night was my first night in my little place. It was a little awkward and uncomfortable at first, but I slept through most of the night and when I woke up, I sat for a minute, looked around, and realized that I could not have done any of this without God. He made everything possible, paved the way for me, brought others to help me, and here I am.

I am not sure yet exactly what all this means, but I feel a peace about it and a certainty that He is leading me towards wholeness, and my purpose, and my destiny. Thank you, God for all that you do for me.

He is placing me in a position to hear Him so I can recognize His powers and walk closer with Him. He has been consistently with me and showing me my broken and doubting mind with every step I am taking before I take each step. He has shown me how my walk must be, and when I felt challenged, He showed me more. God has been taking me and showing me my weaknesses, and I see His strength. He has shown me my fears, and I see His faith. He has shown me my pride, and I see His humility. He has shown me my sins, and I see His grace. He has shown me my doubts, and I see His promises. He has shown me my idols, and I see His truth. He walks with me every minute and straightens my path, corrects my footsteps, and leads me through until my joy becomes real as I see all that He has done for "me."

Below is the random bible verse I was brought to after writing my morning entry.

1 Chronicles 17:16-18

Then King David went in and sat before the Lord and prayed. "Who am I, O Lord God, and what is my family that you have brought me this far? And now O God, in addition to everything else, you speak of giving your servant a lasting dynasty! You speak as though I were someone very great, O Lord God! What more can I say to you about the way you have honored me? You know what your servant is really like. For the sake of your servant, O Lord, and according to your will, you have done all the great things and have made them known."

§

Because you have been walking in obedience even when it was uncomfortable and painful, I have blessed you. Because your faith stood up against your fears, you have been blessed. Because you have recognized my hand in all things happening, I have made room for more. Because you are following my voice, I speak to you. Because you stop to seek me in every decision, I have sent my Spirit to guide you. Because you have sacrificed what was familiar, I will bless what you think you lost. I will not forsake you nor leave you for I see your love, your faith, and your hopes. I answer you consistently because you stop to remember me, and you do this in both moments of peace and of inner turmoil. Your faith in me has been seen and has touched my heart more than you realize.

I am watching you develop into the fullness in which I have created you for and have looked beyond your sins to show you how worthy you are to me. I have seen beyond your crazy and brought you peace. I know you. I know your mess. I know your confusion. I know each fear. I know your struggles. I know your inner challenges and have qualified you because of your faith and obedience. I recognize what you have been through, and I noticed how you pressed into me even more.

Even in your disobedience to your destiny, I straighten your path and sharpen your mind and intensify the presence of my Spirit so you know it is me. I will not leave you where you were because I have seen your heart is perfect towards me. I allow my Spirit to reach you in your stubbornness and have reminded you of the desert you were once lost in. I know you and prepare the Holy Spirit for each moment you start to fail yourself because I know your heart wants to follow me no matter what you have to lose. I have been waiting for you to recognize my touch on each moment of your life.

Because you have been willing to follow me, I am guiding you with a fierceness that will not allow you to falter. I know your heart and that it is for me. I see you at that moment that reasoning and compromise start to lead you through and beyond your own thoughts and responses. I know you. I see your heart. I have heard your prayers to know me like never before. I have heard that prayer in your deepest broken moment, and how you loved me purely even in your brokenness. I saw your praise even through your tears. I will not let you fail. I give you my strength in your weakness. I give you my courage in the middle of your fears. I will guide you for as long as you seek me in all things.

Psalm 40: 1-3

I waited patiently for the Lord to help me, and He turned to me and heard me cry. He lifted me out of the pit of despair, out of the mud and the mire. He set my feet on solid ground and steadied me as I walked along. He gave me a new song to sing, a hymn of praise to our God. Many will see what He has done and be amazed. They will put their trust in the Lord.

§

You are wrestling with the word you have been given though the word has not changed. Still, you find yourself clinging to the alternative for fear of both feeling sorrow and causing it. I have been leading you out of bondage, and still, you fight to stay. I heard your cry from deep in your belly and rescued you, but you still find yourself in temptation to run back. But I cannot complete my process in the hearts of those in that land until all they have is me. You received a verse this morning when you woke with a pain in your belly, an ache in your heart, and your judgment clouded with emotions that you had already been released of. Do not pass this verse off by chance for it is my Spirit that caused your discomfort and brought you to this word. You cannot go back to the ways that are dead for they have done no good.

Mark 4:12

So that the scriptures might be fulfilled: When they see what I do they will learn nothing. When they hear what I say, they will not understand. Otherwise they will turn to me and be forgiven.

§

You have given your testimony and have spoken my words for them. You have shared instructions on how to bring peace to this place of turmoil and destruction. You have shown them my Spirit. You have directed them to seek me wholeheartedly and still they linger in their own thoughts and in their own power to persuade you that changes are being made, yet have not taken the most important step to honor the changes I am bringing.

They speak to you from a place of doubt and linger on their pains rather than seeing yours, and still you battle with this letting go and letting me heal them. You do not have the power to change their minds nor their hearts. That can only come from me and this is no longer your battle. When they seek me, they will find favor. When they seek me, they will have earned the right to follow you. When they seek me, they will be forgiven for hurting my people. When they seek me, they will find me and everything will change.

This is not your battle. There was a reason why you left. Do not be persuaded by what looks good if they have not taken the steps that you gave them, nor followed your instructions. It is easy for a person to say, "I will," in desperation, but you must qualify their worthiness to follow you by the actions they take immediately or do not take in its fullest as is required.

I need you focused now, but you are allowing others to distract you and take your time away from me. This is a crucial time for you, and you cannot lose time nor the opportunity because you are too distracted.

Just because you face opposition, this does not mean that my plan for you has changed. You are at a point of incredible breakthrough where past hurts can no longer hurt you ever again. You are at a point where the road must change and you must follow that path faithfully.

August 3rd

Mark 14:6

Leave her alone. Why criticize her for doing such a good thing to me? You will always have the poor among you, and you can help them whenever you want to. But you will not always have me. She has done what she could and has anointed my body for burial ahead of time. I tell you the truth, where the Good News is preached throughout the world, this woman's deed will be remembered and discussed.

§

You must be intentional about your time with me. I woke you before to show you my power in that hour of invitation. Now you must seek me diligently no matter where you are.

John 10:17-18

The Father loves me because I sacrifice my life so I may take it back again. No one can take my life from me. I sacrifice it voluntarily. For I have the authority to lay it down when I want to and also take it back up again. For this is what my Father commanded.

§

Make room for me. Give me a dedicated space and time that you invite me into your day, before your day begins, and before your day ends. No matter where you are, this must be intentional. No matter the place, no matter the company, no matter the distractions. I will give you visions and the knowing of each step that you must take. Where others may be confused, you will know. Where they may be lost, you will see through everything to discern truth very quickly. You will know my direction in every situation, for you have opened your heart and brought me into your daybreak and where your day ends. I will give you images of the direction that you must go at each crossroad. I will tell you what you need to know in all things concerning you, your purpose, your faith.

I need you to realize how important this is. You are covered by me, and I am the one taking your pain away and bringing you comfort. You are finding new peace each day. Do you not notice the difference between when you start your day with me and when you do not? I am covering you so that you may begin to cover others. You will grow through this connection, in this time that you dedicate to me. Let no one take that time away from you. Do not let others take that time away from me. You must learn how to live like this daily. This is where your protection is.

Beware when the enemy tries to take this time from you for this is your hour of protection where I regenerate my covering for you. Trust me always for I will shield you from all this. I have saved you for a purpose, for my purpose. Throughout your life, I have shielded you. You may have gone through things that nearly broke you, but I was shielding you from the break that had no returns. I do not let you stay broken. I give you my strength. I do not leave you in depression, even in the midst of the struggle, I will bring you joy. Do not be ashamed of your joy for it is my gift to you as you come out of the breaking.

I will show you how to demonstrate revival and rejuvenation and restoration to others. They will see my light in you and need your light, and you will teach others how to live under my covering. Do not feel inadequate for it is my light that empowers you and guides you and teaches you the ways that are right, both for you and for others. You lack nothing under my covering. This is why your time with me is so important. This is where you can tap into my power and authority to give what I require you to give, both to yourself and to others.

You have the power to lay things down for me to bless. You have the power to sacrifice what needs to be sacrificed and I will give you the power to endure all things. You are no longer barely surviving. I have made a way for you to thrive. Be watchful of those who wish to take that joy away from you. Protect my power manifesting in you. Be wary of those that come to you with a list of what they need from you for they will sacrifice very little for you in your time of need. They have a "give-me" mentality and do not understand the power and the joy that comes from sacrificial giving. You need to understand that sacrificing must be mutual and must mutually benefit one another. Both must be willing to sacrifice in order to receive the blessing from God within that connection. Do not allow yourself to become one with anyone who will not sacrifice for you, for I have already brought you out of that.

Every aspect of your life will require sacrifice on some level. Your life is not random, and you must be very selective on what you sacrifice, but even more important, to whom you sacrifice for, lest you lose yourself again. That is not an option anymore for you are coming into your power through me and no one is allowed to take this from you.

Commit your life in the direction where I am moving you and I will guide your path. I will teach you when sacrifice is necessary. I will teach you when you need to guard yourself against others that have not earned your sacrifice, for their journeys may still be long, and you cannot get lost on someone else's path. Live for my kingdom and I will build you your palace. I will make your life what it needs to be, and it is going to be more than you could have ever imagined. Stay under my covering and give this up for no one. Sacrifice what you choose to bless others with, but never sacrifice this.

Your life and everything in it will amaze you. You will not even recognize yourself once I have restored to you what was always yours and will make beauty from your ashes.

Do not regret needing your time with me. You are keeping a promise, a vow that you made at a moment of revelation that I must come first. You allow yourself to become distracted by the feelings that sabotage your growth by focusing on others when others are not focused on what you need. You allow yourself to feel guilty which distracts you from grace. It's okay to need this time with me and you cannot allow yourself to sink into the same emotions that you are crying to be released from. Let it go.

Love God. Love yourself. In this you will be able to love others. Your time with me will propel you into that type of love. The broken pieces of you no longer have a place where I am trying to restore the power of my love in your heart. If you miss these appointments, you miss my word for you on that which will make you whole again. I am working on you right now, healing that which is broken to fix your foundation.

If you respond to the world from your brokenness, that is all they can receive from you. The goal of this time with me is to help you release these things, these feelings, these thoughts. I am dealing with what you have built up on the inside of you from all the people and experiences that broke you. Your time with me is where I am showing you the things inside of you that keep you in bondage to the things that have no value for the next part of your journey. This is where I will guide you in releasing the things that destroy your joy.

When you dedicate your time to meet with me, I will be there. I know every tear you have cried since you were a child. I am repairing those parts of you that you lost since those days and all along your path up to this moment. I am removing what you learned, the beliefs you adopted along that path, and am replacing it with understanding and self-love so that when others see you, they do not see just your brokenness, but rather the strength and the love that I have transformed all of this into. This is the time that I am altering your beliefs that have negatively affected your attitude, for your approach has been tarnished from the behaviors you have learned during those moments of pain, and your guard has prevented you from fully demonstrating who you are in me.

You were chosen as a child and this is the time where I am revealing the good that has come out of everything, removing what you kept that serves no purpose. I am stripping off the self-condemnation and adopted beliefs about your life and yourself that I now requires you to learn from and let go of.

These burdens you carry no longer have a place where beauty must rise. If you do not spend this time with me, you will continue to carry that which must go. You have clung onto all of these pains because you believe that's all these experiences gave you, but no. They gave you beauty that you have yet to see. Because your memories are clouded by the pain, you fail to see that even in the pain, there is a beautiful soul emerging.

There will be the time that I teach you how to express healing, for you will have lived through healing in these moments. You will come to wholeness, moment by moment, revelation by revelation, word by word. I am bringing you to wholeness where all things will work together and serve your purpose. Your pain will serve you. You will no longer be in bondage to these pains for they will come to serve your purpose and bring healing to yourself and to others.

There is power in your testimony but your testimony cannot be that which is stuck in your past pains. I will take the issues that you have adopted that you believed made you strong and show you where your strength truly comes from. I will replace your bravado with true strength and courage. I will replace your idealisms with true love. I will replace your aspirations with true purpose. I will replace all that you think you are built of and replace it with who you truly are so that you will live freely as you gaze into your own eyes. You will no longer be bound to your bondage but will lean to bind what has kept you bound.

All your misconceptions about life up to this point will be replaced with what living truly is. These moments with me will brush away everything that prevents you from following your true path. I will clear the way for you to follow me freely, full of life, full of love, and full of all the beauty that you are. Your light is bursting at the seams waiting to be released, and in these moments is where all the covered layers will fall off once and for all, so that all that remains is what I see in you, in who I created you to be, full of life, full of hope, full of love, full of faith, full of joy, full of my power, full of strength, full of wisdom, full of grace.

This is where you will see me. This is where you will come to know me. This is where you will come to remove that which the world created and become that which I have created. You are no longer a product of what you lack. You are no longer a product of the environments that you found yourself in. You are no longer a product of what others believe about you. You are more than all this. And this is where you will meet you, in my eyes. This will be your place of comfort, the type of comfort that replaces what is broken with what is whole and beautiful. In this place you are becoming. I am changing your perception of who you think you are because of all that you have been through. This is my time. This is your time with me that will lead you into wholeness. The world will no longer see you in your brokenness but will come to see who you are in your wholeness, in all your beauty, in all your power, in all that life has helped you become.

August 5th

Why does God have His hand on my life? I see Him in everything right now. He blesses me daily, but why? What is it about my story and my life that He has chosen me as His own? He fills me with His Spirit and leads me through everything, and the things that I don't have the power to change, He moves in and changes it for me. He calls me forward out of the darkness and into His light, but I know that it is not solely for my sake, for my healing, nor solely for my own happiness. I know this is bigger than me. It is bigger than all that I see and experience.

He gives me strength when I am at my weakest. He gives me grace when I am facing my own demons. He gives me love when I am at my loneliest. He gives me power when I feel the most inadequate. But why? What is it that I have to offer? Why is He investing in me?

His voice calls to me when I cannot hear anything above the noise in my mind. His Spirit moves me when I am paralyzed. He propels me beyond my despair, even when I cling to it, for it has been my identity for so long. He gives me vision and thoughts above my chaos. He gives me light when I am lost in the dark. He calls to me. But why? He is changing my heart and changing my perception of everyone and everything. He is shifting my focus to hear His voice. He keeps giving me a word that I will be the one to change those around me and those that will hear my name. But why?

§

You will be the vessel I use to change the culture of those around you. You are the catalyst. I will use you to change perceptions, beliefs, and hearts so that they rise and seek me. There will be healing that will come from me through you. People will be magnetized toward you because of what you hold inside of you. You have opened your heart to receive me and strive to please me. Your heart has become mine because you reached out for me with a heart that was filled with faith when all seemed lost.

But you cannot stay lost even though you know faith will pull you through. It is time to move above that level in your mind because if you continue to see yourself lost and continue to claim that identity, you will not be able to receive the identity that you are the light. You dishonor me by continuing to believe this about yourself, for I have already spoken a word to you about who you are, who you are no longer, and who you are becoming.

I have pulled you up and out of that and you know it, now take hold of it, and claim your place in my kingdom. You have a purpose to fulfill, to lead others through their darkness, and until you let go of the identity of being lost and broken, you cannot lead others into the light and into their own wholeness. Let it go. Do not be afraid of what I am telling you about yourself, for my grace is shaping you. My grace is shifting you. My grace is changing your perception. Receive that power. Know who you are. Know your worth. Know your light for that is who I say you are.

Do not feel guilty about your healing. This is my gift to you. Do not feel guilty that I am connecting with you, for you are blessed by my presence. Own your calling and do not be afraid. It is time. Claim your true identity.

Your suffering served a purpose so you could speak to the hearts of those who suffer. Your sins were so you that you could reach the hearts of sinners. Your losses were so that you could speak to the souls of those who grieve. Your failures were so that you could encourage those who have forgotten their own worth. Your isolation was so that you could lift the spirits of those who are lonely. By my grace, you have survived all these things so that you can be a beacon of hope to those in desperation.

Own your past for it is your blessing, but do not live in the pain of your past for it is also your prison. You have been set free for a reason. There is greater purpose for your pain, but you must come to the understanding that this is not your true identity but is only your experience. And through these experiences you have been able to see who you are called to be. Own this and let the rest fall away. You do not need to display your brokenness anymore. It is time to display your breakthrough. It is time to be and do who and what you are called to be and do.

August 5th – The Condition Of Your Heart

Isaiah 35: 3 - 6

There the Lord will display His glory, the splendor of our God. With the news, strengthen those who have tired hands and encourage those who have weak knees. Say to those who have fearful hearts, be strong and do not fear, for your God is coming to destroy your enemies. He is coming to save you. And when he comes, he will open the eyes of the blind and unplug the ears of the deaf. The lame will leap like a deer, and those who cannot speak will sing with joy.

§

You must protect your light with all your might. You must shield your joy and your spirit from everything that aims to injure either. Do not neglect your spirit as this is where the light does live. This is where you connect with the Spirit of the Living God. Protect your heart for this is where your spirit lives.

Qualify everything and everyone that moves your heart and analyze how they move you. Do they add to or detract from the joy of your spirit? Watch their words, how do they speak? Is it encouraging speech or is it tarnished by thoughts and language of the world? Does it help to purify your thoughts and your heart, or does it lead you into distraction that takes your mind and your heart beneath your calling? Does it serve your purpose well?

Look at yourself always and qualify your own actions and responses to that which surrounds you. Are they in alignment with the prayers whispered unto the Lord? Are you sabotaging your own answered prayers in response to what surrounds you? Does it allow you to grow, or does it shrink you back into that place of darkness that you were pulled out of? Does it serve you well? Do you see the hand of God in what surrounds you? Does it possess the character of God, who is love? Does it help you become like Him? Does it add to your value, or your dysfunction? How does it shape your heart? This is what He looks at.

Does your heart sing with the joy of freedom or is it constrained by what surrounds you? Events and experiences and people have a power to affect your heart. Do not accept what makes your heart sick for this is where Christ lives. This is your vessel to heaven.

Love, but be guarded in what you love, for that love is what you give out. What are you loving and what are you giving? Be real about what affects your heart, for from there your life will flow.

What is the condition of your heart? Is it well? If the condition of your heart is not well, you need to face it and allow God in to heal it with truth. Your pain is real, and you must be willing to let God in to show you the root of that pain so it can be identified and removed.

What lives in your heart? What lives there affects your spirit and when your spirit is affected so is your life and your thoughts about your life and your true purpose. It can distract you, delay you, and keep you in places that keep you bound to the breaking. Be real with what lives in your heart. Does it take up the space where worship should live? What does it produce?

You must become whole by removing what is broken and no longer has a place. Do not allow the pieces that are broken to interrupt and detract from your healing. You must allow God to transform your pain into wholeness. Do not be a result of what you have gone through. Be the result of what God is doing in you that you will come to know and learn to love you the same way He knows and loves you.

Trust Him and not your past. He is making a way for you to be free in Him. Discard the pain of your past for it has no place where God is trying to fill you. Focus on His presence in every moment that you don't get stuck in the moments, but rather, you are following Him through them.

Are you growing? Are you happy? What is the condition of your heart? It is time for healing. Open your heart to Him, recognize His truth, accept His grace, and allow Him to remove all that has injured you. It is time for healing. Focus on your relationship with God and allow His healing power to flow freely through you. Remove all that stands in the way of your healing. It is time.

August 6th - Worship

It is alright to cry, but you must cry with a clear understanding about where your tears flow, why they flow, and what they flow for. Your crying must be a release and a letting go of your pains. It cannot be the place where you live, and you cannot allow your tears to shape your heart and your identity.

Your identity is found in your time with God, for you are naked before Him and He sees everything in your heart. This is the place where your soul is open and free. You scream here. You sing here. You cry here. You speak honestly without inhibitions here. Worship is the way to release what you hold and that is why nothing can take your time and attention from your dedicated time with God. Through your worship, you bless God with all of your love without a tainted spirit. If you love God with the same intensity that you cry with, then you have achieved worship.

When you recognize His hand in the middle of your hurt, then you have achieved worship. You love Him from the purest place when you worship for you open the connection in that place, and your heart is made new each time. Love grows here. Your time with Him is essential and as He propels you into the future He has planned for you, you must remember this and keep all of your appointments with Him. This is where He heals. This is where He dries your tears. This is where He gives you understanding and wisdom and strength. This is where He fills you with His spirit. This is where He strengthens you. This is where you learn your walk, receive your guidance, and renew your vision of the path He has placed you on. This is where He speaks to you, where He corrects you, and where He demonstrates His love for you. This is where your prayers are raw and real and where you exchange love with God. This is where your comfort lives.

Your time with God is essential. Your worship is essential. When you give Him your love, He shows you better love. Focus on His goodness and He will remove your pains. He will replace your pain with love and protection. He is your safe space, where the real you can be you.

August 7th

1 Corinthians 14: 1

Let love be your highest goal, but you should also desire the special abilities the Spirit gives you, especially the ability to prophesy.

§

You have been given a special portion of revelation that has helped pull you out of desperation and continued to guide you through this challenging process, navigating out of the dark and into my hands and my light.

Because I have brought you through this, much will be required of you to do for others what has been done for you. You need to understand what I have given to you and multiply it amongst my people. You have talents and abilities and capacities beyond what you think you have, and you are right, they are not just yours you carry, but rather mine has been added unto you.

The world needs what you have beyond your capacity, and what the world will receive will be beyond your capacity. You will represent me to those who either do not know me or are currently seeking me in the same desperation you first sought me. You must do well with what I have given you and guard your blessing from those who might attempt to diminish your blessing for their own motives.

Do not hide your talents. You may think there is nothing special that you possess, but you do. Your way with words communicates to souls much of what they cannot hear from others. Do not be ashamed that you have these talents and abilities to speak, to communicate, to reach hearts, for this is a blessing and your special gift that I have placed in you for my purpose. It is time to take that gift and gift it to the world.

You will not just write. You will teach. You will preach. You will counsel. You will lead others to me for they are calling for me and you will help guide them. Do not wait to do your work. Do not settle for good enough, for this is beneath your calling. Your thoughts and issues no longer have a stronghold on you, and you need to recognize this and release your grip on this for it is time to give what you have been given.

Be faithful to your calling, and anything else that interrupts your process and distracts you from your calling must fall away, and it is you that must release it for this will be your greatest act of faith. I will strengthen you where you need strength. You have more than you need. You have everything you need.

Do not be preoccupied with what you think is missing, for where I give power nothing lacks. Expand your reach. There is more in your process than even you can see and this is all for a greater purpose. Do not be afraid of your calling, it is what you were made for. You have always had the ability to sway a room either way, and you have seen this power in your worldly environments. It is now time to use that power for good, but more importantly, to use it for me.

You have always been sought for counsel and even those who have sought you did not know why their secrets were freely given to you. There was always a reason. You must recognize this, for you have even helped them without knowing the outcome. It is time to expand your reach. Your life was as it was for a reason. Be thankful for what you have been through, for what you have been through will take you to a path of great success amongst my people and will draw others to me.

Stop complaining about your past and learn the blessings that come from your past, for your experiences will be a tool that will move you to your purpose. It is all connected. It is time to bury your complaints, bury your past, and take with you only what has given you growth from both. You have more than you think you have. Do not worry about what you lack but lean into what you do have, for you have much.

Your past brings you anxiety and fear if you give it the power to change your heart in the moment. Your present brings you peace when you allow yourself to appreciate where you are and when you recognize the power you held onto to get here. I have been with you every step of the way. My instructions to you are real. Do not be ashamed that you have heard my voice while others wandered and wondered, for your faithfulness to follow what you did not understand has been seen in the heavens and I am raising you up now. Take hold of my hand now.

Do not become weak in your walk. Focus your mind with intention even if it is required a thousand times a day, for you have much and it is time to pursue your calling with a knowing that it is there. All I have given you is there. Reach for it. It is time.

A word was spoken over your life and that word is permanent. It cannot be changed. Lean in. Press in and press on for you are called to greater things. Do not put effort and strategy in the wrong direction for you know you are being called to more for me. Something great is being prepared and you must now reach for it through faith and not lack. Your process is working on your behalf and that which needs to move, I will move as long as you continue to reach in and reach out in faith knowing your truth. You have made it through much and it is time to multiply what you gained from your much and bury what no longer serves your peace. It is time to make peace with your past and move onto your path. You are where you are supposed to be.

August 10th

What have I lost along the way, and where and how did I lose it? This is an important question as I find true healing, not a temporary healing that can be shaken. What have I lost along the way? I have lost my confidence, my joy, my creativity, and my peace, but what I miss the most is my peace.

§

It is time to take inventory of your life, the steps you have taken, the choices you have made that brought you to a place of a lost self who lived in sadness, isolation, grief, and sorrow that had not been consoled. But when you do this, you must also take inventory of parts of your life where you felt real joy so that you begin to recognize what you need and reconcile with what you think you lost. You must allow yourself to discard the hurt and begin to replace it with joy again. It is not an easy process, but you must. And when you do recognize what hurts, you must be willing to make peace with it and let it go. You cannot be filled until you are empty.

It is time to rebuild yourself so that you have the strength and the wisdom to live a full life, for this is why Christ died, that you may have life, and live it fully. This is where you will find the value in your experience. Finding this value is necessary in order to achieve a major part of your purpose in bringing others to live life fully to mend old wounds until their scars can no longer affect their vision of themselves. As you make decisions towards healing, you must always qualify each step you take by asking if that notion or person will add value to or detract from the person you are, and the perspective you have of yourself.

Your experience is not your identity, but it does add valuable perspective that will push you to growth that you may be an example of coming out of somethings and living in my light.

As you qualify people in your life, this too must be your approach and you need to be willing to be honest with yourself and with them on what they give to you that could affect your perspective on who you are. Do not allow others to condemn you for not providing what they lack for themselves. You are not responsible for their needs, and they are not responsible for yours. I am the One who can provide true perspective and value in who you are.

You have allowed others to determine your value and your worth and you still seek validation though none of them are qualified to judge you. You are more than all of this. You are more than what others believe they see. Only those that can see your light are qualified to follow you, for they must be able to support that life and that light that will serve others. It is time to take a deep dive to remember what you lost, identify how you lost it, and take it back. It was never anyone's right to take it away from you. This is important as your future actions in the kingdom will require you to earn a place in the hearts of many by how you live to serve them well. You will need to learn how to honor each life and propel others to a self-love that will also be shared with the world. This is how a world changes.

I have restored you and am ready to give you what you lost but this requires that you never go back to who you were in the darkness. This is why it is crucial for you to ask yourself what have you lost, how and where did you lose it, because you cannot go back and repeat these cycles and patterns. Your wholeness is more important than just you. You still have a hard time claiming your worth. You know it, but have a hard time claiming it, and you have a hard time requiring honor for yourself from others. Because of this, you tend to repeat cycles and patterns that are detrimental to you and the life you are called to live.

You must learn to receive what you deserve, and to do this you must know your worth beyond your belief in what you think you are worth based on your experiences and what others made you believe. Your circle needs to change, even now, for it is time that you learn to take hold of your true value, your true light, and your true right to joy and peace. For this is the life Christ died for, that you might live and live fully.

This is the life that will serve the kingdom well and demonstrate the truth of knowing me and living life with me. I want you to see life as it is meant to be lived. You need to see everyone in the right light and properly. You need to see yourself in the right light and properly. There is a good life waiting for you and it has been set apart for you, but you need to see your true value so that you are able to receive that life well and live it as it is meant to be lived.

Expect more, for more is waiting. When you walk into a room expect more, for more has been set apart for you, and if the room does not serve you well, it is not the room you should be in. Expect more of your place in this world, for the world is waiting for you to take hold of your place that you may lead well. It is time to make it your mission to figure out what you lost, and it is time to take back what you lost from those events and from people that shaped your perception on who you are and what you deserve. Expect more and take back what you lost.

Do not feel guilty for taking back your joy, your peace, and your confidence. If what you come across attempts to bring you back to that false perception of yourself and what you have through shame, guilt and condemnation, then put it down and keep walking, for they no longer have a right to affect your perception of who you are and what I say you are worth. It is time to take hold of what is waiting for you. Expect more.

It's not over, it's just re-beginning, restoring, replacing, refilling. It is time to no longer tolerate less but reclaim what was lost. It is time to claim your confidence that you are worthy. It is time to claim your joy that you would live life fully. It is time to reclaim your peace so that others will see my hand on your healing and your life.

August 11th

Job 22:21-23

Submit to God and you will have peace, then things will go well for you. Listen to his instructions and store them in your heart. If you return to the Almighty, you will be restored, so clean up your life.

God is everything. He is your strength. He will bring you into all that you need, for He has been paving the road on which you will walk. He will align your life, your heart, and your mind to follow the instructions He has provided you He will restore all that you have lost, tenfold.

§

I have brought you this far and will take you further than you ever imagined. I will remove the barriers set before you and restore all that has been taken from you in a single moment.

You will know my hand in everything. You will thrive and you will prosper and see all that I have set aside for you, for you have sought me first in all your ways. Your decisions have been based solely on my guidance and you refuse to act without my word over your life. You will break down all barriers that stand in your way with greater strength than you have ever had. You will see my hand in all things as you travel the path I have set for you.

Do not fear, for I will not let you fail. I will not let you fall under the inner struggles you have been carrying. I hear you. I know your cries. I know your fears. But nothing can come against you and succeed at taking you down. You will see my hand in everything. All that you face, you will find the strength to overcome. All that you fear will have no power over you.

You will overcome the giants you are facing with greater ease, for you have reached for my wisdom and my strength in all of your steps. I will take what you have buried inside from the fear you had to face. My wind will push you to overcome it. You will be required to face it all and overcome it all. Your potential will grow with each thing you face, and you will see my hand in everything.

I will manifest all that I have promised you as long as you face and overcome all that you fear. All that you ask for will be given to you so long as it is part of what I have ordained for your life. I will not give you less than all that I have set aside for you. Focus on this thought always. Let his thoughts permeate your thoughts with an intense knowing that my love provides all that you lack, and you will lack nothing. Face everything knowing this, and you will see my hand in everything.

Your faith and your commitment to follow my promptings will be rewarded with more than you have even thought to pray for. You will be blessed by what I have set aside for you. Let this motivate your walk with me. I am in the midst of investing in you, for your hope has been focused on me. I have heard your cries. I have seen your fears. I know what you need and will always lead you right to all that I have promised you in that hour when you were at your weakest.

I will strengthen and feed all your hopes. I am faithful to you always. Never forget your place, for I stand beside you, and if I stand with you, then the place you stand in must fit my presence. Though you will face things that make you afraid, your fear will not overtake you, for I stand beside you always. What power can overtake me? There is nothing. And if it is I who stands firmly beside you, what has the power to overtake you? There is nothing. You will see my hand in everything.

Your future is in my hands, and you will begin to take hold of all that I have set aside for you, and all things are being restored to you. Something is happening on the inside of you that is making you dance in praise for you have seen me work at the moment your prayers left your lips. You pray and I answer. You are witnessing my hand on your life and are recognizing the power of your prayers. This is not your imagination. This is as real as I am. So how real do you say I am? You have seen me deliver on what I promised you, prayer after prayer. You have seen my hand in everything.

There is no room for doubt, for you have seen me through your faith and this grows every day. Never fear what you face, for you have seen me work in your life with intensity and I have brought you through all that you have faced. You have seen my hand in everything.

Take hold of all that I offer you. I am lifting you up out of the fight you have been in for years. I stand beside you, and you will not lose the fight. Focus on me and my love for you and you will overcome all. Your battle no longer has the power to overtake you. What was taking a space in your heart to break you no longer has the power to break you. Greater am I who is in you than he who is in the world. You opened your heart and your mind and invited me in, and this is now your rod of strength. You have felt my touch. You have heard my voice. You know my presence. You have known my power. You have seen my vision. You follow me for you have seen my hand in everything.

This is your breakthrough. Seize it knowing it has been set aside for you. Nothing has happened against you, but rather, for you so that you could recognize me in all things. My strength carries you. My love fills you. My knowledge speaks to and through you.

Do not be troubled. Do not be overcome. Rest in this knowledge, for I speak this to you to guide you through the years that are falling away. I am sharpening your mind. I am strengthening your heart. I am shaping your spirit and working out what no longer belongs. So, make room for what has been set aside for you.

You have broken out of old ways of thinking and being and did not understand how or why, but you followed my promptings faithfully and the struggles did not overtake you. You are being restored and your restoration is a blessing. I am raising others that will come into your life to bring you to that next level, necessary to get to your miracle. Trust the process.

Know that my hand is in everything concerning you and is working towards your promises and are a direct response to your prayers. There is power in your prayers, and you are overcoming everything you thought was bigger than you. You have overcome things you thought you would never overcome. Remember this as you face everything else going forward. I stand with you and my hand is on your life.

Do not let fears overtake you. Plow forward into your destiny with the power you have been given to overcome. You will make it through all that stands against you, with all that stands within you. These things will fall away. Recognize these things but do not fear these things.

Meditate on me for I stand beside you, walk before you, and make your path straight. Focus on me and you will rob everything else of its perceived power. Do not become distracted by your fears. Intensify your focus on my promise, my path, my promptings. You know my presence and I stand with you. There is no greater power than this.

Fear is only an indicator that qualifies something you will overcome. Focus on overcoming and not the fear. Press through. Do it anyway. For greater am I who is in you than he who is in the world.

You have taken steps of faith, and for this, you were made able to overcome. Do not focus on the voice of fear. Focus on my power that brought you through all of your fears that have now lost its power. You have seen my hand in everything. You have developed much and grown far more than you realize. Let your praise in this overpower the voice of fears that you will face. Face them. Sharpen your focus and place your faith where it belongs.

Where there is a voice of faith, there is no room for fear. Fight the voice that says you can't and know that you can do all things through I who strengthens you. This is your truth. Pray through your fear. Pray through all that you face, for this will take away the power of that which you face. Pray through everything you fight against.

You are getting stronger for there is power in your prayers, and you have been killing the fears within you one by one. Your faith is your power to overcome all things, for you know who stands beside you. You see my hand in everything.

You must see yourself for who you are only and let everything else fall away. Know who you are and who stands beside you. I know you and you need to see yourself right. Know your worth. Know your value. Do not settle for less than you are worth. Do not let your fears define you, for greater am I who is in you than he who is in this world.

I know what you have been through. I know what you have come out of. I know the strength it took to pull out of it. I know and it is time that you know. Don't sell yourself short based on what you fear, for you have overcome much more than this. Know yourself and what you have overcome, everything else is less than this. You're worth more than this and you must remember who you are. When you do, in that moment, you will pull strength from this truth, for you have overcome much and much more than others could ever have made it through. Do not allow anyone to take that away from you.

August 12th

§

Let nothing hinder you from moving forward. Your purity is necessary. Your full power must be seen in excellent light and all your actions must maintain excellence. Be wary of focusing on momentary stimuli, for your spirit can be tarnished in that moment. The purpose of sex is not physical, it is spiritual, and you cannot reduce yourself to a lower standard in your spirit, for what you invite into your physical being, you also invite into your spirit and the two become one.

Your souls become linked and what their soul carries, you adopt. Your validation cannot be found in this experience, lest you reduce your true value. Sex is oneness and unity that your spirits intertwine, and a soul tie can be created. Sex cannot be for simple pleasures for there is a greater impact to your soul than you realize.

When you unite in sex with something I am trying to free you of, you delay that separation from the thing to which you are no longer bound to in spirit. You need to be stronger than that in order to get your power back. You need a greater understanding about what you give away when you give it away so freely, to someone who has not been ordained for you to have.

Do not allow yourself to be bound up with another, lest your power be taken from you as you are trying to move forward. Intimacy is powerful and can change your perception and alter your path and delay your purpose. Do not give it to anyone that is not worthy of a soul tie and has not been brought to you by me for this will delay your purpose in ways you will not expect. Do not follow old patterns and perceptions for you are worth more than that. And before you know it, you begin to adopt their beliefs, thoughts, and attitudes. This is the most intimate part of you. Sex is not nothing. It is not meaningless. It is not transparent. It is deeper than you realize and creates and renews bonds that are never supposed to be.

You have the potential to paralyze your mind through this joining and your mind must remain focused on excellence and your becoming. Qualify your relationships as you qualify all other parts of your life and all your footsteps. I am working on and shaping your character so you can finally have what I want you to have.

August 13th

§

Enjoy this day and be content. Your life is changing, and it is no longer as you know it. Everything has changed, but I have come to you, and for this you can rest in my promises to bring you hope and joy. You lack nothing and nothing of this world can give you what you need. Be happy with where you are at. What you lost is not lost, but what you gain will be better than anything you have found.

Press in closer to me. Be still and know that I, who loves you, stand beside you and walk with you. Do not place your hopes in what you lost. Do not pity yourself with things that have passed. Do not carry this torment, for I am bringing you more. I am opening up the heavens to bring you all that you lack. Enjoy the journey.

I have stripped you of your pride and restored your humility. In this there is growth. At the right time, I will pull you up and promote you. This is a process, and you must always seek my hand in your process, and you will see your blessings. Life is changing and growing, and you will be amazed at what has been set aside for you. Take hold of the journey.

I have given you talents and abilities that far surpass what others have. Be not concerned about how you appear to the world, for I have opened eyes to see your light even if you don't see it for yourself. My hand is working over your life. Trust in me and I will bring you much more than you could ever imagine. Your sorrow will fade away to nothing. Your joys will abound, and your past devastation will be no more.

Release what hurts you immediately and trust in me for I am with you. This is your greatest blessing. There are many who search their whole lives and do not find me because their hearts are not focused on me, but rather on what I can bring them. This has not been your heart. You have sought me with the heart of a servant, and for this you will be rewarded. Do not worry about anything, for I will bring you everything you need.

Your worship has been heard in heaven and your light has been seen on this earth. Your blessing is that my presence lives within you. Do not be disappointed in others for they do not know what you know. Put me first and do not let anything or anyone come between you and your walk with me. I will fill your heart. I will meet all that you lack. I will help you discern what really matters and help you see beyond distraction.

I will show you what you need to know about your path and give you a discerning eye and fill your spirit with my wisdom that you will not get lost. I will help you pass through what you should leave behind. I will sharpen your focus so that your perspective of each moment and each step cannot be tarnished. I will tame your pride and hold your tongue that you do not get lost in your own accomplishments.

<blockquote>
I am your source for everything.

I am your source for healing.

I am your source for wisdom.

I will fill you up.

I am your source for life.

I am your source for light.

I am your source.

I will fill you up.

I am your discernment.

I am your grace.

I am your path to happiness.

I am your source.

I will fill you up.
</blockquote>

You reached for me, and I have pulled you up. You reached for me with need and I have satisfied your desperation. You are free. You are free from your desperation. Faith has set you free. Your focus on me has set you free. I am your source. I will fill you up. I am bringing you beyond just healing. Set your mind higher for I am not a small god who brings you just enough. I am bringing you more than you could ever imagine. My prayer fills you. My light fills you. My visions of your life fill you. I am your source. I will fill you up. Be not afraid for I am with you.

Mark 5: 34

Your faith has healed you. Go in peace and be freed from your suffering.

§

Keep focused on me and I will always provide for you. Do not be persuaded by what others say you need to be. I am guiding you now. Be still in those moments and pull for my voice. Hear me. See me. Sense me. And know that I am there pulling you past all the distractions. This is what separates you from others. I am your source, and I will fill you up. There is no demand in life greater than this.

August 14th

Colossians 3:12

Since God chose you to be the holy people he loves, you must clothe yourselves with tenderhearted mercy, kindness, humility, gentleness, and patience. Make allowances for each other's faults and forgive anyone who offends you. Remember the Lord forgave you, so you must forgive others. Above all, clothe yourselves with love, which binds us all together in perfect harmony. And let peace that comes from Christ rule in your hearts. For as a member of one body, you are called to live in peace, and always be thankful.

§

You are a light in this world. This is who you are and what identifies you amongst others. You cannot hide this about yourself for this is who you are. Do not live otherwise. This must guide your steps always. For as you are the light, you must live in the light and be the light for everything and everyone around you. This is where your beauty comes from. This will never age out. This beauty will live in your eyes, be shown in your actions, and all will recognize where this light comes from and bring a people to me who gives you light.

Do not forget this, for this is who you are called to be, and anything that dims that light has no place in your heart and in your life. You are not normal for you are light. You must recognize this, especially in moments where darkness threatens to snuff out that light. You must take hold of this identity for it is who you are. Your light is seen in the heavens just as it is seen on this earth, but what you don't realize is how bright that light shines in the heavens.

No matter how you see yourself, that old identity is no longer yours. You have been clothed in much more than you realize, and your presence changes the atmosphere. Remember who you are always. Do not look at your past and disqualify who you are. Your past does not define you. You do not need to carry those hurts. I am bringing you understanding of what those experiences have brought you in blessings. In this, your past darkness becomes flooded in light.

You have been through much darkness, and along that path, whether you realize it or not, you have been blessed in those places, by those people, and through those events with who you are, and you are the light. This is where your power lies. This is just who you are. Recognize your power and let your light shine. See it. Show it. Share it. It is your shield against all that is dark that threatens you. It is your purpose, to bring this light unto all those you meet. I created you in this way that you will bring light into the dark. People look to you for this light.

This light represents your joy, your peace, your ability to lift the spirits of those around you. It changes the atmosphere. You change the atmosphere. This is you. For my light lives in you. People are drawn to this not understanding why. They are drawn to me through you. You change perceptions by shedding light on situations. You help others to see what they cannot see in the dark. My power lives within you. This is who you are. You are the catalyst because I have made you the light. See it. Show it. Share it.

People call you for comfort, for light brings warmth. People call you for understanding for light displays all things hidden in the dark. People call you for guidance, for light shines on the path to knowledge. Don't worry about what others will think because you know who you are. And in their time, they will find themselves, in me. I will bring you to a people for my own purpose that they may discover theirs. But ultimately, it is not you who has the power to change them.

Your purpose is to see it in yourself, your situations, and the people you come to meet. You show it in your demeanor, in your generosity, in your ability to overcome adversity. You share it by imparting clarity, speaking with a joyful heart. You share it in your laughter, it is distinct for it carries light. It is contagious. It has the power to infect the sullen, the down, the depressed. You share it in your ability to love, even when love is not appreciated. It is contagious. It infects their hearts, their minds, their beliefs about themselves and who "they" are. It leads them to a greater light in their own journey of self-discovery.

But you cannot always guide them lest your own light dim. They must seek greater light. They must seek the source of your light for their own torches. They must begin their own journey within themselves to become the light they have seen in you. You preserve the environment, but you are not responsible to provide everything in that environment lest people become dependent on you and never begin their own journey. So let it shine as you walk through but keep moving. They will follow.

§

A lot of what is happening on the outside of your life begins on the inside, and from here is where you will produce. Your belief that I am working in every aspect of your life is necessary to remain firm in that belief or you will find yourself returning back to what I have had you put down.

It is easy to fall into that trap because you are used to reverting without real change. Examine your decisions closely, and examine the relationships that you have had, and the relationships you will have. My Spirit will lead you in all your decisions and you must not fall prey to old patterns, lest you become crushed beneath what you are asked to carry. I have not changed my mind on where I have you now. Do not be swayed by love that has passed for that season is over.

There are consequences on your destiny for denying me in this situation. You may not see the blessing in this experience yet, but it is good. You are in an internal battle between returning to your default or pushing past the boundaries to what I am laying out for you.

You have spent many years in the wilderness, alone and without the comforts relationships should bring. Step forward and declare your right to happiness. Step forward and declare your right to the promise I have for you. Do not be swayed by the past for it is passed. You have an ache in your gut because you are bound to the tradition of what was, by guilt, not by my promise.

I still have work to do in you. And you cannot be distracted by that which detracts from you. You know your purpose has moved beyond that which is now behind you. You do not have to justify this choice for this is my justice on your behalf. Do not settle your soul on the default reaction to what is now past. You were called out of this the moment your cry was heard in heaven.

You are entitled to more for the suffering you have already endured. Come to me with all your dilemmas. When you do, I will guide your decisions. You do not have to accept any offers that lead you back to what was your default response. The chain of events that led you here can never happen again, and this is the moment to decide to step out on faith to the promise that has been prepared for you.

What has passed does not have the power to bind you to the past. You have been released of your obligation to cater to the whims of the winds. Your movements are guided by my hand, and there is no other choice. Be bold and declare this. It is time to change and follow something new. What is coming will bring you closer to who you are called to be.

August 15th

§

I have been working on you and you have been working towards alignment with my purpose for you and your life. In order to move forward, you need to examine your character and qualities that mirror Christ. I am trying to get you to lay hold of your true identity, and though you are in your infancy stage, this too has its purpose for this is where you find your need for me. In this stage you are believing me for everything and do nothing without me.

I have been with you on your walk and will not let you fall, but your eyes must rest on me. Be still, stand firm where you are, and be grounded in my spirit no matter what you are facing. You cannot be still and still do. Do not become impatient with the process for there is much that is happening where I am working.

I am working in the hearts of those whose hearts have been hardened, but you cannot put your hand on this, for they too must find their need absolute in me and not in you. They have yet to seek my voice though you have commanded them this. They have yet to see my hand in this for they keep looking to you for what is coming. The timing to return is not right and my word has not changed.

Do not leave your process to walk someone else through theirs. You cannot alter your life to pursue someone else's journey with me. The Holy Spirit is operating but they have yet to see. They have glimmers of my presence but have yet to fully receive me. They seek for their need to be met through you and seek the voice of others before seeking my voice in its fullest.

Do not drop this standard in your process, lest you teach others to drop theirs. I am waiting for their response. Their faith is fickle and not firm. Their faith should not rest on you, for you are not the source. Letting go has its blessing. The blessing is in the breaking. Though you have seen the blessing in the breaking, they have yet to see my hand in all that is happening, for their focus is on you.

Instead of allowing me to work in their circumstances, they put their own power into a thing and delay the power that needs to free them, for they do not seek my power, but attribute the power of change to you. They question my methods and my process because they fail to seek me for their own process. Their hearts are not leaning into me for they are overwhelmed with you.

You cannot be the source in this hour, or what is taking place will only be temporary and they will never know me as I am trying to reveal myself in their own journey. The Holy Spirit will guide them when their focus is solely on me. You have been faithful to seek me and follow me, and in this you have received guidance and direction. For the sake of others, you must follow my promptings to release them to me so that I become their source. Everything else is irrelevant. They need to develop their relationship with the Holy Spirit, or you will always be unequally yoked. This is not allowed for you in this season.

You find yourself off-balanced and back in indecision because you are swayed by your belief that it is in your power to save them, but this is not your power nor your purpose. You are not called to save. You are called to show and release. Receive and release.

You cry out for peace yet invite the distractions that hurt you. You can never be just fully open-minded because you are not focused in this state, and you must remain focused. Pay attention to your unsettled spirit when you confront this dilemma, for I speak to you here and show you what is good for you and what you must reject. You cannot just receive whatever comes unto your ears for you have already heard my truth. Discernment in necessary in all matters at this point on your journey.

Be wary of the words that come to you for you do not know the spirit that comes with that word and the vessel has not been purified by the Holy Spirit. It is unclean for your taste. Do not devour the words lest you eat a false hope. If you are too open, you will become weakened by the need to fulfill a promise that has burdened your spirit and you will become lost again.

Though good intentions drive the words spoken, they know not what this action proposed will do to your spirit in the long run, for you will be closing your spirit off from mine. You need to qualify thoughts, emotions, and the energy that comes to you from everyone and look closely at its origin. Is it originating from the mind and thoughts of mine in which I have already presented to you? Does it align with my purpose? Does it heal or hurt you? Do you find yourself bending your will for something that has not been blessed by my Spirit?

You must protect this and ensure that what you are allowing into your mind and into your heart does not hurt your process towards healing. Is this helping you or anyone else? What are you holding to so firmly that my power has no room to work with? Choose well for your choice has an impact on someone else's purpose that has yet to be discovered.

They must seek me wholeheartedly, but their hearts are currently at battle in the pursuit of you. Do not open yourself up to everything that is presented to you. You must guard yourself lest your progress regress. You must qualify what to keep and what to release. I will not take your will away no matter what you choose, but be warned, being open is not necessarily good for you.

You are delaying what has already been decided, for you have opened up your heart to what disagrees with the word you have already been given. They will heal, but not until they step into their own journey with me, and their focus is solely on me. You are taking their focus away and are delaying their purpose from manifesting in their hearts.

The Holy Spirit is trying to tell you that what you are trying to choose right now is not a part of your future and this is why your own spirit is not settled. The Holy Spirit surrounds you when you are in alignment with my call on your life but will step away when you take what does not align with this purpose.

August 16th

§

If I move you to be a blessing, be a blessing. Do not doubt my motives in your life for I am good. I am working in the beginning and the middle and the end. I am working for your good. I am working. This is part of your legacy. You must let go of your fears in this matter and do not be anxious for this is a critical season in your life and something powerful is taking place. This is what draws you there.

Part of your anxiety is that you have had to experience and endure violations and abuse of your beliefs and you can lose sight beneath what you carry, but do not allow this to interfere with the plans I have for you. Do not lose your spirituality under the burden of your thoughts for thoughts are fleeting, but what enters the spirit lingers.

You have access to me and my spirit. Seek what you desire for as you have been deeply connected to me in spirit, it is my Spirit that has led you there. This is fated and not negotiable. There are basics of spirituality that you have yet to discover, and this is part of your path to the discovery of these things. Your foundation must be built on who you are as a spiritual being for this is your essence. You were spirit first, and in this time, you will rediscover that part of you.

What you have experienced in the past is not the same as what you are experiencing now. You know this already. Do not be preoccupied with anxieties that have developed from your past, for you are being shown much more in this season. You have access to get back to the basics of spirituality. You will recognize this in the conversations you share.

I will show you how to tap into the well. This means a lot of things to a lot of different people and in order to speak to the masses, you must understand them in the spirit first. If you go back into the history of the spirit and recognize this from the angle of all different cultures, you will see what is common in spirit and recognize what has been generated and directed by man.

People worship the one they call God in various ways and their hearts do connect. They worship through prayer and through meditation to the spirit, but their practices differ culture to culture, and you will learn to decipher connection to the spirit versus what man has elected to practice. And just as you do not want others to judge nor condemn your own experience of intimacy with me, so you too must not judge nor condemn the experience of intimacy with me that others have connected with me through their own worship.

There are many that consider themselves religious but have a belief that they must do or say things to attract my love and their vision of the experience of me is narrowed to that belief, therefore never truly experience the connection to my Spirit. For the connection is not found in practices, but rather, in their perception of who I am and who they are in this connection. Practice is made by man.

Perception is inspired through your connection. Practice does not confirm nor affirm my touch on your life, for my touch is spiritual and is experience, not the action of getting there. Faith and the fruit of it is the experience of me in the most intimate of ways. Worship brings people out of preconceived notions that have developed over life experience into the experience of my spirit. Worship is for people, not for me. Practice is for their own process of achieving the experience. Practice does not denote spirituality for practice is made by man, for man's own reasoning on how they come to achieve the experience. This is an illusion and is diluted for the focus becomes the practice and not the experience of intimacy with me.

My desire is the intimacy in the relationships that all develop with me. This is where the blessing is. Culture can tarnish this. People can tarnish this. Practice can tarnish this. And all of this can tarnish their deepest experiences with me because it becomes based solely on culture, people, and practices that once led them to the experience but that is not the reality of how people become connected.

My touch cannot be found in how a culture practices. My touch cannot be found in the people that surround them. My touch cannot be found in the practice that one acts out. My touch is spirit, not culture, not people, not practice. My spirit is in the depth of your own. You are about to step into something more than you have ever imagined because your spirit has been planted in the truth of my Spirit, and not how culture denotes your practice to knowing God. Since I am spirit, you connect with spirit. And Spirit is everywhere.

My Spirit is in every culture. Their practice does not define nor direct their connection to the same spirit you have connected with. It is intimate and this is where transformation occurs. This is why cultures and people are passionate in their own practices, but their connection is not from practice, and you have learned this by opening yourself up to the experience of my Spirit and have not strapped yourself to a practice of a specific culture.

Worship brings you into my presence, and worship is the opening up of your spirit to receiving my Spirit. This is why your life truth flows freely during your worship hour. Do not look low for who you are, for your spirit does not come out of the things that are low. Validation is not found in things that are low, from culture, and from cultural perceptions. You are validated when you connect with your higher self, which is spirit. Worship is where you find your highest self.

Meditate on things above, not on the things of this earth, for you cannot be affirmed by things of this earth. True affirmation is only found in self-discovery of the true spirit that lives in you, and this is why worship is important. Worship brings you into my presence and is where you see who you really are.

It is time to say to the world, "If you can't see me, you are not worthy of me, me in spirit, me in truth, me in who I really am." Get into the face of God for God is spirit, you are spirit, and this is where you discover you.

August 17th

§

What you went through all those years was to bring you to this moment of consciousness where you are aware of the freedom that is necessary to get your life back. You cannot invest in relationships that do not give a return on your investment. You are too valuable to settle for less now. You are too valuable to accept less than you give now. If they do not know your worth, they cannot contribute to the value in your life on your journey, for faith in your personal value will be the passion that drives you to build it in others.

You need to focus on the awareness that this moment has brought you and on the clarity you have on what is happening in your relationships. Do not let yourself fall beneath the level of value you have already brought yourself to through your connection and relationship with me. Do not look to others to validate your worth. This has been your message for weeks.

Do not get lost in your need and excitement for others. You are too close to allow anything and anyone to bring you back to the bondage of not knowing your own worth. For you are worth more than you are accepting. Stop tolerating less, lest you find yourself back at the you that you have grown out of. You do not need them, they need you. You have already gone through what you went through and done the work to be where you are now. Do not let others who have not earned the right to derail you make you forget who you are, what you're worth, and who walks with you. You are not missing anything. They are missing the blessing of knowing you and being chosen by you.

So, what does not give to you, you need to let go of. This was only a test to see if you truly know your worth, for you are worth much more than mediocre relationships. You must demand excellence where you are concerned and anything less than excellent has no value for you at this point in your life, on your journey, and towards your purpose.

Let my Holy Spirit guide you through these waters and seek me in all your ways, so your path and your purpose are protected. You must recognize the pattern of dysfunction by seeing how a relationship is one-sided. Do not pursue. Be pursued. It is your time to receive. It is no longer your time to give in to things that do not give back. Your time is valuable. Your attention is valuable. Your spirit is valuable. And those who do not see it and honor it do not deserve you. Because when you allow the wrong people to take from you and take part of your spirit, you have less to give to the right people.

What you gave was a gift, but it is time to leave it there. Remember, you do not need them, they need you, but you have yet to recognize this. So, step back. Honor yourself and you will receive honor. Put yourself first, and others will put you first. Do not go back into old patterns with different faces and different people. Recognize the pattern you tend to repeat, step back, and only allow yourself to connect with those who honor you and offer excellence to you and for you.

You tend to give and expect nothing back and then walk away upset that you did not receive what you had hoped for or deserved. Qualify who is on your team and who you have allowed in. Release anything that your spirit cannot and does not receive good from. Others withhold from you because they see you are willing to give without reciprocation. They give you the minimum that can be given to keep you there but do not earn your presence and the blessings that your presence brings.

You belong to me. Do not give away to those not worthy through action or inaction what is honored and loved by me. Remember what I said to you about who you are, and where you are going for not everyone has earned a place on your journey. Your partnerships can no longer be to meet temporary needs. There is more at stake than this moment. You are no longer lost. You must come first.

Do not settle for less than this lest you become distracted trying to prove who you are for validation from others that have yet to know themselves. You have given, now step back, and let go. Let me bring to you whom I deem worthy of walking with you. Do not pursue. Be pursued, then qualify what you hear, what you see, and what is demanding of your time, energy, and focus. If they are showing that they are simply a distraction and do not give to your spirit, then it has not earned your time, energy, and focus.

Let your silence speak aloud what you have not said, and they will know. Do not allow yourself to work at becoming something for someone though they do not put efforts into becoming something for you. What is meant for your good will come to you. Everything else does not matter. What does not measure up does not matter.

You are not ordinary, and mediocrity in others does not matter on your journey. There is protection on your life, and everything that is not worthy will be removed or will be reshaped to meet your needs of excellence or it does not matter. Remember this.

August 18th

§

Be still in the morning as you seek me, and I will guide your steps. I will not let you fall nor fail as long as you remain focused on my path for you. I will make your steps sure and grounded in what is good for you and will not let you stray from all that is promised to you. I will guide you always in all ways. I will move in the hearts of those that need to move with you and for you.

Always stop and seek the answers I have for you and your life. Always seek my voice and you will know which way to go in every moment. Do not be idle in seeking my path for you. Do not become distracted by the blessings I have placed on your path. You are being blessed, but the blessing is not your focus. You have more power than you realize, for you are connected to me. You are connected to purpose, and the tools that feed your purpose cannot be your sole focus.

You must tame your desires and keep focused on me. Your greatness can only be manifested and cultivated in that environment for which you are called to, but the environment is not your source of sustenance. Aim your life and follow where I lead you. Your greatness cannot be aimed at what serves no purpose to your growth. Be wary of what you want and focus on because there is danger in the power you give a thing that can take from you.

Be sure you know what you are investing in and ask why it is there at this moment in your life. Honor the life you are given and do all with integrity. Live your life in such a way that is honorable. Your character must be honorable. Your journey is incredible, and you need to be surrounded by people that are solid, secure, sure, and strong for you. They need to give to you spiritually and emotionally.

There is a calling on your life to impact generations and you cannot focus solely on something that will die, for your destiny is a permanent calling and there is no room for error. Know that you can truly trust and always place your trust in me and my purpose for your life. Do not lose focus on who I have called you to be.

August 19th

§

    You have been losing your commitment to your time with me for you have been distracted by so many things that have been relentlessly affecting your soul. You have had momentary setbacks that have taken you to dark places and caused you to hide your face from me, for you find your own eyes distorted by deep anger. And you are not focused when you find yourself in the pits of emotion in response to things that have been said to you and of you. You become distracted by the thing I am pulling you away from though I am guiding you to something absolute in your purpose.

    Your emotions have been given a power more than they should, and you have already been given truth in all this through the word I have already spoken over your life. Do not base your decisions on what you feel. Base them on the word that I have spoken to you in the midst of these feelings. Let the word lead you, not your feelings about what you are facing.

    In the midst of your challenge, you came across a mirror, and in that mirror, you saw the light literally leave your eyes. The color changed. The shape changed. It showed you exactly what this situation and the emotions attached to them does to your spirit. I am trying to separate you from the things outside of your purpose for they take you out of alignment with my Spirit. For you are spirit first and you are a spirit of great power but you are opening up to and allowing others to take away from this truth.

    You have to become you and in the realest sense of who you are. You are not ordinary, and you need to live a life worthy of your calling, with a commitment to that which elevates your spirit and gives you absolute room to flow. I have been speaking prophetically to you about who you really are and the pages that have been written thus far demonstrate my truth and above this, show my hand on your life.

    You are not ordinary, you are ordained. I walk with you for you are highly favored and it is time for you to rejoice and get excited for what I am about to do in your life. But you must first release what draws your focus away and maims your soul. I have already spoken and command that on this day, you are to take your joy back. Though joy is confronting you, you cannot see it beyond your distracted spirit. You cannot be moved to joy under the heavy burden that has been placed on you but is not yours to carry.

Your mind and your soul are burdened with the battle of just trying to survive that you are not reaching towards the life of joy that I am trying to set before you. You are distracted by that which destroys your mind and tarnishes your soul, and you can barely hang onto the joy set before you. You can see it in the distance ahead, but you are focused on the trials behind you that persistently and relentlessly pursue you.

Though you are in the wilderness, you are being stretched beyond that which breaks you. This is why you have been blessed with a numbness. That numbness is sustaining you through an atmosphere that intends to destroy you. Do not become destroyed by the distraction and press forward, lean in, and trudge on. Keep going. Keep praying. Keep working. Keep reaching for your joy and rejoice in the wilderness, and in an instant, you will arrive.

Your path is being paved with more than you can imagine, but this is being done ahead of you, not behind you. Your past has no place here. You need to stop clinging to what I am taking out of your hands. You are blessed. You are highly favored. This is how you need to see yourself and start living a life according to and worthy of this. This is the day to take hold of it. It has to start with you. Do not fight against this change. Your blessings begin here.

I have already told you what you must do to grab hold of the joy I have prepared for you to lift you out of those emotions that have been slowly destroying your heart. You are a movement, and you can no longer carry burdens that are not yours that dissuade you from your purpose. You need to stop believing things about you that live in your past. Your past is passed.

Take your light back, for your light is required for greater things. Your light will touch someone you haven't even met yet and will touch those who will move many more across nations. Get out of the shallow and go into the deep. As you continue to move forward with me, you can no longer relate to who you were before. I am doing something new in you, and that means that your environments must change to truly take hold of where I am bringing you.

Your walk is different. Your talk is different. Your perception is different. Your goals are not the same. This can be scary but press on and go deeper. Old connections do not understand your walk with me for they have yet to take hold of their own journeys. This is not a negative mark on them, but it is also not your responsibility to bring them to me. They must walk their own journey. It will not be easy, for you always want to take care of others. That is the leader in you, but ultimately they must own their own identity, walk their own path, and find themselves in me.

I have my hand on you and what was once familiar does not work in your present Because of this, you struggle to continue to accept it, and put hope in it. Everything is deeper and that which is shallow you can no longer stand in. You have come to a point where you must make a firm decision either to go back to where you are in control of your life or commit to following the promptings and the path that only I can lead you to and through. You cannot follow the flow that moves against the word you have been given, for this is the flow that leads to your restoration.

Do not be confused. Follow the word. Do not dishonor the revelations you have been given concerning your life. Do not let feelings of desperation move against the flow of the spirit. It is time to do what I have called you to do. Go deeper. Press on. Move forward. Leave what is behind you behind. Your limitations are based on other's beliefs about your limitations and boundaries though you have already seen beyond the mountain.

You have already received the word that leads you to my flow. Worry about nothing, pray about everything. Your soul is unsatisfied with what you see, for you have already seen what I have promised you. You are not swayed by reason from others, for your faith has already led you through. Do not fight the flow. It hurts and you are drowning in the hurt because you refuse to release your grip on what hurts you and refuse to take hold of the hand that is bringing you up.

Live by the spirit, not by your flesh. Recognize what diminishes your spirit and deflates your hope. It is time for growth, and you can no longer grow in the shallow waters where you once lived. My Spirit brings peace. If you do not feel the peace, it is not good for your spirit. It is not me. You need to learn to love your life and seek change even in the circumstances you find yourself in. Embrace the part of your life that has brought you pain and recognize my hand in developing you through it all.

There are places inside you that needs to develop trust that even the pain has served its purpose if it brings about true change. My hand has directed every step you have taken and has taken steps to change the pain into a moment of glory that will bring you to a permanent happiness that cannot be shaken by what you have gone through. Knowing that you have gone through it is glory in itself.

Do not allow your circumstances to alter your belief in all that is beautiful on the inside of you. You have learned to seek me in all things and your faith has allowed you to follow my call on your life. It is time to act upon the command of living your life to the fullest, for I have given you this life to live. Honor this blessing and protect your breakthrough. In this, you shall place all your hope. Expect more.

August 21st

Father do not let my mind wonder and wander from your thoughts to those that others place in my mind through their words. Keep me focused on what you are calling me to do. Let my ears hear beyond my own thoughts. Tell me what you would have me do, so much so that my mind cannot take me in the wrong direction. Take my doubt and give me a sure foot to follow you to where you are leading me to. Do not allow doubt to cloud my , but only allow your Holy Spirit to guide me and my steps. Let me not fall into traps that would have me do otherwise. Remind me of my calling that I would fulfill what you are calling me to do. Give me the strength to follow you when I am tempted to change my mind.

§

You are not hearing my word clearly, for you keep hearing the voice of others and allowing them to change what you have heard. You are being persuaded by the voice of reason from those who do not understand your walk with me nor your journey. Recognize my Spirit for I have come to you. Remember your calling. I am not done restructuring who you are and if you rush into going back, you will stunt your growth and dishonor my command that change is necessary.

You have barely scratched the surface of the power that has been placed in you and have yet to recognize the purpose for which you hold this power and the reasons this power was given unto you. Do not stop just yet. Keep pressing forward for there are somethings you still need to learn. There are things working on your behalf that will amaze you and there are forces working on your behalf that you have yet to see. Home is not the same home that you left and there is still work to be done. Honor still needs to be established in the holes that have been dug.

Proximity to this will only lead you back to what was before what can be established. Do not make yourself so available. You have been stopped from doing this for a reason and the season has not yet arrived. There is truth about your season and your walk with me right now that you cannot neglect nor reject. It is not yet time. They are still too familiar with what was and who you were that they cannot see who you are becoming.

I am working on hearts and minds and changing perceptions, but there is still work to be done that is necessary to harness the power of change so that change can be permanent. They can no longer see you this way for you have changed beyond their current ability to see you right. You are still under construction as well and your faith cannot fall back into the familiar with an attitude of just seeing what can happen. Do not let your faith become common with what is still mediocre, for it will restrict my Spirit from flowing through you. Honor still needs to be established and that which is familiar will prevent honor from flowing as it needs to.

You are worth more than what is familiar, and you need to recognize the season when honor still needs to be established until honor has become truth. Stay close to my Spirit and rise above what you hear for the time has not yet come. Returning now will only make room for old patterns to return. This will bring you back to what is familiar, but you are no longer even familiar to yourself, for you have become more than the place you used to sit in.

There are irrelevant questions that are clouding your connection, and conversations have taken you back to a dark place. This is meant to show you that it is not for you. I am still working in you and if you allow yourself to return to old promises, the new life-long promises cannot take its place. Amazing things are happening, but others cannot yet see it in its fullness, for their mind is clouded by what is irrelevant and tarnishes the revelation that is being given.

It has yet to take deep root. It is still on the surface but needs to take deeper roots. I am trying to move, but the questions are only producing darkness on what has been brought into the light. There are too many questions that are allowing destructive patterns to continue. What is to come has not yet arrived. This is my work, and I am still working. Do not continue to wonder where all this leads. Trust is all you need to carry.

Faith is your weapon in the dark and I have brought you too far to fall back into old patterns. The questions arise where faith is not present. This is why you find yourself deeply offended, because faith is all you have, and faith is everything to you. You recognize that your journey is built on faith, and you take offense towards those who have no faith in what I am doing. But this is not your battle, and expectations for you to provide their own faith brings you offense. They have yet to establish their own faith in the process for their own journey, and it is not in your power to give promise in their lives that only I can give.

It matters not what the destination is, only that my hand is working for their good and no matter what happens, it is me that has the power to work in their lives for their good, even if their good has nothing to do with you. There is healing that still needs to occur. They cling to their pain and desperation, but do not allow the power of the Holy Spirit to remove their pain and desperation. There is promise of a new beginning more powerful than the pain which brought you all here.

Healing is coming but is not fully here yet. Restoration is coming, but it must occur in each individual through faith alone with a "no matter what happens" belief that God is working for the good of all. There is breakthrough coming but it is not yet time for old patterns and beliefs still exist.

The journey is incredible. Take hold of the journey and let it carry you on your path. You left everything to follow me and for this, something new happens every day. Do not let old perceptions and old patterns take you back to the old darkness that I am working to remove. I am working so that they may see you right. And it is not yet time. Work is still happening in all of you.

August 22nd

§

There is a time and a season for everything, and you must be able to detect my Holy Spirit in each season, for all time. Do not let emotions run your life nor allow your feelings to dictate your steps, for you have been raised above it all already to hear my words and see my signs.

Seek always my Holy Spirit in all you do and let me guide your steps. Dedicate your time to me that you do not miss my call nor miss my promptings for your life. Man cannot offer you direction for it is only done by what man seeks for his own needs. Do not allow your environment to shape your thoughts. You must direct your thoughts to the path that I have laid out for you, for you have been chosen for so much more.

The world is changing, and you are needed to pursue my Spirit so that my Spirit can reach your world through you. There is movement happening in the forces around you that you have yet to fully grasp, but that requires your heart to become a beacon to many, for it is your heart that I have chosen to lead a people through. You have become distracted and distant from me because of your distractions. Whether your distractions are good or bad, they are equally a distraction.

I am building you up, yet you are distracted. You have been taken out of bondage and oppression to taste the freedom I have for you. Do not put yourself back into bondage by following your emotions, for the plans I have for you are greater than what you are following.

Your distractions served a purpose in its season, but the season has come to an end. Stop reaching for it, for it is gone. At the appointed time, I will bring you the right love, with the right spirit, that will bless your life and bless your purpose, for freedom alone is not your purpose. Even freedom becomes its own trap and creates a bondage that will keep you from living a life that is true to you. In that life true freedom is freedom that is blessed.

I am leading you to that freedom, but you must take hold of my word in this moment, and reach for me with all your heart, and I will lead you to all that is good. You are being blessed, but the blessing must come through the transformation of your mind and your heart, that it rests solely and solidly on my love for you. For my love is good and always puts you first. My love will lead you to all that is good and will bring peace to your soul no matter the season, nor the environment. I am bringing you freedom and peace and so much more.

There is victory set aside for you on the path which I have laid out for you, and it is good. All that you have been through has put a fire in your belly that emanates off of you and brings light to those who have a hidden unsettling in their souls. This is part of your purpose, to expose that unsettling and demonstrate the power of my peace, for you have been through much and still carry a certain peace with you. But this peace must be tended to. This fire must be tended to. You cannot become so distracted that you do not tend to your own flame lest you lose your peace.

I am leading you to peace, as you will offer peace to a people that silently struggle without. People busy themselves to hide the struggle from themselves, and you cause them to slow down and see deeper. You cause them to recognize what is unsettled in their spirits and this will ultimately lead them to seek peace, but peace comes only through their own relationship with me.

What you have overcome has been much and still you carry a commitment to peace, and you carry a joy about you. You know where that comes from, and it has built a deep curiosity from others that are striving for that same peace. You have sought it day and night and you must continue to seek it, for it is part of your purpose. You have fought much and still found peace.

Regroup, reset, and take inventory of where your peace lives or where your spirit sits in each moment. It is in this time that you are tending to your flame. Your ability to do this is what makes you special. You can stop in the middle of chaos and seek my peace until your fire burns so bright that you feel it throughout your soul, and you can begin to face the world on fire again.

Forget what is behind, for what is behind you had the power to shake you, and you have outgrown that environment, for you can no longer respond to those in that environment with the same spirit. Your spirit has grown beyond all that. I did this for you in your hour of need. I lifted you up and pulled people out of your life that would have killed your spirit. The environment that you were in would have killed your spirit, but I am working.

You see my hand in the separation so that you can move forward. There is more in store for you if you continue to follow this path. It is important. Do not worry about what you need, for I will provide it all. You are chosen. My hand is on your life. Be not afraid of what is behind you, for I have worked it all for your good. Know this as you remember your past, for I have brought you peace amongst the chaos. This is my gift to you.

I know where you come from, what you have been through, and what has shattered you deeply. I know. Others may see your strength, but I know what you had to fight to maintain it. Everyone else sees your joy, but I know what you had to lose to get it. Everyone else sees your light, but i know the tears you have shed to keep it. I know you.

Though these things are part of who you are, I know all that you are made of. Take my word on who you are now as you remember all that broke you in your past. You were able to love me, seek me, and praise me in your brokenness. Your intimate moments have given you peace and joy beyond your brokenness. I know you and give you your strength. I give you your joy. I give you your light.

Do not forget the power that brought you there. Do not forget the power that gave you your power lest you fall astray in your success. Always seek my hand in everything you encounter, and ensure it is my will in the moment, in the people, in the opportunities that fall at your feet. Do not lose sight of your need for me in your life and every step will be a successful step towards your purpose.

I will lead your life in the stillness. Do not disregard your time in the stillness. Do not neglect your time to be still in my presence. I will bring you focus and peace in all you do. Be still and listen for me always. Be still and hear me. I will show you what I have for you. I will show you what is good for you and what you must let go of. Trust the process. Be still and trust my voice over your life.

I am building a life for you better than you can build for yourself. Seek me in your success like you did in your brokenness. Rediscover your need for me the same way you have needed the validation of others. You pursued that validation with everything. Pursue me with everything now, for I will bring you everything you need. I carried you through your desperation and you have found peace. I have dried your tears and you have found joy. I have heard your cries and you have found purpose, meaning, and life.

Your testimony has revelation in it that will serve a nation, a people. Your testimony will be a defining moment in someone else's life. It will serve as a catalyst to someone else's ability to find joy. I have placed this in you for this purpose. Do not be afraid of what is behind you for it is all filled with this purpose. You are chosen. You are blessed. You are filled with purpose.

Regroup, reset, and get back into position. Be still and I will speak to you all the things you are made to be. I am speaking to you your purpose. I am speaking to you the reason for your life. You have been ordained for this. You have been created for this. This is who you are.

August 24th

Psalm 119: 25-32

I lie in the dust, revive me by your word. I told you my plans and you answered, now teach me your decrees. Help me understand the meaning of your commandments, and I will meditate on your wonderful deeds. I weep with sorrow, encourage me by your word. Keep me from lying to myself, give me the privilege of knowing your instructions. I have chosen to be faithful. I have determined to live by your regulations. I cling to your laws. Lord, don't let me be put to shame! I will pursue your commands, for you expand my understanding.

§

The words you have been given have the power to change your life, but you need to see the person I saw when you started this journey. I have been showing you all that you are, and this means that you can no longer entertain people that only know who you were.

It is time to move forward and recognize what it is you hold inside that now has the power to change your life and the lives of many others. You don't even know the person that you were, for the changes inside you no longer reflect her. This is a revelation that is meant to guide you the rest of the way. There are some that see who you really are, for they look at the spirit of you and reach you through their own. They see the light you don't always see in yourself. These are the people I have brought to you for spiritual growth and development, so you learn to love who you really are and not who you think you were.

They are a reflection, kindred spirits, mating in the soul. You see them and are drawn to them, just as they see you and are drawn to you, spirit to spirit. Their perception is not clouded by your circumstances, but rather, who you can be once you start believing you are worth the true presence of who you really are. These people are my blessing to you in this season, and this is why your spirit is at peace in their presence. Do not allow your mind and thoughts of what is past to prevent you from connecting to them.

They are waiting for you to see yourself the same way they see you so you can freely flow in your true spirit.

Go back in your journals to discover who you are. I have spoken truth plainly to you. These words are not your own fabrications but are blessed conversations with the Holy Spirit to bring you into a full understanding of who you are. Totally and completely – you. The eyes of your understanding need to see who you are, accept fully who you are, and own completely who you are, before you can move forward into the blessings set aside for you.

You have cried and were heard. You have thought less of yourself and are being reminded of your value. Do not look past this revelation for it is the most important one you need to grasp in your heart in order to fulfill the kingdom purpose. What you allow to change your perspective on who you are will have a lifelong impact on your pursuit to fulfill your purpose. Be watchful for what changes your perspective on yourself. Be selfish. Stand firm in your true identity.

This is possible only through your relationship with me, in my truth about the core of who you are, and the destiny tied to your name. When I make myself known to you, you begin to see who you are in me and there is power in knowing who you are for there is power in me. I am your bridge. Keep pressing in to cross the bridge into who you are called to be. No matter what others may say to and about you, there is no relevance to who I say you are. It is time to believe the word about who you are that has already been given to you.

It seems like this is repetitive, but you must become convinced, no matter how many times you have to hear it. There is so much depending entirely on you coming into this knowing.

> *"Loyalty is such a deceiving word, and you have to watch out for insecure people who will use this notion of loyalty to keep you beneath your destiny. You have come to a place where you say, 'I'm going to be loyal to myself and loyal to who God has called me to be, and if being loyal to you brings me down, I have got to cut this thing off."*
>
> TOURE' ROBERTS

Remain committed to only that which raises you up and doesn't manipulate you with loyalty at the expense of your destiny. Let nothing stand in your way of becoming. You are not the same person anymore and if something keeps trying to pull you back, break it off. Keep moving, no matter what.

August 25th

§

You have been through many changes. Many circumstances have been part of your journey that you have had to fight through to hold onto your faith. You woke up this morning with peace at knowing you are one step closer to wholeness because you have allowed yourself to let go of what no longer works for your life and who you are becoming.

You have recognized that what used to shake you so violently has lost its power on you. I am getting you ready. You have not been alone in your fight, and I have reached for you at many stages on your journey to remind you of who you are, who you are no longer, and above all, who you are becoming for the sake of the kingdom.

I have spoken to you in the darkest hours and brought you strength and clarity to see beyond all that threatens to cloud your mind and shake your spirit. You have never been alone. You have found comfort in those dark places, and I have used every means possible to bring you into the comfort of my embrace. The word has led you to me. The word has led you home.

For the first time in your life, you know, understand, and appreciate the comforts of home. You have been searching for this for so long that at times it was uncomfortable. There is peace in these walls I have brought you into. The silence is beautiful and refreshes your soul. That is what home is all about. You have found a space that allows you to pray freely and fully. These walls give you freedom; Freedom to be in my presence, freedom to dig for the well that refreshes your spirit, freedom to be you, without shame.

These walls have given you the safe space you have been looking for to pray your blessings into becoming your reality. You see this daily. These walls give you a voice that the heavens hear. This is your sacred space. You connect here. You repair here. You rejuvenate here. You are at home.

If you find yourself in a space that does not give you peace and freedom to be you, it is not home. You have been taken out of spaces that confined you, attempted to define you, and took from you, your peace. That is not home. You do not belong there. It may bring peace to others, but it is not your place of peace. Though you are passing through and transitioning in the new space, I have made it home so that you recognize what home needs to be, needs to feel like, needs to provide you, all the time. It needs to be a place that renews your spirit, always.

So, as you sit in a space, take careful observation on what it does to your spirit, in this you will recognize if it is a place you are supposed to be in. This is a space I have given you. I have led you there for the purpose of bringing joy to your soul that once drowned in desperation. Go there with courage and faith knowing I brought you there for a reason, for a season that your spirit needs. If for no other reason, it is a space to rejuvenate.

There are connections to your soul there that drive you to reach higher, to live fully and free. There is kindness there and this is why you were brought there, even if it is just a season, it is just what you need right now. No one knows what it took for you to get here, but you are here. You are where you need to be. This is your high place, a place where your heart can reach beyond all your limitations. This is a place where you have a discerning heart that can see beyond what the world will show you. You hear from me here. No one knows the work it took to get here, but here is where you need to be.

You are becoming in this place, and it is protected by the heavens for your becoming is essential to the purpose which has been placed on your life. It is time to take this to a new level. It is time to start taking what you have been given and sharing it with the world. You will start with your small circle and the circle will grow. The more you receive, the more you will give, and the greater your circle will become. What you are birthed with in this space will bring the same comforts and peace needed to change spaces and homes beyond that which your eyes can see, but it is so.

There is a responsibility that follows you for this very reason. Tend to that responsibility, remember this responsibility, for you will come to a time of deep questioning, but do not let it shake you in the same way you have been shaken before. Return to this space to reset and remember what you are doing and why you are doing it. Do not worry whether you are qualified or not, for there is power beyond your own that qualifies you for more than you realize.

You will be faced with choices that can take your life in different directions, and this space will allow me to speak unto you what choices you shall make, and I will make it so. You will be given authority to make decisions that affect the whole. Treat this authority with reverence for me, for it will have great power, and your decisions must be shaped in my hand so that your purpose is what helps you rightly exercise that authority. Take ownership of this authority and do not just give yourself nor your space over to just anybody, especially to those you have been called away from you for purposes beyond your needs.

Your needs will be and are being provided for by me. Take authority over your purpose, your voice, your choices, and the gift in which you have been given for reasons beyond you. You can no longer adjust who you are, for you are more than what others see, and you are more than even you can see. Believe in your authority for it is being shaped in my hands. This is your validation.

You have the authority to change everything around you. It is time to take what has been birthed in this place and share it with a world in need of what you have found and have been given. Prepare yourself for it is coming. What you have been holding in and keeping safe in these walls will begin to invade those around you and it is time. It is you. You are the catalyst. It is coming.

You are in the right place of preparation for what is coming. Open yourself up now. You are no longer bound to your silence and your pen will speak loudly in dark places that will ignite a change in others who are chosen though they know this not. They will know me, and they will respond. What you have birthed here will change more than you can imagine. Believe anyway. Your heart has been shaped here. Your mind is being shaped here. Your purpose is being shaped here. Your commitment to discernment is being refined here.

I have removed you from the voices that were preventing you from hearing these messages but have opened up your heart to hear my truth about who you are and the life you are being called to live to change so much more. You are in the right space and have sacrificed much to be in this place. It is not forgotten. Though you doubt, believe anyway.

You will heal others, for I have healed you. You will change lives, for I have changed yours. I am providing all you need so that these things shall become at the sound of your voice, for you have heard mine. Though you doubt, believe anyway.

You sent your word to me, and I have been healed.

§

You are experiencing a new perspective that has been washed of all that has dirtied your vision from the pain and grief you have had to endure. You are being given insight on all things concerning your life, your experiences, and all that you sense of what you are currently going through. I have been speaking truth to you with a greater intensity so that you will be set free from a limited vision that is based on past pain. And pain has passed.

This is why I have been pursuing your thoughts so intensely. You cannot lose sight of the word I have given you when I changed your perspective and based it solely on the insights I have been speaking unto you. There are forces trying to change your perspective on just what they see but have yet to see me with the insight of their soul, therefore cannot tell you the truth, for the truth comes only through me and the spirit in which I give them to see.

Do not allow yourself to disregard the insights which I have given you based on man's sight. What I have shown you is truth and is your current revelation. Do not walk by sight, walk by faith. And your faith should be based on what I have spoken directly to you, and not by what others urge you to see with your eyes. Your spirit has been receiving directly from me, and the lessons of your past are part of your new perspective. It is in going back and seeing what was done, what has changed, and what is now coming that you find healing.

You must manifest the word that has been spoken to you. This is insight that cannot be shaken for it has been divinely given to you. This is your truth no matter what anyone else may think or wish for you to think. Know that your insight has been divinely inspired and you need to set your mind entirely on this. You see something others cannot see, and you cannot escape what you know. I will not let you fall from what you have seen, back into what can no longer take hold of you.

You know that you know that I have reached you. I have spoken to you. I have made a new covenant with you and in this you cannot doubt. You must recognize when the thoughts of others invade this sacred space where the word is housed. Your heart cannot be shaken, for this is the place the word must live.

August 28th

§

I am developing something incredible and amazing in you so the world can see me in you. You are being blessed that you too may become a blessing, and you must learn to believe in your worth, that you accept the blessing without pride. Just know that I am with you. It is your faith that brings me unto you with blessing after blessing.

Though you are experiencing things that may scare you, be not afraid, for I have brought these things as blessings and miracles that will bring you joy unlike anything you have known. I am setting you up into a place where you can breathe, where you can be free, where you can be you. You may be questioning your emotions in this place but be sure-footed for this is the path I have made for you. It is I.

Do not be afraid, for you have seen my hand at every turn where your doubt threatened to overtake you. You have seen the shift in an instant each time your mind began to believe otherwise, but still, you hold faith that I am breaking rules and barriers for you. I am taking you further than you realize and the limits you believe are there, are no longer.

When you placed your life in my hands, I began shaping everything for your good. Be of good faith for it is I moving mountains on your behalf. Get excited and let go of the guilt for I am breaking rules to bring you to what is next. Keep reaching beyond the invisible lines, limits, rules, and boundaries, for it is I.

I have removed the borders to bring you up. It may be uncomfortable for a moment because you do not recognize this joy and strength. You have never seen nor felt it with this level of intensity, but it is so, for I have made it so. See my hand in all things, seek me and I will make it clear for you. You are astonished at what is happening and you become nervous and begin to harbor guilt for experiencing this new joy, but be not afraid, for it is I.

I am making resources available for you in measure of your faith and there is no room for doubt. Don't pay attention to the rules right now for these rules and restrictions are bondages that are not yours. Your growth beyond this is critical for there is more increase in store for you so that you will see my hand and know that it is I. You have no limitations in this season for it is now the season for blessing and where my blessings exist, no limits apply.

What I bring together, no one can part. What doors I open, no one can close. What doors I close, no one can open, and I am shaping and paving your path. Do not trust the voice that is limiting you right now, and place your faith in the season for it is I. I am making the way known to you, so your doubt dies in an instant when you remember the season. Be of good cheer. My hand is on your life for you have given yourself to me and you have dedicated your heart to my cause and for this, I am providing everything you need to keep moving forward and toward that goal without limits.

Relax your mind for I am with you. Enjoy this moment. Enjoy this season. The tears are gone, and I am bringing you joy so that you will recognize my hands on your life. You feel the peace for it is I. Do not trust what others see or say because everyone else is blinded by rules that do not apply in this season. Let your heart soar without guilt for I have made the way known to you, and it is good.

Confront the norm and do so in faith for it is I. You are breaking through barriers with my strength. You are changing atmospheres with my spirit. You are activating ability in others with my light. See yourself in me for I want you to see who you really are, for it is I revealing all things unto you. Take heed of my promptings, they come with peace. I am reflecting to you the power that exists within you through spirit and soul, spirit to spirit, soul to soul. I am showing you your truth. Just look to me and you will see beyond the restrictions and boundaries.

This is your breakthrough. So, break through the limits. Break through the rules. Break through the doubts that threaten to overtake you. Break through religious systems and traditions that do not pertain to this season which I have brought you to. Be of good cheer, for it is I.

I have given you the faith to break through it all. Let faith win and defeat doubt. You have the power to push out old environments that limited you. Place faith in this for it is truth. Trust the journey. Enjoy the journey for you see me working in it all. You will continue to be blessed according to your faith. Let your faith be bigger than every mountain you face. Let your faith reach beyond the span of everything you see. Let your faith propel you beyond your adopted beliefs about limits that are no longer yours. Push. Break through. Move past it all with faith. There are things that I have brought into your life in this season that will help push you through the barriers so that you are no longer stuck in the middle of transition but make it to where I am taking you.

Let your faith lead you and be of good cheer, for it is I. It is I opening doors. It is I changing hearts. It is I positioning you for greater things. Do not doubt, for it is I. There are things and people assigned to your life that you are now connecting to. Don't be bound to what once limited you. You are supposed to win this battle and it is with your faith that will give you the strength and stamina to push you to win.

You no longer fit the box you once placed yourself in. Do not feel guilty about this. I have made the connections that don't connect become your past. I am making the things that do connect, connect through what is right to where you truly are, though you have yet to see it. I am shifting everything, and everyone connected to you to bless you. So be of good cheer, for it is I.

I will move the mountain. I will break the barriers. I will take out what does not work and replace it with what connects to your soul, that your soul may soar with the power that only faith can bring. So be of good cheer. Be of good faith. Break through the limits, for it is I moving in your breakthrough.

August 31st

§

There have been words spoken to you by others that have caused you to doubt the words that have been spoken to you by me. You have begun to question the validity of my word over your life, but you must not allow their doubts to sway you into unbelief, for they know not what has been said to you, why it has been said to you, nor what all this means as you move to a greater purpose.

Bring your thoughts and your focus back to your purpose and look back on what has been said to you, why it has been spoken, and what was revealed to you for greater purpose. What has been produced in these pages has been what has connected you to all that is higher than the human mind can comprehend. Do not believe that your gift was self-made and self-serving, for all this has been inspired by that which is holy and has been put on your heart for more than your own healing.

It is time to finish what has been started so that all will know that these words were given to you for all. There are people that will read these words and know that healing comes and will live on that promise that I am speaking to them directly. You are nearly there.

There is strength in these pages. There is love in these pages. There is an absolute peace in these pages for the hearts that need it most, and for the hearts that still teeter on unbelief but play a prominent role on healing my people. Do not let the enemy infiltrate what is holy, what has been given unto you, for it can ultimately affect much more than your own belief.

The words in these pages will transform hearts, and inspire others to fulfill their own purpose, find their own worth, and bring order into their lives that will transform nations. You need to press in and finish what has been started no matter what it costs you. For what you lose will be gained over tenfold of what you lose. Own the message for it has been given to you to speak out to all who will hear it.

Be committed to the end and let your testimony produce the power it has to produce in others. There are tears that have been cried unto heaven that will be dried in these pages. What you are doing requires faith for the future, and what is in the past, must remain in the past. It is time to turn the page and grab hold of the future that has been promised to you, and it is good.

No one knows your brokenness except those who have been broken. No one knows your fight except those that are just discovering theirs. These words are for them. There is healing here for them, and you must finish it. You must press in. You must move on. You must embrace this with everything in you and let your heart speak into the pages for it will speak into the hearts of those who have been waiting for it. Finish it.

I am leading you to others who will read these pages and become united in the fight for inner freedom that will change a nation. There is favor on your life for this reason. Do not let circumstances cause you to doubt my presence, for my presence is real, and is real in you. Renew your mind. Reconnect to the power that propelled your change to begin with.

It is time to pull it all together and finish what has been started. This is for you. This is for them. This is for my Holy Purpose. Do not let others in to manipulate you and cause unbelief. The success of what I am doing in these pages is not dependent on what others believe. It is based on what you believe, and your belief is stronger and more powerful than all their unbelief put together.

Follow the promptings in the words spoken to you. Release what does not belong. Press into faith, for this will change your entire world, and it is good. Nothing can pull you outside of your destiny except your own unbelief. This will be your weapon to survive all attacks on your destiny. Do not become offended, become your purpose. Put up the walls that need to be put up. Guard your heart from those who do not understand your path. You do not need to prove yourself to anyone, lest you get lost in the search for vain and meaningless validation from those who have yet to discover meaning within their own hearts.

Your belief and your faith will speak to the ears of those that desperately need power in their own belief and faith for transformation. You will be the example of how my power transforms a heart into absolute faith and absolute healing. Do not be dissuaded by others. Press in. Move forward. Finish it.

Focus on me to the very end and I will give you the new beginning that has been birthed within these pages. A beginning of life and love beyond measure and time. A promise fulfilled in my inspired word over your life. A strength and a peace that you have been fighting for. A joy and a wholeness that is solely yours. From that place, you will bless others. From your purpose, you will become a beacon of hope to the lost, and in this, you will find the fulfillment you have been searching for all of your life.

The words embedded in you, you have carried long before you ever knew you needed it or would share it. It is what drives you to respond to others. It is what others see in you that draws them to you. There is more inside you and in these pages than even you realize. There is a battle for your belief. Fight with all you have and finish it.

Do what I say you can do. You have already won this fight and it is time for your faith to take you to the finish line. Do not stop. Do not settle. Push. Press in and finish it. There are forces fighting on your behalf. This is your favor for there is no influence greater than what now stands behind you and empowers your heart to fulfill your purpose.

You have found peace in these pages for you have been aligned with your destiny. You have found joy in these pages, for your sorrows have been defeated here, for my hand has been in your healing. I have been with you form the start and will be with you to the finish and beyond, into your new beginnings, and into and through all that is next. Stand firm in your belief and forge ahead. Do not look back, the past is not your burden any longer. Press in. Follow my promptings, for what I have for you is good. You are closer than you think. Finish it. It is time.

Turn the page and let go of your past. Press in. Move forward. Finish what has been started. Reach deeper for the destiny that has been promised to you, for it is yours. Seize it, for it is good. Claim life over yourself, for there are other lives connected to you that need you to finish this. Do not be shaken for you know who you really are and what you will do. Keep going. Finish it. The victory is already yours.

September 1st

When she reached out for the hand of God, He healed her.

§

Tender one, do not worry about what others think about your state of mind, your illness, your grief, your sins, for they know not the strength it took for you to get where you are, with the clarity of mind and the purpose in which you now walk.

When I came to you, you were drowning beneath the overwhelming depression and the all-consuming grief. You were drowning in loneliness and shame, but you had the faith to cry out, and in that cry, you found the strength. Your vision was restored. Your mind became clear. Your heart began to sing. From there you were able to hear and feel the Holy Spirit and in this came your healing. I reached down and rescued you, healed you, and brought you out of your stupor. I raised you up, restored your creativity, and in this, recovered your forgotten purpose.

You are no longer bound to that which broke you, for you have been brought out of that darkness and no one knows what you had to cling to, to rise up out of your bondage again. You do not have to accept the thoughts of others anymore, for it is none of them that pulled you out. You are being guided. You are being led. You do have my hand on your life, and I am making a way for you to rediscover your joy.

It has been long enough for you to be living in the bondages of the breaking. The breaking has passed. Look up child, for I am here, and will continue to guide you. I will not let you fall nor fail. I will restore your spirit to absolute belief again. You are worth too much to leave behind in the ties and situations that are no longer yours to be bound to.

Let who once lived in desperation go now, for her time is now gone. Allow the one who lives on hope come alive, for this is her time. Take hold of her spirit and rise. Reach for the promises that you have been given, for all that you reach for will be yours for the taking. You are so much more than you think you are.

Reach higher, for the limits have been removed. You are no longer in the process of healing for you have been healed. You are now in the process of claiming your power and owning your restoration. You are now becoming who you really are. You were created for more than the life you left behind. Do not let others in your life touch you and take your peace from you, for they do not know what you have truly suffered to get here.

They see the surface and repeat your words, they throw bricks and try to shame you into believing you are less than you truly are, but they do not know what it took to get to where you are now. There is strength in your overcoming, and you have overcome. You are no longer a nuisance nor an inconvenience. Stop basing the idea of you on how other people have treated you, for they do not know who you truly are. But I do. And I have come to tell you, you are more than the old identity which you claim, and which once claimed you.

Release her, for she is not yours any longer. Do not allow yourself to be trapped by the thoughts others have on who you should be, for you are more than those thoughts that have become stale and useless. Let her go, for she is no longer you. She was just part of your experience, but you are being called for more.

Do not let others stop you, for they do not know what it took for you to get to where you are standing now. You are already free from your suffering and sorrows. You are free from your shame and your sin, and it no longer has hold on you. I am bringing you help to remember who you really are. Release the one who you no longer fit, and who does not fit you.

Mark 5:34

He said to her, "Daughter, your faith has healed you. Go in peace and be freed from your suffering."

§

You have forgotten who you are, because you were so focused on who you needed to be for others. You are no longer she. You are my child, and I call you daughter. Claim her, for she is you, and you are she, and all other identities, self-imposed, and called on by others are no longer you. You cannot live the rest of your life in the shadows of the girl that once was broken, bound, and forgotten. Rise up and take your place, for you are called daughter to the Most High. Daughter of the Holy One. Daughter of the God of Everlasting Life.

You are being called out of the old you who was bound to the lower terms of a you who no longer is. She is no longer your truth. Your brokenness is no longer your truth. Your grief is no longer your truth. Your rejection is no longer your truth. Your isolation is no longer your truth. Your sorrow is no longer your truth. Your sin is no longer your truth. Let her go now, for she is gone.

You are not what you suffered. You are more, so much more. Take hold of who you are, for you are called daughter.

The truth has been spoken to you. Claim it, for it is yours.

"Jesus brought her back to tell her the truth. She was bleeding on the inside, and she did something on the outside. But God didn't just want to fix what was happening in her body. She heard about Jesus, and that freed her from her suffering. But when she heard from Jesus, it freed her from her shame." Toure' Roberts

September 2nd

§

Do not doubt the path you are on. This is the path I chose for you. There is a reason your path has taken this turn. It was immediate, for it was predetermined before you even knew. There are hearts tied to your destiny and I wanted you to have this because I love you, and I trust that all that you have gone through will serve another.

Celebrate this day. The revelations you are seeing were planned and set aside for you long before you realized it. I chose something before you could see it. Build on it. Be not afraid, for this has been chosen for you. This is where your joy waits, for my hand has been on you for a very long time.

I have seen past everything you were going through because I knew this would be your destination. There is destiny here and you knew it the moment you let your guard down and began to follow this path which has been predetermined. Do not allow your past to influence you now that you know, for you have now seen what is waiting. Celebrate this day and be glad in it.

In order for me to bring about what has already been written in your future, you have had to go through what you have been through in your past so that you would be ready for the blessings that have been waiting for you. For this reason, your heart has been set in stone against the past that could have changed your path. This is the reason all of your messages have been telling you to press on, for what I have for you is good.

My hand is on your life, and I have brought you here. This is your confirmation for the things that have been pressing on your thoughts. I will take you higher than you have ever been and show you what life should look like. You are covered by my grace, and this is your path. This is your plan. This is your destiny. Keep following it. Set your foot firm in this path, for it is preordained. It has been at your core long before you knew it, but you have known it longer than you realize.

I have set you in the midst of this, for it is good. There is power on this path, for it has been blessed for you. This is the one you have been led to. Stand firm and celebrate the path you are on now that you see the destiny assigned to this path you have been set on.

What door I have opened, no man can shut. And what door I have has closed, no man can open. You now have the key that has been set aside for you. Open the door, for it is blessed for you. In this room, you will discover the most important parts of yourself and come to own the joy that is your core. Do not let someone else change your direction, for it has already been decided. Protect your core. Protect your path. Protect your blessing, for it is blessed by my hand.

This is why you find peace here. You have felt the peace here and it is not your imagination. It is real peace that will allow you to produce from this place that you now stand in. You will no longer produce from the past now that your path has been revealed to you. You will produce from what has been set in your future. Do not bring what has passed and has been what you relied on, to sabotage where you are headed. Protect your path, for it is good.

Do not trust emotions that tie you to your past, for it is time to let those emotions go. It is time for you to start doing according to what has been set in your future, for it is your destiny. This is a life-changing defining moment. Own it.

You are destiny to those who have needed you, but this is future and not past. There are those waiting on you for you to take hold of your destiny, to take hold of your power, to take hold of your path. They have prepared for you and wait for you to recognize what has been set aside for you to take hold of. You have been hearing messages about your future, you have reached the door to that future. You have had a feeling planted firmly in your spirit for it has been assigned to lead you here. For this reason, you have not been allowed to revert and return to what must be laid down in order for you to pursue the light that is waiting for you to take hold of, and it is good.

Your pain had a purpose and it brought you here. Your fears had a purpose to ignite your faith despite your fears. There is healing and wholeness here. Take hold of the here and now and move forward with confidence.

You don't need another revelation. You don't need another sign. This is your confirmation that you are where I have called you to be.

Do not question it any longer. Have a faith so bold that you live from this revelation fully, for it is good. Stand against everything that tries to lead you away from this place I have brought you to, for there is purpose here assigned to your name that will propel you to fulfill your destiny. This is the day that I have made. Rejoice! And be glad in it, for my hand has shaped this moment, made your path straight, and will lead you through everything that will try to stand in your way.

There is divine power pushing you through. Be not afraid to follow the path that has been laid out for you. It is time to change your core and take hold of what I have set aside for you. You have nothing to be afraid of. There is power here, greater than anything you can see, and it will bring you into the most amazing version of who you are.

You went into seclusion to get yourself together, Because you have heard this word and followed it no matter what came against you and your calling to move forward, you shall be blessed. The seclusion gave you clarity about who you are and has allowed you to let go of who you were and gave you the faith and power to pursue who you are called to be.

Do not fall back, for what is behind you must stay behind. Take hold of this, for it is truth. Put everything else in my hands, for you can no longer carry it. Pursue your path with boldness and hold your head high knowing that you have been led to this place, this position, and this path. This is your path to restoration.

You are called to be here. It takes discipline, but you must practice discipline and allow my presence to saturate your spirit that your steps do not fall back to what is behind you. Press in. Push forward. Reach for my promise over your life. Pull from the power within you and let your light shine radiantly on your path. Surrender to this word for it is good. This is my will over your life.

Part IV
The Becoming

September 3rd

Ecclesiastes 8:1

How wonderful to be wise, to analyze, and interpret things. Wisdom lights up a person's face, softening its harshness.

§

You have been given much to this point which has led you through the dark and into that which has brought you light. This is what you carry now, and it matters not what others see, but more that you see what is reflected back at you when you look into your own eyes.

Where you saw lines and darkness as a place on your face where your eyes sat, you now see light in its place. You carry much more than you have before.

Where parts of you were broken, you have been restored and made whole. You are being shaped every day.

What used to confuse and confound you, you now understand and see beyond what is in plain sight. You have been brought to a capacity of greater vision and clarity that you can now see spirit beyond the flesh of a thing.

Where you have lost sight, you now see clearly.

Where you were once blinded by the thing you thought you needed, you now seek and see purpose in all that can and cannot fill the need to meet your purpose.

Where you once saw lack, you now have sustenance that feeds your soul.

Where you were once burdened beneath all that you carry, you have been lifted up and out of, until all that weighed you down fell off and out of your grip. You have learned what to cling to and what to release. There is power in your transformation.

Where you were once wounded, you have found healing.

Where you once found death, you have discovered life. Your eyes carry now carry new life.

Where you once laid down defeated and in desperation, you have learned to rise and walk with a new spirit that no longer knows defeat.

Where you were once lonely, you have found a divine relationship that feeds the needs of your spirit.

Where you were once paralyzed by grief and sorrow, you have been given healing and joy.

Where you were once rejected, you have found self-acceptance.

Where you were once drowning in shame, you have found true redemption.

Where you were once numb, you have learned to feel deeper and differently.

Where you were once weakened by what you have lived through, you have found your greatest strength.

Where you were once neglected, your voice now carries the biggest influence.

Where you were once lost, you now have direction.

Where you were once defeated, you have found victory.

Where you were lost and last, you are now first and lead the way for others.

Where you were once insecure and inadequate, you have found confidence and meaning and true value in who you are.

The Becoming

You are light.
You are His reflection.
You are restoration.
You are understanding.
You are clarity.
You are the vision.
You are the spirit.
You are the purpose.
You are the sustenance.
You are the transformation.
You are the healing power.
You are new life.
You are freedom.
You are strength.
You are victory.
You are love.
You are joy.
You are acceptance.
You are redemption.
You are the deep.
You are the influence.
You are inspiration.
You are wholeness.
You are confidence.
You are valuable.
You are the flow.

You are all that I have made you. Live it. Own it. Know it. You have overcome. You have become all that I meant for you to be. This is your truth. Live it. Own it. Know it. For it is so. You have been shaped into all this for I now live in you, and there is no greater power.

September 4th

§

You did not come here to stay the same. You are in the middle of your becoming from places that tried to take all that you are. Hold fast and firm to your transformation and do not let anything cloud your mind that threatens to take you back to where you came out of. You have been filled with the Holy Spirit in this new place and I have partnered with you during your transformation.

Despite everything you have had to face and endure, I have helped you stand taller and gave you the power to press on. Because you believed, I have blessed every step that you have taken. What has been embedded in you will begin to touch the world around you and you must stay focused on what you allow to consume you, for what you consume, you will feed to others.

You must take hold of and keep your peace for peace is what you will offer. Your environment and the people around you must contribute to your light and inner joy, for that is what you will give out in the places you will find yourself in, in the future.

You have been allowed to see all of your pain, so you know what causes that pain and keeps you there. But you are no longer a kept woman, consumed by the pain, for it is not your pain to carry. You have been restored, for you will give others the tools and insights that will lead them to their own restoration.

You have experienced trauma so deep that when you are faced with someone experiencing this same level of deep trauma, you will be the beacon of hope that will lead them out of the depths of their despair and into my presence, for an absolute healing, and where brokenness has no place.

Do not let what once broke you take you away from what is now building you into the woman that will inspire others to build from their own brokenness. Your change will be so real to them that they too begin their own transformation that will change others. You have gone through the fire and your heart has been purified in that fire, for you will be the spark that will ignite the fire in others. Protect your flame, for it is needed to light the way.

Your faith and beliefs have been challenged through the greatest opposition, and you have overcome it all with your faith and belief. They are the weapons that you will bestow on others that are lost in their lack and desperation. In spite of what you have gone through, you have come out and overcame it all from the strength of your faith and belief that I have empowered you with.

You have experienced confusion to the point that you believed everything and nothing at the same time and that conflict nearly broke you. But because you cried out for clarity, you have received revelation after revelation that will take others out of the dark and into the light that they too will see with eyes of true understanding.

Do not feel sorry for yourself for you have been blessed with much, and what meant to break you has given you the power and strength to push through and has propelled you to become the woman that others strive to become in themselves.

You have been at war with the darkest parts of yourself and others for a very long time so that you could see the power of your own endurance and your own inner strength, so that you will inspire others to overpower their own demons, both inside them and around them. There is a force within you that has trampled dark hearts, forged through dark spaces, and defeated everything that came against you, so that you can inspire the warrior within others to defeat the enemies that threaten to steal their own joy. And joy is a great strength in the midst of war and adversity.

That is the power of belief that you cling to that took you out of the environments that were meant to break you, and in this you have discovered your value, for value is what you will instill in others that have forgotten their own worth. Your mission is to remind them of who they are.

You have experienced the deepest heartbreaks of rejection, so that you would learn what love needs to look like, feel like, and be like, so you will recognize it when it is ready for its place in your heart and in your world. You have learned that the love others offer you has to equal to the love you have for yourself. In this too, others will learn to discern what is good for them and what must be let go.

Your faith tells you that when you are ready, it will come, and if it is worthy, it will stay for the rest of your living days. You have learned not to settle, for you have learned how to truly love you, that you will teach others what is worthy of who they are and what has no place in the spaces of their own hearts.

Your testimony has the power to transform lives of many. It will inspire. It will lead. It will ignite the fire that changes minds and environments in the hearts of many after you. You are becoming and coming out of all that held you back, and you are a force that I have created to change the lives of others. You are part of my movement to change the world, one heart at a time, one mind at a time.

You are being made into the change that others need within themselves. I am with you, and in this, is your power to change all the environments that you stand in, in the people that stand around you. You carry much more than you realize, but the moment you take hold of what you carry, everything will change, and that is the power and realization that you will deliver to others.

No one can take that away from you, for that is what you will give.

You see things differently and there is more to you than you realize. Other people recognize this power you have, but until you recognize your own power, you cannot teach others to tap into theirs. So, take hold of who you are and what you carry, for this is what you will build in the hearts and minds of others.

Be at the ready to stand in your full power, for it is greater than even you realize. That power will change many. Accept your favor for you will connect others to their own favor. This is your movement, for you move with me in every step, in every thought. Move in favor and increase the environments you stand in. Inspire others with who you are, by simply standing in the room. You bring power into that room. It permeates the space so pay attention to what you carry into that space. Change the room, bring it up to you. Do not let the room bring you down, bring it up to be worthy to walk in.

Never forget who you are and what you carry for you carry much and that will change more than you realize. This is the time to take hold of who you are, what you carry, what you give out, and all that your presence affects.

The power in your stride moves mountains. Own that power for it is needed now to transform much. You are the key to the change that needs to happen in the broken, the desperate, the lost, the lonely, the forgotten, the rejected, the neglected, the abused. There is a world waiting on you to step into who you are. Step in. Take hold. Produce in others what has been produced in you. There is power in your presence. Own it. There is healing in your heart, give it. There is change in your transformation, share it. There is greatness in who you are, deliver it.

September 5th – True Meaning Of Submission

Submit yourself to the Will of God for His plans for your life are good and will nourish your soul.

Follow His call, His will, His voice, for He has prepared a path for you that will take you out of your bondage and free your spirit to be everything you can be, without limits. There is pure freedom in your submission, because He loves you as a father loves His only child.

He protects and covers you in this love, and what you give will be returned to you and multiplied beyond measure, when you understand the power of submission. It is not a form of bringing yourself low, but rather an act of tapping into the power He has for you to change your life and make it amazing.

His covering will bless you. There is peace here. There is joy here. There is love here. There is freedom here. There is power here. When you follow His promptings in your life, He changes it into everything that it will need to be more than you ever thought it could be. He removes the limits here. He breaks down the barriers here. He destroys all that oppresses you here. There is power in alignment, for what He has for you is good. Everything changes here. There are miracles here.

Submission is connection to Him, His power, His spirit. Submission is connection to a love greater than you can imagine. Humans have turned submission into ugliness and abuse, but that is not what submission truly is. There is comfort in the covering of God. There are blessings here. There is beauty here. There is wholeness here.

It is not something you have to strive for. It is a divine relationship. It is where you are able to lose yourself to find yourself. There is a greater you here. What He has for you here is more than you can build for yourself. Submission is not giving up your freedom, it is discovering a freedom beyond everything you can see. Submission is not making yourself lower than everything else, it is discovering the value and worth that you truly are.

Submission is not losing parts of you to bring you harm, it is losing the parts of you that keep you in patterns that do bring you harm. There is protection here. There is grace here. There is deep love here. Submission does not take from you; it provides for you. There are gifts here. There is friendship here. There is deeper connection to all that is beautiful here.

Submission does not bring you harm, it provides all the help you will ever need against that which brings you harm. Submission does not rob you of your voice, it empowers your voice to reach beyond your own boundaries.

Submission does not take away your abilities, it feeds into your creativity and expands your mind to all that is unseen. People struggle with the concept of submission because the concept has been distorted by people with ill intentions.

Submission does not make you the lowest form of you, it raises you up to become more than you can imagine. There is true value here. You learn to understand your worth here. You discover your own power here. For He covers you here. He connects with you here. He communicates with you here.

Submission does not take your free will, for you will always have that, but it does freely give to you that which will bless you. There is freedom from your own limitations here. There is freedom from fear here. There is freedom from oppression here. There is hope here. There is belief in greater things here. There is strength here. There is possibility beyond your own power here. There is wisdom beyond your own understanding here.

Here is where you discover who you truly are beyond all that you ever believed. Change your concept of what it means to submit to God. Erase all that has distorted your views on what it means to be in relationship with God. For what He has for you is good, if only you are willing to connect with Him.

September 14th

Luke 8:16-19

No one lights a lamp and then covers it with a bowl or hides it under a bed. A lamp is placed on a stand where its light can be seen by all who enter the house. For all that is secret will eventually be brought into the open and everything that is concealed will be brought to light and made known to all. So, pay attention to how you hear. To those who listen to my teaching, more understanding will be given. But for those who are not listening, even what they think they understand will be taken away from them.

§

Now that you understand who you are, you have a responsibility to remain authentic to who you are while still interacting with others and leading them through their own journeys. You cannot afford to stay focused on just your own purpose and beliefs, while navigating them through their own, lest you lose them before you win their hearts. There is power in your presence that is different from everyone else, and that alone is the only power you need. Do not overpower beliefs, challenge them. Speak your truth and step back to allow my power to permeate their beliefs, for it is my power that will challenge beliefs in the hearts of those who have heard your truth.

You have yet to see your full potential, and you still battle your own old beliefs, so step back and allow my power to work in your circumstances and all your relationships, for I know who I have placed in your circle and the hearts that you have been placed in. Love alone has the power to change hearts. You do not need to force it on others, nor should you lose the passion to pursue what I have placed in your heart to pursue. All you need to do is believe that I go ahead of you and work on your behalf. Do not give up. You are not giving in; you are where you have been placed for my purpose. I have placed you there. You bring my light. That is who everyone should see.

Don't get bogged down in who you are, but rather, remember why you are who you are. You do not need to fit in. You will raise the room to meet my purpose. You are there for a reason. Be the light. Hold onto your light. This is who they need to see. Change will come through the light that they see. You are shaking things up with your light. Don't worry about the impact you have, for your impact has already shaken the room. You have already changed hearts and if you step back, you will see what has already been done.

Your light has already changed rooms you have walked into. That is who you are. You are light child, so let your light shine. This is where your power is. Your light comes from me. This is my gift to unto you that you will carry into the world, and those that come to know you shall be touched by my light. In that truth is where the changes come to life. So, step back and let your light shine. Let it shine and all that is hidden in the dark shall come into the light.

September 18th

§

It is time to understand the world that you live in, for often you will find that you don't quite fit in. That's okay. You are not meant to fit in everywhere you go. You are more than the environments you enter. What you carry is meant to be different than the world and the people. What you carry is meant to change these environments, people, and the parts of the world that you will touch. This is your protection from the things that could harm you, so you must understand the power that you hold.

You bring an incredible energy into these atmospheres you enter because of what you carry. Your mind has been opened, your heart has become discerning, and your spirit has learned how to soar, and all things must come up to where you are. You will bring breakthrough. So, sometimes you have to be separated from the things that you will change, by being different from the things that must change.

You will change the broken and the desperate. What you carry will help make them whole. The world cannot give you what you need, for it has been broken by a desperation that has yet to be satisfied. Do not be insecure, for what you carry is more than what you think you need. It is time to see yourself in this light, for your light must inspire change. Do not try to fit in, you were made to be different for a reason. Embrace the beauty that you are. The world needs that exact beauty that you bring into the fallen world.

Through your words, you will change minds, and in your silence, you will change hearts. What you speak will echo in the minds of those who have been able to hear you, and your silence will create reflections that will be adopted in their hearts. You are different. And it is beautiful.

You have come into the power that you are meant to be. You are deep, and those who stand in the shallow cannot understand you. You move the waters that they sit in, and not everyone knows how to handle this movement, for it is different. Do not fall under the weight of rejection, for it is you that must qualify what is allowed in your deep. This is meant to protect you from those who are shallow and have the potential to change who you are, how you see, and what you believe. Remember the truth that has been revealed to you in the deep.

You have experienced the deep stirred by my power, and it has brought you understanding that the world cannot yet see. And you are responsible for leading those who are not ready, into the deep, but you must stand still and wait. They will come to you in their own time just as you came to me in your own time. Remember this, for it is a struggle that you have already overcome, but you only overcame when you were ready on your own to go deeper.

Do not let yourself become less to lead others, lest you become less than who you now know you are. Stand still in the silence of the deep and wait. They will come. Do not seek attention of those in the shallow, for you have substance beyond the shallow that only the deep can sustain. You have evolved and grown beyond the shallows. Let those in the shallows stay in the shallows until they are ready to experience the deep within themselves, for that is when they will be desperate enough for change. And in the end, that is all that matters – change; A change in thinking, feeling, being, so they too can stand still in the deep and wait in the silence to change the world around them.

You were brought into the deep because what you carry changes the deep. I have placed you there to separate you, for what you carry must be protected. You carry my light in you and that light must be protected, for it is my light that will change how others see the deep. So, stand still, wait, and let my light shine around you in the silence of the deep.

You are different. You are light. Embrace the beauty of what you have become by being clothed in my light. This is your atmosphere. You are the atmosphere that changes the shallows as you pour into the world what you carry. You are right where you are supposed to be. Embrace where you are, for you were placed here for your protection, for what you carry must be protected.

Your tears filled the deep, and from this, came true understanding. You have been healed in the waters of your tears. With each tear you cried, you filled the waters until what you were standing in became the deep. With each tear you cried, you shed the pain, you released your grief, you let go of the sorrows that you carried until you were surrounded by all that you once carried and could see everything with eyes that were clear and no longer drowning in tears.

The release gave you understanding. The release gave you life. The release gave you clarity. You have become strengthened in the release. You are more than that which attempted to break you. You have conquered the shallows. You have conquered the shame, the pain, and the rejection. You have conquered the grief, the loneliness, the sorrow. You have conquered the shallows from the depth of each tear and turned what was meant to break you, into your becoming.

Protect your deep, for it is your place of peace. The silence of your waters is the place of true understanding. Here your pain has become your purpose and there is an inner power pushing you all the way through. I am pushing you. I am fanning the flame within you, that you may take it unto the world and those that still sit in the shallows. I am stirring in your waters to make all your tears beautiful, for the release has become your blessing.

September 20th – Relationship With The Spirit

Colossians 3:10

Put on your new nature and be renewed as you learn to know your Creator and become like Him.

The Holy Spirit comes upon you morning and evening and in between. When you reach for Him, He will be there if it serves my purpose. He reveals what needs to be revealed and guides you through all decisions and circumstances that are assigned to you, for this purpose. It is a blessing to have this relationship with me and the Holy Spirit is your connection to this blessing. You must learn what it feels like when He is upon you and recognize what it feels like when you are being misled by something other than He.

Live by the Spirit, and you will not be led astray and into the things that could derail you or deter you from fulfilling what has been promised.

Because you seek Him, you will find Him. The Holy Spirit responds to your calling. He knows you and every step you need to take to become all that you are meant to be. Be still and feel Him near. In this stillness, you will hear His voice, see His revelations, and come to know where He is leading you.

To do what you are called to do, you must come to know when He is near and speaking to you, and when it is not Him. Be still and learn to recognize His presence until you know what it feels like when He is near, what it sounds like when He speaks, and what His guidance looks like when He is directing you. He knows you and you have the power to know Him in the same way. He will always move in your purpose, so you must know your purpose at the core of who you are until it is your entire essence.

You shall abide in Him as He will abide in you, until your voice becomes one, your visions reflect the other, and your steps are equal in stride, direction, and purpose. You have unlimited power within you when the Holy Spirit is carrying and covering you. When you are walking in His power, there is weight in your steps, a light on your path, and sight through all that is dark and unseen.

Your relationship to the Father and the Son is revealed to you through the Holy Spirit. All that needs to be revealed to you will be revealed through your relationship to the Spirit. Honor His presence, for He brings you truth and protection. In Him is discernment. In Him is guidance. In Him is revelation. And through your relationship with Him, all this becomes what lives in you, and this is where wisdom reigns above your own thoughts and desires. He will lead you well when you know His voice.

September 21 – Walking The Path To Purpose

The door has been opened for you to move towards your destiny. Now that you understand the darkness you had experienced, and the blessings that came from it, you can move onto the next level of who you are.

Remember these lessons for change is constant. Living through, learning from, and letting go will be constant. As you begin to recognize what you are letting go of, and the purpose it has had in your life, you will learn to reach for what has been set aside for you.

Your decisions must be a directive from the Holy Spirit so that you can surrender what is no longer good for you. Lay it down and if it is meant for your destiny, the doors shall be opened to it. If it is not meant for your destiny, He will shut the door by way of how your heart responds to it. And if you are in alignment with the Holy Spirit, your heart will know what must go.

He will show you which path to take, for He knows what is good for you. You can lay down your guilt, for He has freed you by way of Jesus for the sake of your purpose and anointing. And whom He takes away from you in this process also falls under the covering of God and their path too, has promise attached to it. This is not random. There is purpose in motivating these changes and changes must happen to fulfill the destiny for you all.

Do not remain in battle based on what you perceive as the norm. Your alliance with the Holy Spirit has broken those boundaries to open the door to new beginnings. Do not worry how people will view you but be mindful of how you deliver the change. Your actions in these moments will affect their perception, not of you, but rather the God that you serve. So be gentle and kind, compassionate and understanding. Love even those who have hurt you. Serve those who have abandoned you. Give to those who have denied you. Accept those who have rejected you. Forgive those who condemn you. Love from a heart that has healed beyond the hurt, and in this, they will know the God who lives within you.

You will falter, and you will fall. You are not perfect, but through faith in knowing that you serve a greater purpose, you will be persistent to becoming better than you were before. You will make choices that others may question, but only you and God know the heart that faces those crossroads alone. You will struggle making the right decisions and will make mistakes along the way. You are not called to be perfect, as it is not the perfected ones that will need you to be the example of God's amazing grace and divine calling.

Let them know of their own calling to new beginnings that will amaze them and give them the answers to their own heart prayers. Speak your truth and demonstrate how His grace has carried you, changed you, and restored the soul that was once lost. There is purpose in these changes that will take each of you higher and closer to where you are required to be. God can heal the hurt, but anger will prevent the connections to the destinies for each of you. His covering rests upon you all. Be bold when you speak your truth so that all will know what true grace looks like.

There is promise of peace and better tomorrows that are set aside for each of you. It may hurt when you have to face your truth, but true change only comes from honest self-evaluation and recognizing the parts of you that you must lay down, and the parts of you that must change. True change always hurts, when it comes from a heart of true repentance. In this you will start with a new identity and learn to honor who you once were knowing she has shaped who you are becoming. Starting over may be scary but live on the promise of peace and better tomorrows. It is meant for the good of all.

You will have to separate from relationships, connections, and places once that part of your journey ends. You will grieve the loss of them all. When you have to separate from someone, do so with compassion, knowing that each of you has a journey that must be honored, separate from the other. Give thanks for their presence and impact they had on your life, honor them for who they were on your journey, and let them go with love. His hand will be on you both. Seek to see His hand in everything, even in the separations though you may grieve.

When you separate you will have moments of doubt because your heart longs to see the good in everything and everyone, but God will keep your heart at bay for reasons beyond your own understanding. And through your faith in His hand, you will be able to stand firm on His promise that He brought you there for a reason, for a season. And though you may not know the reason, when the season ends, follow in faith, pursuing His truth each step of the way.

You will be the catalyst for change even when change will challenge you. Your faith will give you strength to withstand the emotional storms, endure the hard questions, defeat unbelief, and hold fast to hope no matter what. And for this, you will be blessed with peace beyond your own understanding.

Where you begin to doubt your journey, He will give you signs that you are on the right path. Where you began to fall under defeat, He will give you a reason to stand on hope. Where you began to question your own motives, He will give you truth that it is His promise moving you beyond people, places, and seasons. He will strengthen your faith beyond your own understanding.

You will be blessed by this, and you do not need to feel guilt, but honor the changes. As soon as God knows you are ready, He will give you the strength to take each step.

September 22nd – There Is More

When God gave you these messages, He meant for them to touch your heart to change your patterns, shift your perspective, and lead you to a direction of promise. There is more.

Your transformation was just the beginning and was meant to shift your view away from just yourself, your life, and your needs to produce a passion for what is meant for many. There is more.

He knew that what was in you and developing and becoming would contribute to the changes needed in this world. There is more.

God has protected you, provided for you, and positioned you to influence others in a positive way to encourage change, growth, passion to becoming a greater influence on their own. There is more.

You have fed the hungry with your word that has been given to you to provide them with sustenance for their own souls. There is more.

You broke out of your patterns, your places of comfort that caused you to become complacent, and adopted passion and commitment to pursue your purpose. You were meant to demonstrate what this looks like, how it is done, and the power that moves you. There is more.

You have sacrificed, given of yourself fully, sought the strength that moved you through each uncomfortable step so you could stand before God and others to show how His power has shaped you. There is more.

You have made difficult decisions, destroyed the inner thoughts that damaged you, discovered your destiny so you could help direct others to discover their own. There is more.

You have been required to release what you have carried, rejected what has broken you, and been restored by His love and His word so you could inspire the need for restoration in the spirit of others. There is more.

You have walked hard miles, woken up to the word, and discovered your self-worth so you could strengthen the weak, open up the path, and wake others to who they truly are. There is more.

Though you battled dejection and grief, you have demonstrated what strength amidst your sorrows looks like and have inspired others to defeat their own giants and inner demons, to help produce in them their own desire for God amidst their own chaos. There is more.

You have become light unto the lost, loved the lonely, and led others to lean in and let God lead them out of their own loneliness and lack until they learned to love the life they have been given. There is more.

You have shaken up the norms of your own societies, shifted the focus from problems to solutions, and shown how sacrifice can multiply your blessings from belief in something bigger than yourself, to help others see how faith in the unseen has blessings attached to it. There is more.

You have committed yourself to compassion, even under your own inner grief and communicated through your actions how God's covering carried you through. There is more.

You have held onto your pain, but still honored the Father, followed after the Son, and housed the Holy Spirit in your heart so you can show others the path to healing, and hope, and still, there is more.

Never underestimate the power that is inside you that pushed you through each heartbreak, hardship, and the losses you have had to endure. What you fail to see about yourself is that there is so much more.

September 25th

Ecclesiastes 5:18 – 20

Even so, I have noticed one thing, at least that is good. It is good for people to eat, drink, and enjoy their work under the sun during the short life God has given them, and to accept their lot in life. And it is a good thing to receive wealth from God and the good health to enjoy it. To enjoy your work and accept your lot in life – this is indeed a gift from God. God keeps such people busy enjoying life that they take no time to brood over the past.

You have been blessed despite your doubts.

You have found joy despite your depression.

You have found healing despite your brokenness.

You have found faith despite all that came against you.

You have found hope despite your disappointments.

You have found love despite your inner pain.

You have found freedom despite your bondages.

You have found more despite what you lacked.

You have found Him despite sitting in darkness.

This is a reminder to live the life He has given you to live, and to live it fully.

You have found clarity despite your confusion.

You have found help despite being alone.

You have found friendship despite the walls you put up.

You have found transformation despite the forces that have been pulling you down to stay the same.

You have found peace despite the battles you face inside.

You have found life despite experiencing death that overwhelmed you.

This is a reminder to live the life He has given you to live, and to live it fully.

You have found sustenance despite your desperate hunger.

You have found acceptance despite your rejection.

You have found comfort despite the pain you carried.

You have found opportunity despite what you lack.

You have found wisdom despite your ignorance.

You have found destiny despite your aimless journey.

This is a reminder to live the life He has given you to live, and to live it fully.

You have found passion despite living in numbness that overtook you.

You have found courage despite your fears.

You have found His light despite the darkness you lived in.

You have found purpose despite all that held you back.

You have found beauty despite the ugliness you felt inside.

You have found victory despite the losses you have had to face.

You have found happiness despite your sorrows.

You have found redemption despite your shame.

This is a reminder to live the life He has given you to live, and to live it fully.

September 28th

When you pray from a heart that yearns for the touch of God, He hears you. You are connected to Him by the Spirit, and here is where He speaks to you and answers your call. Here is where His peace finds you and fills you. There is nothing else like it. While all other good things in life can bring you joy, that is just surface joy, but His Spirit will bring you a joy that touches every part of your soul. It will move you beyond every challenge you face and will take you to peace that surpasses all understanding.

You have been awakened to your truth through the touch of the Holy Spirit. He has spoken to you the calling that God has placed on your life and has led you this far, and He will continue to lead you all the way through. Seek God out of your heart and remember always that it is His strength that carries you. His wisdom that provides discernment on what shall remain with you and what shall leave. His love flows through your veins and here is where your identity flourishes.

He nudges you to redirect you when you begin to wander off the path and reminds you to keep following the path that He has led you on. He speaks to your needs and brings sustenance for your soul. He turns hearts towards you and helps you to see the value in all. He restores your faith when you feel the beginning of failure or challenge. He brings you courage and power to make it through change. He takes your hand with the love of the Father, and He leads you to all that is good for you.

You recognize when He is with you now and know when He has stood aside to allow you to see Him, to seek Him. The knowing comes quicker now, and you find that you no longer settle into the spells of sadness for very long. You must see your growth and focus on what you see, what you feel, what you know in those moments that He is near, and in those moments that He has stepped aside to allow you to see your own glory.

You have been searching for fulfillment in your spirit for a long time and now find comfort in His presence. You have found fulfillment in your relationship to Him through your spirit and have learned to step back to allow His power to work in your circumstances. You have released control and have adopted His faith that all things work for your good. What is meant to be, will be, and what shall not be, you have learned to release. This has been your growth.

You have allowed your expectations to rest on Him and have learned to receive the good He has for you. You learned to release the hopes that held no truth for you. You have found that there is peace even in the hopes that produced nothing. You have learned that there is more.

You learned to trust God and that His timing and His sustenance is all that matters and continued to believe that His will for your life far exceeds all that you could hope for or want. This has been your growth.

You have learned to lean in and let Him lead you. You wait in expectation and excitement to see the breakthrough, and have learned to trust that no matter what, you still believe that whatever happens will happen in the way it should for your good. It has been a struggle to discern His voice. It has been a struggle to maintain your faith when what you hoped for has fallen away. It has been a struggle to keep your joy through those disappointments, but still, you pressed in and believed. You have adopted His trust beyond your own understanding.

You have learned that your obedience does not take away from you, but rather, gives to you all that you have needed. You have learned that following Him in every step did not take away your freedom, but rather gave you the liberty to walk through everything in His power. This has been your growth. You leaned in and let God, and He responded with the fierceness of a lioness protecting her cubs. You have seen Him remove your pain. You have seen Him take away your sorrows. You know you are secure and safe in His hands. You have seen Him comfort you in all things and have adopted His peace beyond your own understanding.

You have learned to rest in Him. You have learned what this means during times of your greatest tribulations. You have invited Him in to change the atmosphere when your own inner chaos turned the air heavy. You have learned to breathe Him into your spirit when you felt most suffocated. This has been your growth. You have opened up your heart to allow Him to move in you and through you, in your mind, in your heart, and throughout your spirit, even through your shame. You let Him in to change the air that you breath into that which fills your lungs with hope. You have adopted His hope beyond your own understanding.

You have learned that His purpose ignited the fire in your belly and have seen your passions stirred up even in your dejection. You have learned to reach for Him with all your might as you fought the urge to return to the old you who fell into patterns that were destructive to your spirit. This has been your growth. You call out to Him when nothing makes sense. You trust Him when everything comes against you. You keep moving when all you want to do is run into hiding. You have adopted his courage beyond your own understanding.

You have learned to rely on him in prayer for everything. You have learned that healing in the spirit, in the mind, in the body all comes from Him. You have learned to depend on Him for strength when you were at your weakest. You have learned to give Him all your pains and fears. This has been your growth. You have seen Him move in you and in your circumstances. You have seen Him change hearts and minds. You have seen Him still the waters around you to allow you to stand. You have seen Him calm the storms of your mind and recognize when He is there. You have adopted His strength beyond your own understanding.

You have learned to humble yourself to receive His word and His guidance. You have learned that your need of Him outweighs all other things of this world. You have learned to be aware of His presence when all that you presently face threatens to break your beliefs down. This has been your growth. You see the deception before the lies overtake you. You see the truth amidst the lies you tell yourself. You have recognized the lines that separate your truth from His truth in who you are, what you have, what must stay, what must go, what is good, and what can harm you. You have adopted His truth beyond your own understanding.

You have learned to hear His voice when you are lost. You have learned to identify what leads you astray and back into the spirit of defeat. You have learned to recognize His light on all that attempts to remain in darkness. This has been your growth. You have placed faith in all that He has shown you. You have stretched yourself beyond what is comfortable to allow what He is bringing into your life to move you forward. You have searched for His light in your darkness. You have gained confidence in His word over your life and know that it is good. You have adopted His wisdom beyond your own understanding.

You have learned to receive His love when you felt less than worthy. You have learned to be led by the Spirit of God during your shaping. You have learned to trust the changes that were happening with a knowing that His love will protect and cover you. This has been your growth. You have submitted to His love and accepted Him into your heart. You have allowed Him to overwhelm you with His blessings birthed from His love that has changed you. You have learned to speak from this place of love. You have learned how to respond from this place of love. You have learned how to comfort from this place of love and have learned that what you love can no longer break you. You have learned to place your pain in His hands and seek His comforts when everything hurt and nothing consoled your soul. You have adopted His love beyond your own understanding.

You have learned to strive for His courage when all you saw instilled fear in you. You have learned to listen for His voice amidst all the voices that would have kept you in fear. You have learned to overcome fear with faith. This has been your growth. When all seemed bigger than you, you stood up in Him. When all seemed to come against you, you stood up in His strength. When all seemed to swallow you whole, you reached for the hand of His saving grace. You have learned to trust the word He has brought you about your life, your purpose, your worth. You have learned that He will meet your every need and take away what does not feed you. You have learned to accept only what is good for you and reject the false hopes that could have destroyed you. You have learned to let go and let God. You have adopted His faith beyond your own understanding.

You have grown in Trust.
You have grown in Peace.
You have grown in Courage.
You have grown in Hope.
You have grown in Strength.
You have grown in Truth.
You have grown in Wisdom.
You have grown in Love.
You have grown in Faith.
You have grown in all that is good, and all that is God.
You have grown.

September 29th

When you first recognized His hand on your life, you sought a true understanding of your position in the life and the relationships that had you bound. You learned how to allow the pain to build what is beautiful. He has seen you at moments where doubt threatened to overtake you and watched how you clung to Him and His word. While you stood still in the middle of the challenges you faced, you did so with your eyes upward towards the heavens waiting earnestly for His guidance and His strength. You did not doubt that it would come. That is faith.

You stood in faith no matter what you have had to walk through. You have reached for Him with greater purpose and intensity when all threatened to consume you in the fire. He watched you pull strength from Him. He watched you demand the faith necessary to keep moving forward. He watched you stop in the middle of the fire to feel for Him, and to hear from Him, and you would not move until He told you to move. You were willing to suffer the burns that would come if it meant that it brought you closer to Him. That is faith.

He saw you press in when all that was pressing against you threatened to suffocate the life out of you. He watched you stand firm in His word, always seeking His guidance, and waiting for the signs that His Spirit would provide for you. Your relationship with God was elevated through all this. You had no preconceived demands that determined your walk with Him. You walked toward the darkness despite your fears. He watched as you pushed forward with the hope that His courage would give you the momentum to keep going. That is faith.

You are not ordinary, and your love for Him is not ordinary. He sees your heart and it is good. For this, He called you unto Him and gave you all that you needed to make it through all things. You reached out from the struggle, walked through the fires, stretched yourself further out of your comfort zone, and all was done in faith. You prayed and knew that He would answer. You called and knew that He would come to you. You never failed to need Him. You never failed to seek Him. You never failed to know that only He had the authority over your life to tell you where to go next. That is faith.

He heard you as you praised him through your pain. He watched as you looked for Him in the deep. Though you knew not where you were going, you followed Him anyway. Your faith was manifested to new levels each time you had to face all that you had to face. He watched as you would close off the world and its distractions even though you thought you needed more from the world. You reached for Him instead. You stopped on your journey to seek Him, to know that your steps were being ordered, and refused to move until you received His word. That is faith.

He watched you in your weakness, pull strength from all that threatened to break you down. He saw you when you sacrificed what you believed was everything to you, that you would fulfill His purpose. He saw that nothing else had a place on your journey unless it aligned with His call on your life. He heard your praise even in your storms. He saw you dig deeper when all that was on the surface threatened to bury you in the shallows. He saw you go deeper to find Him. That is faith.

He saw you believe when all that you saw provided nothing real to hope for. He saw you stand up and plant your feet when the shaking threatened to knock you down. He saw you cling to Him when everything in your world was falling short. He heard you praise Him for the breaking. He saw you demonstrate His love even in the things that threatened to build hate and division in your heart. He watched as you looked beyond what the eyes can see, and you found promise and hope anyway. That is faith.

He watched as you recognized when you were getting lost and sought to find him in the dark. He saw you stop and feel your way through to reach Him even when the world demanded that you keep moving. He heard your heart amidst the chaos in your mind. He watched as you pulled your heart up for Him when your thoughts threatened to silence your prayers. He watched as you found His power to silence all other voices, in expectation that you would hear His. That is faith.

He watched as you questioned your every thought and qualified that it came from Him, discard what came from your own hopes, and kill what was not His. He watched as you laid down the treasured pains that you carried, with a knowing that what you leave at His feet, He will restore for you. He watched as you leaned on Him for all your needs. He watched you focus in on Him when everything and everyone around you vied for your attention, and you refused to move until you saw His Hand in the things that called to you. That is faith.

He watched you wait for His voice. He watched you recommit your heart each time you felt that you were being led astray. He watched you stand still in the silence when everything around you was screaming. He watched as you took each step no matter the terrain, the instability of the ground that you walked on, and found your steadiness in His Spirit. He watched you stand when you wanted to fall. He watched you walk toward Him when your fears caused you to want to run back. That is faith.

He watched you pull compassion up though you were buried in bitterness and resentment. He watched as you pulled love out of the wells that were dried by hate and division. He watched as you summoned hope from the voids that housed all your sorrows. He watched as you demanded healing from the things that broke you. He watched you reach in for His power with an expectation that you would receive it. That is faith.

He watched as you recognized that He brought you through all this, made you stronger in your weakness, filled you with hope in your disappointments, surrounded you with comfort while drowning in grief. He watched you recognize that His hand was what pulled you up, His love filled you, His power pushed you, His word encouraged you, and His light led you. You never stopped believing that He lived within you, that He ordained your steps, that He was shifting the world around you in your favor, and that no matter what it looked like in the moment, that all things were working for your good. That is faith.

Epilogue

So much has happened since the last sentence was written that has amazed me in the most profound ways. What started out as a journey towards healing has become so much more. I have been awakened to my purpose, found a strength I never knew I had, and my connection to God is ever increasing. I am no longer just becoming but have found the wonderful spirit within who loves deeper, laughs louder, and has learned the true value of being.

I have a greater love for humanity because I understand the darkness that lives within each of us when we fail to recognize the light we carry. And that if given the guidance to find it, and the chance to embrace it, we can each have a greater impact on the world around us. I now know what forgiveness truly is, to give it and to receive it. And I can honestly say, because of this, I love from an unburdened, untarnished, and a balanced place.

I have a greater appreciation for all experiences, both the most challenging ones and the ones we find the most fulfillment in. There is growth from it all, and that if allowed, can take us to greater levels of self-awareness, self-acceptance, and a profound sense of self-love. From here, we feed the world around us.

I have a greater appreciation for life, for I have lived through death of the spirit, of the soul, and of the relationships that have fed me. I have lost loved ones too soon and know that the greatest tribute I can give to them is to embrace living with all that I am so that my life makes a difference in the lives of others. From here, I act with compassion, for I know that every soul has its own journey.

I have a greater appreciation for who I am in spirit, for here is where I meet God. I am guided, protected, refined, and redefined. I am stronger, wiser, and more aware of how who I am can trigger the evolution of another soul or contribute to their struggle. Because of this connection, I am always reminded that I have a greater responsibility to those around me, and that I can gift to them what has been gifted to me.

To say I have changed is an understatement. I have become.

Here I am, and I am unstoppable, surrounded by a love and power that is undeniable. I am risen from the ashes, now glowing with the flames that tried to take me out. I am a fighter for the underdog, with a heart bigger than it has ever been before. The Great I Am lives within me; therefore, I am, and I am always becoming.

No matter what I have lost, I am whole. No matter what I have suffered, I have gained. No matter what I lacked, I have more than many. I am a force to be reckoned with because I am a warrior that has won many battles. I am a love that will never be forgotten because I love from a place that has known His love in the most intimate way. I am a fire that will always burn brightly because He is the light within me. I am the defender of those forgotten because He chose to remember me. I am unbreakable, unstoppable, and unforgettable. I know my worth. I am.

Because of this, and because of the personal guidance God has given me, I have a responsibility to humanity, to help develop them on their journeys, to plant the seeds that will feed the growth to who they are becoming. I have a responsibility to demonstrate how God's love changed one single life that was once broken, survived the becoming, and now represents a higher self of being.

Thank God for all that I have been through. I wouldn't change a single step on my path, for He has shown me who I really am, and for the first time in my life, I know where I am going, I know why I am here, and I know I am not alone.

About the Author

Melanie Joy is the eldest of ten. Yes, ten. She was raised on the little Island of Guam, a US territory in the middle of the Pacific Ocean. She has a passion for connecting to people and with nature, and now that she lives in Washington State, she has the best of both worlds. This is her first book.

www.ingramcontent.com/pod-product-compliance
Lightning Source LLC
Chambersburg PA
CBHW071110160426
43196CB00013B/2531